Foundational Concepts of Decolonial and Southern Epistemologies

GLOBAL FORUM ON SOUTHERN EPISTEMOLOGIES

Series Editors: **Sinfree Makoni** *(Pennsylvania State University, USA)*, **Rafael Lomeu Gomes** *(University of Oslo, Norway)*, **Magda Madany-Saá** *(Pennsylvania State University, USA)*, **Bassey E. Antia** *(University of the Western Cape, South Africa)* and **Chanel Van Der Merwe** *(Nelson Mandela University, South Africa)*

This book series publishes independent volumes concerned primarily with exploring peripheralized ways of framing and conducting language studies in both the Global South and Global North. We are particularly interested in the 'geopolitics of knowledge' as it pertains to language studies and aim to illustrate how language scholarship in the Global North is partially indebted to diverse traditions of scholarship in the Global South. We are also keen to explore interfaces between language and other areas of human and non-human scholarship. Ultimately, our concern is not only epistemological; it is also political, educational and social. The books are part of the Global Forum, which is open and politically engaged. The Global Forum fosters collegiality and dialogue, using the technologies essential to productivity during the pandemic that have served our collective benefit. In the book series, we experiment with the format of the book, challenging the colonial concept of a single monologic authorial voice by integrating multiple voices, consistent with decoloniality and the democratic and politically engaged nature of our scholarship.

Full details of all the books in this series and of all our other publications can be found on http://www.multilingual-matters.com, or by writing to Multilingual Matters, St Nicholas House, 31–34 High Street, Bristol, BS1 2AW, UK.

GLOBAL FORUM ON SOUTHERN EPISTEMOLOGIES: 3

Foundational Concepts of Decolonial and Southern Epistemologies

Edited by
Sinfree Makoni, Anna Kaiper-Marquez, Magda Madany-Saá and Bassey E. Antia

MULTILINGUAL MATTERS
Bristol • Jackson

DOI https://doi.org/10.21832/MAKONI8851
Library of Congress Cataloging in Publication Data
A catalog record for this book is available from the Library of Congress.
Names: Makoni, Sinfree, editor. | Kaiper-Marquez, Anna, editor. | Madany-Saá, Magda, editor. | Antia, Bassey Edem, editor |
Title: Foundational Concepts of Decolonial and Southern Epistemologies/ Edited by Sinfree Makoni, Anna Kaiper-Marquez, Magda Madany-Saá and Bassey E. Antia.
Description: Jackson, TN: Multilingual Matters, [2023] | Series: Global Forum on Southern Epistemologies: 3 | Includes bibliographical references and index. | Summary: "This book brings together 11 prominent scholars and political activists to discuss and explore issues around postcolonialism, decoloniality, Theories of the South and Epistemologies of the South. These wide-ranging discussions touch upon issues from academic research methods and writing conventions to global struggles for justice"— Provided by publisher.
Identifiers: LCCN 2023030049 (print) | LCCN 2023030050 (ebook) | ISBN 9781800418844 (pbk) | ISBN 9781800418851 (hbk) | ISBN 9781800418875 (epub) | ISBN 9781800418868 (pdf)
Subjects: LCSH: Decolonization—Developing countries. | Developing countries—Intellectual life. | Sociolinguistics.
Classification: LCC JV236 .F68 2023 (print) | LCC JV236 (ebook) | DDC 325/.3—dc23/eng/20230801 LC record available at https://lccn.loc.gov/2023030049
LC ebook record available at https://lccn.loc.gov/2023030050

British Library Cataloguing in Publication Data
A catalogue entry for this book is available from the British Library.

ISBN-13: 978-1-80041-885-1 (hbk)
ISBN-13: 978-1-80041-884-4 (pbk)

Multilingual Matters
UK: St Nicholas House, 31–34 High Street, Bristol, BS1 2AW, UK.
USA: Ingram, Jackson, TN, USA.

Website: https://www.multilingual-matters.com
Twitter: Multi_Ling_Mat
Facebook: https://www.facebook.com/multilingualmatters
Blog: www.channelviewpublications.wordpress.com

Copyright © 2024 Sinfree Makoni, Anna Kaiper-Marquez, Magda Madany-Saá, Bassey E. Antia and the authors of individual chapters.

All rights reserved. No part of this work may be reproduced in any form or by any means without permission in writing from the publisher.

The policy of Multilingual Matters/Channel View Publications is to use papers that are natural, renewable and recyclable products, made from wood grown in sustainable forests. In the manufacturing process of our books, and to further support our policy, preference is given to printers that have FSC and PEFC Chain of Custody certification. The FSC and/or PEFC logos will appear on those books where full certification has been granted to the printer concerned.

Typeset by Nova Techset Private Limited, Bengaluru and Chennai, India.

Contents

	Acknowledgments and Gratitudes	ix
	Foreword	xi
	Prologue	xv
1	Introduction *Sinfree Makoni, Anna Kaiper-Marquez and Bassey E. Antia*	1
2	Theory from the South: Thinking Out Loud About Decolonization *Jean Comaroff*	12
3	Epistemologies of the South: Justice Against Epistemicide *Boaventura de Sousa Santos*	41
4	Upending the Inhuman: Decoloniality, Postmodernism and Afrocentricity *Molefi Kete Asante*	66
5	The Politics of Language, Memory and Knowledge *Ngũgĩ wa Thiong'o*	88
6	uBuntu, Nite and the Struggle for Global Justice *Drucilla Cornell and Souleymane Bachir Diagne*	104
7	Foundational Concepts and Struggles for Dignity and Life *Catherine Walsh and Walter Mignolo*	121
8	Decolonizing Methodologies: Research and Indigenous Peoples *Linda Tuhiwai Smith*	159
	Epilogue: The South Writing Back *Clarissa Menezes Jordão*	182
	Index	187

'When we use the term "indigenous" or "methodology" or "theory" or "decolonizing," it does not represent a narrow idea about one possibility or one pathway for one type of configuration of being indigenous or being colonized. I believe we have to keep our ideas open. Don't close the door. In our world – the indigenous world – it is really important that you don't close the door because in closing a door, you close the hope for a people who have not yet made it to the door. Leave an extra chair at the table because there is a people that are making their way to sit at the table' (Linda Tuhiwai Smith, this volume).

Acknowledgments and Gratitudes

Successfully completing a writing project and seeing it through to publication in a timely manner, when we need to attend to many other commitments, including completing PhDs, changing jobs, and running academic and research units, requires the contributions of many people who give of their time. The Global Virtual Forum is composed of volunteers from across the globe, including Africa, the United States and South America, to name a few, who also are at different stages in their academic careers. The Forum is therefore an exercise not only in cross-regional exchanges but also in intergenerational and interracial communication.

Despite our geographical diversity, we share one feature. We are all committed to exploring and expanding alternative ways of conducting research, disseminating knowledge, and finding productive ways of engaging with the many different societies with which we are affiliated. Issues of mobility are of central significance for the participants in this remarkable project because members and participants of the Forum have all lived (or live) in more than one location. In a sense, we are all intellectual nomads and understand what it is to be both insiders and outsiders.

I am proud to say that this is our third volume in the Global Forum on Southern Epistemologies series, published by Multilingual Matters, and many more volumes are at different stages of production. I would like to express my gratitude to my colleagues who organize the weekly sessions on Fridays and, at times, twice a week (Fridays and Saturdays), which have become our trademark. I also am grateful to my colleagues who lead the production of each volume, transcribing and editing the volume, and to the scholars who selflessly give of their time to discuss their research and share their work. I have been enormously enriched by this iterative engagement with so many different people, and I look forward to more.

I also am grateful to the Dean of the College of Liberal Arts, Clarence Lang, and the Senior Associate Dean, Scott Bennett, for funding the graduate students who participate in this project as well as for the additional funding that renders it possible to engage in activities related to the project, including transcribing and editing the sessions.

Finally, I would like to thank Cecil Vigouroux, John Joseph, Alastair Pennycook, and Jason Litzenberg, who have all commented on different drafts of this volume and to Multilingual Matters for believing in us. I also would like to thank Anisa Caine who beautifully designs and paints our covers at what must be irritatingly short notice.

There is no template that we follow in assembling each of the volumes. Each volume has its own intellectual trajectory but is influenced by the preceding volumes and helps to shape subsequent volumes. In this series, we are not only interested in producing a variety of volumes related to our themes of decoloniality and Southern epistemologies but also to expanding and reframing the notion of what constitutes an author, a scholarly book, and even what is meant by a 'book'. Through our work on this series, it has dawned on us that, unless the notion of what constitutes a book is radically revised, a decolonial agenda and scholarship will never be fully realized.

Sinfree Makoni

Foreword

As the reader will appreciate, this volume represents a significant advance in ongoing projects of decolonizing language and its study as linguistics and/or sociolinguistics. Rather than merely adopting the deconstructive and oppositional stance of reflecting on language from a southern perspective, the project that sustains this volume has much in common with Fanon's concept of *sociogeny* in which he identified the suffering of the colonized as, on the one hand, more than ontogenetic (involving a coming to be of individuals as beings) and on the other hand, more than phylogenetic (involving the coming to be of individual beings in contact with other individual beings). Fanon's (1967) *sociogeny* as a political-therapeutic proposal, refers to the interconnection between the external institutional, objective dimension of coloniality and the internal subjective plane which Sylvia Wynter characterizes as a qualitative mental state that produces the sense of *'what it is like to be'* colonized, racialized and southernized.

In academic terms, the epistemological issue of not having *southern* knowledges (from an onto-epistemic, and not necessarily geographic South) valued and recognized as academic knowledges often incites resistance in the form of attempts at oppositionally and assertively insisting on the value of southern knowledges. However, this often tends to be done using the academic means already available, institutionally, such as written journals and publications. As time has shown, by using already available and already institutionalized means, the southern knowledges thus produced risk falling harmlessly into 'market niches', of interest only to those already interested in such knowledges, thus losing their transformative potential.

In her consideration of Fanon's sociogenic principle, Sylvia Wynter (2001) called attention to the fact that this principle goes beyond the traditional nurture–nature dichotomy and portrays humans as creators of culture that then fashions and creates humans. It is then humans that, through the epistemic and ontological categories they have culturally produced, produce concepts of humans and of their knowledges: 'although born as biological humans we can experience ourselves as human only through the mediation of the processes of socialization effected by the invented *tekhne* or cultural technology to which we give the name culture'.

Hence, what is as important (if not *more*) as resisting and opposing hegemonic political and onto-epistemological structures which are *objectively instituted*, is to reconstruct *subjective* structures of feeling to modify the feeling of racialized academics as to *what it is like to be* colonized and *southernized*.

This then involves NOT using 'as is' the existent objectively instituted cultural categories ('academic', 'rational', 'scientific', 'formal', 'literate') to produce *new* knowledges and *new* subjective experiences of *what it is like to be* a racialized producer of academic knowledge. An academic *of* the South, yes, but not necessarily only *for* the South, and *in* the South.

The strategic option is then to make use of alternative means and categories of knowledge production, not yet objectively institutionalized as 'academic' in Eurocentric terms, but also objectively institutionalized and academically practised in the South, such as face-to-face oral discussions, collective conversations and dialogical narratives.

The *double consciousness* of the black Americans, accustomed to seeing themselves through the eyes of the hegemonic white that Du Bois (1903) described, is not dissimilar to the present sensation of academics of the South who have to see their knowledges and their cultural categories of knowledge production as being of lesser worth than those of the North, and of only local and not 'universal' interest.

Confronting the problem of double consciousness and sociogeny, and reflecting on Fanon's political and therapeutic indications, Wynter takes recourse to the conceptualization of a *transcultural* space in which cultural concepts categorized as *quantitatively* different by two conflicting cultures can, in confrontation, be reconfigured and understood as *qualitatively* and *contextually different*. It would then be the case of not a simple *replacement* of one 'better' category/concept by another, but more significantly, and more *transformatively*, it would consist of *translating* contextual differences, understanding the *similarities* of value of certain concepts/cultural categories in *different* contexts. This would permit the perception that, for members of different communities, each of these *objectively* institutionalized elements produces radically different *subjective* effects – different feelings of *what it is like to be*.

So, rather than merely *replacing* previous institutionalized and objective colonial cultural categories for categories which, though also objectively institutionalized, are not valued because they are considered marginal or peripheral, this volume makes the option to *translate* knowledges of the south into *transcultural* categories such as transcriptions of conversations moving between the conflicting categories of oral/the written, formal/informal, academic/popular, narrative/argumentative.

The subjective sociogenic aspect of *what it is like to be* in the case of racialized academics is often not given adequate thought. Current theories of epistemologies of the South and decoloniality speak much of the invisibilization and silencing of the racialized, colonized other. Similarly, Du Bois' concept of the imposed double-consciousness of the racialized North American black tends to highlight the invisibilization and silencing of the colonized in relation to the hegemonic other. What these various theories tend to pass over too quickly is the other side of the double-consciousness of the colonized other: while this other may indeed, in interactions with hegemonically 'superior' others, see herself through the eyes of this 'superior' as worthless, invisibilized, silenced and a mere consumer of knowledge, in interactions with her peers, this is not the case; to her peers she is indeed visible, existent, voluble and produces knowledge capably. After all, in order for there to be a *double* consciousness, as an imposition of an external consciousness over an internal one, an internal conscious has to, *does* exist and politically and sociogenically needs to be recuperated.

Politically and strategically, inspired by the Fanonian concept of sociogeny, one could move from being content with one's being on a plane of *existence* to elaborating strategies and forms of *re-existence*. Where existence refers to the predominance of the subjective feeling of *what it's like to be* a racialized academic otherized within the existing status quo, subject to external institutional means of knowledge production and dissemination, *re-existence*, in contrast, refers to promoting the subjective feeling of *what it's like to be* simply a competent academic, that no longer sees the knowledge it produces as also racialized. The transformative substance of this gesture lies in moving beyond the dichotomy of a sense of unracialized being *for one's peers* versus a sense of racialized being *for hegemonic others*. This gesture implements a sense of unracialized academic being *in all situations of academic knowledge production and dissemination*.

In the case of racialized academics of the South, this other consciousness or sense of being is indeed present and appears, in epithets such as knowledges *of the South*, *Southern* knowledges or *Decolonial* knowledges. However, the current volume forms part of a project that goes beyond epithets and seeks to attain the sociogenic plane producing new and sustained structures of feeling of *what it is like to be* an academic producer of knowledge beyond racialization.

Through its choice of exploiting multiple *other* and multimodal forms of academic knowledge production, this volume represents an ongoing effort to think and produce language, knowledge and being otherwise.

Lynn Mario T. Menezes de Souza
Universidade de São Paulo

References

Du Bois, W.E.B (1903) *The Souls of Black Folk: Essays and Sketches*. Chicago: A.C. McClurg.
Fanon, F. (1967) *Black Skins, White Masks*. New York: Monthly Review Press.
Wynter, S. (2001) Towards the sociogenic principle: Fanon, identity, the puzzle of conscious experience, and what it is like to be 'black'. In M.F. Durán-Cogan and A. Gómez-Moriana (eds) *National Identities and Sociopolitical Changes in Latin America* (pp. 30–66). London: Routledge.

Prologue

Foundational Concepts of Decolonial and Southern Epistemologies gathers a stellar, global group of scholars and theorists whose virtues include transcending disciplinary decadence and refusals of epistemic apartheid. Disciplinary decadence involves reductive disciplinary thinking in which practitioners treat their disciplines as either an exclusive standpoint on reality or, worse, reality itself. It a form of non-relational commitment or prejudice in which all else is epistemologically closed. A similar feature happens with epistemic apartheid. That involves the segregation of knowledge with a small set of hegemonic exemplars functioning as legitimizing all others. It, too, is, in short, decadent.

The importance of transcending the pitfalls of disciplinary decadence and epistemic apartheid is evident in what is at times called the decolonization of knowledge. Decolonizing knowledge requires addressing epistemic colonization; it requires, in other words, taking head on the practices and misrepresentations by which knowledge is colonized. In what has become known as decolonial thought, the demands addressing 'coloniality', the normative life of colonialism in which grammars, practices, commitments facilitate the enduring effects and rationalizations of colonization. As colonialism in this context is specifically *Euromodern colonialism*, this means addressing its concomitant organization of life along its themes of degradation and dehumanization – namely, Euromodernity's anthropological presuppositions, its distorted notions of freedom, its justificatory practices, and its appeals of redemption. Among these normative presumptions is the supposed neat separation of normative, especially political, and epistemic life.

As is well known, physical violent control over a people rallies an array of unsustainable material resources. It's far more efficient to discourage the critical capacity and imagination of a people to the point of them believing their subordination is, in a word, ontological. By that is meant an absolute conclusion of what there is. Believing things cannot be otherwise, what is there left to do but accept the dictates of the system?

Euromodern colonization of knowledge is manifested in most sites of hegemonic knowledge across the globe. They take the forms of (1) racial and ethnic origins or of history, (2) coloniality of the norms by which knowledge is produced and received as legitimate, (3) market commodification, (4) disciplinary decadence, (5) solipsism and (6) appeals to redemptive narratives of colonial history and continued practice.

The first is straightforward: People from the 'North', presumed white but in general refer to lighter peoples from the East to the West, are the originators of thought and the production of knowledge. The absurdity of this position is exposed through its temporal appeal to the idea that humanity didn't begin to think until about 2,500 years ago. As our species is about 300,000 years old, with most of its time spent on the African continent, the northern epistemological 'miracle' appeals to a racial thesis: lighter people think; dark ones don't. As light-skin homo sapiens didn't emerge until about 8,000 years ago, what, one wonders, was dark humanity doing for about 292,000 years? An additional consideration is that hominins have been around for about 2 million years, which means a lot of creative and technological activities preceded the emergence of the species we call 'us'. Given all that, the idea of history beginning when a race or lighter set of races emerged among us defies facts. The empirical demand is obvious: seek and ye shall find. Given the abundant archaeological and written evidence, the task is clearly more than an empirical one of seeing. It is also one of interpreting and learning the conditions for the appearance of what has been proverbially hidden in plain sight.

Coloniality of norms blocks sight. They are premised on presuppositions not only of what is but also what *must be*. Locked into the logic of 'can't', the many contributions and relationships by which humanity reaches beyond itself are foreclosed. There is, in effect, the notion that knowledge and truth emanate from some onto others. The fallacy of this position is that it seals the knowledge producer from affect and connection; the contradiction of knowledge without learning follows. This self-reductive notion leads to the idea of a self that stands as reality-onto-itself, as what the ancient Latins called 'substance' in their translation of the Greek notion of ουσία (*ousia*). While useful as a hypothesis, this metaphysical idea has been a disaster as its proponents joined forces in producing what became the rationalization of the Euromodern world. The idea of a self-contained being, extended to the idea of a people who need no others, pushes knowers out of relations with others beyond themselves. A form of epistemic arrogance follows in which there is no one else from whom to learn.

The isolated subject is a prime figure for what became The Market. Markets have been around for hundreds of thousands of years, as our species and other hominins practices of exchange or trade attest. What is different – and peculiarly distinct – about the form of colonization inaugurated in the Euromodern era (or error) is the rallying of absolutes from metaphysics to religion to theology to the self to produce purified notions in which even concepts are closed. Thus, markets fell prey to The Market, an abstraction through which the paradox of business premised on the elimination of other markets followed. A market against markets functions as an economic god. Without room for others, all must be swallowed up into its logic, which means no exceptions for other forms of life. Instead of knowledge of The Market, there is the market of knowledge – properly, The Market commodification of knowledge. As a colonial force, capitalism – whose god is The Market – renders knowledges that challenge it as devoid of 'capital'. This shortcoming eclipses reality and truth to through making exchange value the condition of knowledge appearance. What follows is that Euromodern colonialism carries, in part and parcel, a convergence of commodification, dehumanization and misrepresentations through practices of rationalization in which there is investment in lies as truth and the invisibilizing of truth under the mythopoetics of fiction.

The relationship of all this to disciplinary decadence is, then, in the colonization of learning communities into those of mandatory closure. As with the reductive self, disciplinary decadence has the self-contained discipline, the organization of knowledge practices that turn away from relations, from reality as an ongoing practice of reaching beyond the given, to the discipline itself as all that needs to be learned. Rendering the discipline in effect an idol or a god, what is left to do is mere 'application'. This practice, in which the methodological offerings are treated as if created by a god, becomes a fetish in which there is radicalized inwardness of disciplinary practice follows. Made concrete in the study of social reality or, less pretentious, people, societies, and ways in which meaning is communicated, wherever such practitioners encounter people who don't fit into the presuppositions of the discipline, the response is to ask what's wrong with the people instead of critically examining the discipline's limitations. W.E.B. Du Bois formulated this problem elegantly. He called it the knowledge production of "problem people'.

Treating a discipline as 'complete' leads to solipsism, the attitude in which the discipline becomes 'the world'. Moreover, with such reductive thinking is also an urgent need for legitimacy. There is therefore the rationalization of the practices as in themselves justified, which means all contradictions and any notion of error become *external*. The system – in this case the discipline – must be redeemed at all costs.

Now, one can clearly transcend such practices. If turning practices inward to the point of near implosion is the problem, clearly the response is to turn outward; if rendering others irrelevant is the problem, then making others relevant is a solution; if noncommunication is the problem, then communicating is a necessary antidote. The communicological challenge is, then, one of transcending the hubris of the self-contained self. It is the humility of learning through practices of communication. One must reach beyond oneself for the sake of reality. And where reality is the ongoing communicative practice with others, it is clearly never complete and thus must be related to instead of conquered and colonized.

Liberatory thought begins not only with Euromodernity letting go, learning no longer to be full of itself, but also, in kind, for the rest of us to do the same. Anyone taken too seriously ceases to live.

I begin with these reflections to contextualize the virtues of this important collection of critical intellectuals reflecting on decoloniality in the context of the Global South. Even that geopolitical designation must receive critique, since, as the various authors remind us, the Global South is not a place but a set of relations through which people appear in a myriad of ways premised on relations of power good and bad. The Global South could be located geographically anywhere in which practices in which it is constructed are conducted.

Think, for example, of the colonialization of knowledge creating a crisis of justification. If Euromodern production of knowledge was in the service of dehumanization and degradation, doesn't this entail a crisis of justification? How does one justify justification *epistemologically*? The five set of epistemic colonial practices from racialization to secularized theodicean redemption outlined inaugurate a crisis in which presuppositions of North versus South and legitimate movement from East to West must be addressed through a global perspective in which knowledge emerges from everywhere. What is this but a shift from the Euromodern geography of reason?

I regard *Foundational Concepts of Decolonial and Southern Epistemologies* as a contribution to shifting the geography of reason. Eurocentric forms of knowledge are, as Molefi Asante advocates, decentered. The project isn't anti-European or anti-white but, instead, anti-Eurocentrism and anti-white supremacy.

As I've already mentioned, a virtue of this book is that it does not practice epistemic apartheid. Instead of sectarianism or Balkanism ('my country', 'my nation', 'my people'), there is the rare gathering of intellectuals who facilitate the meeting of ideas as well as peoples. There is fidelity to the idea that if decolonization is to make any sense, it should at least be the liberation of humanity.

Liberating humanity involves addressing the irony that our imprisonment is not externally imposed. Even dehumanization is a human effort. This metareflective realization pertains as well to practices of liberation. Thus, even decolonial theory must be held into account. The editors and authors offer a critique of decolonial theory in addition to offering ways of transcending it. Going beyond decolonial theory involves the constructive project of figuring out what to build instead of exclusively focusing on what to tear down. This is in stream with an observation Jane Anna Gordon and I offered in our edited volume *Not Only the Master's Tools* (2006) in our discussion of Audre Lorde's famous dictum that the master's tools won't tear down the master's house. Our addenda were twofold. First, so-called masters don't build houses. Second, we should understand the fecund or generative features of the tools brought by the colonized and enslaved, many of which fattened the Global North and without which such beneficiaries may have been nothing more than afterthoughts of a larger human story. This leads to, third, the observation that the generative tools of the colonized and the enslaved could be used to build many different kinds of houses, those premised, as Frantz Fanon argued, on new concepts through which to set afoot a new humanity. If there are many houses, claims to mastery lose their force and received the deserved verdict of their greatest fear: their irrelevance.

The Global Virtual Forum is among the new houses devoted to this project of building new concepts to set afoot a new humanity. Organized by an extraordinary group of scholars and public intellectuals with a background in linguistics, this group is actively undergoing what I call a teleological suspension of disciplinarity – a willingness to go beyond their disciplines to communicate with whomever or whatever will offer a way of addressing the challenges humanity faces in the 21st century as we also try to shake of the shackle of colonial stratification. A collaboration of the Pennsylvania State University in the US, the University of Oslo in Norway and the University of the Western Cape as well as Nelson Mandela University in South Africa, the project's focus is to provide equitable access – de facto communication and relational commitments – across the globe to decolonial transdisciplinary scholarship grounded in Southern Epistemologies. The project's transdisciplinary instead of *inter*disciplinary commitment is connected to the transcending of disciplinary decadence. Interdisciplinarity, after all, is at times avowed when a collection of disciplines or subfields locked in disciplinary decadence gather. Like ships passing in the night, they could speak alongside instead of in communication with one another.

Rejecting colonial metaphysics, communicating with one another requires an admission of the incompleteness of each contributor. The result is, through an embraced humility, the understanding that it is impossible to have genuine communication and remain the same. To communicate is not only to affect but also to be affected and transformed.

In similar kind, reading is an effort to learn from others, which means also to be affected. Read actively, Dear Reader, as Jean Comaroff from South Africa, Boaventura de Sousa Santos from Portugal, Molefi Kete Asante, Drucilla Cornell and Catherine Walsh from the US, Ngũgĩ wa Thiong'o from Kenya, Walter Mignolo from Argentina, Linda Tuhiwai Smith from New Zealand, Clarissa Jordão from Brazil join Sinfree Makoni from Zimbabwe and Rafael Lomeu Gomes from Brazil in critical conversation beyond their national designations for an urgent understanding of what it means to go beyond the privatization of global power (colonization) into opening the gates for a public understanding and commitment to the task of building conditions for dignity, freedom, health and livable lives.

Lewis R. Gordon

1 Introduction

Sinfree Makoni, Anna Kaiper-Marquez and Bassey E. Antia

This is the third volume from the Global Virtual Forum (GVF), hosted jointly by the Pennsylvania State University, United States; University of Oslo, Norway; and University of the Western Cape as well as Nelson Mandela University, South Africa. The GVF is an existing multi-person global project initiated in 2020 by the African Studies Program at the Pennsylvania State University. The project's focus is to provide equitable access across the globe to decolonial transdisciplinary scholarship grounded in Southern Epistemologies. It accomplishes its mission in three interconnected ways: (i) via virtual weekly forums with scholars and activists; (ii) with publications of the discussions; and (iii) through its itinerant Global Southern Schools, the first of which is organized jointly by the University of Connecticut, United States; the Pennsylvania State University, United States; and Nelson Mandela University, South Africa.

The GVF contributes to current debates on the geopolitics of knowledge, illustrating how scholarship in the Global Norths is partially indebted to diverse traditions of scholarship in the Global Souths. GVF organizers, speakers and participants foster collegiality and intercultural dialogue, using the technologies imposed upon us during the pandemic to our individual and collective advantage. The nature of the GVF is insurgent, democratic and political as it seeks to facilitate and develop global networks born in social and cognitive struggles. Its horizontal organization offers equitable space for sociability and professional development for graduate students, professors at different stages of their careers and non-academics contributing to scholarship from their areas of social and political experiences.

The term 'Global' in the GVF refers to four dimensions. First, it refers to the diverse countries of origin or the regions where the organizers and members of the GVF come from or are based (e.g. Ghana, Zimbabwe, Kenya, South Africa, Sudan, United States, Nigeria, United Kingdom). Second, 'Global' in GVF refers to the diverse regions of the globe where in our regular attendees live and work. Third, 'Global' refers to the plethora of regions where those who access the GVF videos come from (e.g. Norway, Russia, Israel, Kenya, Ukraine, Malta, Sweden, South Africa). This diversity reflects the true global impact of GVF. Finally, the sociocultural and political issues addressed in the presentations are also from diverse parts of the world.

GVF's series of volumes, entitled Global Forum on Southern Epistemologies, are published by Multilingual Matters. Each volume is subsequently turned into a short video using material from the appropriate sessions. Throughout these volumes, we assert that the Souths are not restricted to the geographic South (Lane, 2023; Pennycook & Makoni, 2021). Just as there are centers and peripheries of the Global North, so too are there centers and peripheries in the Global Souths. We pluralize Souths to capture the diversities within the Souths. We further contend that the Global Souths are not geographical locations but instead, orientations, politics and a cluster of ways of thinking. Arguably, neither Northern nor Southern theory is an unambiguously discrete domain. While we should avoid homogenizing the Global Souths, we should concurrently acknowledge that Eurocentric knowledge is also hybridized and is always 'creolized' (Comaroff, this volume).

The first volume in this GVF series (Makoni *et al.*, 2022) is called *Decolonial Voices, Language and Race* while the second volume is entitled *Shades of Decolonial Voices in Linguistics* (2023). In this third volume, entitled *Foundational Concepts of Decolonial and Southern Epistemologies*, we explore the decolonial and Southern epistemological perspectives of 11 seasoned scholars, based on their engagement in seven separate chapters. The seven chapters in this volume are as follows:

- Chapter 2: Jean Comaroff – Theory from the South: Thinking Out Loud About Decolonization
- Chapter 3: Boaventura de Sousa Santos – Epistemologies of the South: Justice Against Epistemicide
- Chapter 4: Molefi Kete Asante – Upending the Inhuman: Decoloniality, Postmodernism and Afrocentricity
- Chapter 5: Ngũgĩ wa Thiong'o – The Politics of Language, Memory and Knowledge
- Chapter 6: Drucilla Cornell and Souleymane Bachir Diagne – uBuntu, Nite and the Struggle for Global Justice
- Chapter 7: Catherine Walsh and Walter Mignolo – Foundational Concepts and Struggles for Dignity and Life
- Chapter 8: Linda Tuhiwai Smith – Decolonizing Methodologies: Research and Indigenous Peoples.

In their respective chapters, the authors explore the nature of peripheralized knowledges and examine how knowledge in the Global Norths is partially indebted to knowledges from the Global Souths. In his chapter, Molefi Asante goes a step further by arguing that knowledge from the Global Souths could be further developed by adopting 'Afrocentric orientation' (this volume) to complement decolonial initiatives.

Text and Knowledge Production in Neoliberal Universities

One objective of the GVF is to challenge the nature of academic production as it is central to the Western scholarly enterprise in neoliberal universities (Deumert & Makoni, 2023). Decolonial scholarship cannot be successfully achieved in the Western academy and in neoliberal universities unless we challenge the notion of what constitutes the 'text' that sits at the center of Western scholarship. In the publications from the GVF, we challenge the ideology of a 'single monologic authorial voice by integrating multiple voices' (Makoni et al., 2023: ii) consistent with our vision of decoloniality and Southernized scholarship. In GVF publications, academic publications are presented in many different formats and modalities. Edited volumes are based on the transcriptions and interactions of each recorded Zoom session including the interactions between the participants and the presenter. However, it is important to note that the automated transcriptions from the recordings often reflected bias against pronunciation and diverse accents that are not standard American English. Non-standard American accents or other varieties of English, such as African English, have long been regarded as 'incomprehensible.' The texts presented in this volume are the outcome of a complex process of listening (the video recorded presentation), transcribing, rereading and re-listening. After this process occurred, we sent these updated transcripts to authors to ensure that what we heard was what they intended.

Along with the transcribed presentations, the chapters also consist of questions and comments made by participants, either orally or via Zoom chat. Songs, poems and other forms of performative interventions were also welcome in our sessions. As we understand them, these forms of intervention contribute to disrupting our understandings of (monologic) academic texts and reframe what is considered as 'legitimate text.' By including these diverse contributions, 'the text makes visible the multidirectionality of conversations and challenge the linearity of texts' (Deumert & Makoni, 2023: 7). Finally, in addition to the multidirectionality and polyphonic nature of the conversational chapters, each volume is multimodal as it is accompanied by a link to a short video consisting of the highlights from the recorded sessions with the contributors. These additions further disrupt conceptions of academic text being in one language and one modality.

Contributions of Volume Three to the Exploration of Global and Philosophical Movements

A unique feature of Volume 3 is that it brings together some of the most established scholars and political activists who have researched and written about global decoloniality and Southern epistemologies over an extended period of time, and who have systematically explored the complex relationships between their respective ideas. In this volume, we establish a dialogue between the different authors' positions on decoloniality and Southern epistemology and explore implications of their stances on the politics of knowledge production. For example, recent past discussions about decolonization were motivated by students from demonstrations related to *#Rhodes Must Fall*, *#Fees Must Fall*, *Black Lives Matter*, *Idle No More* and *Missing and Murdered Indigenous Aboriginal Women* (Shilliam, 2022). These movements and social struggles, which de Sousa Santos might say are based on 'different ways of knowing,' brought attention to global issues related to social justice and played a critical role in bringing scrutiny to the nature of social and intellectual production, particularly in universities.

The struggles spurred by these movements are global in nature, as is evident in the following quote from Linda Tuhiwai Smith in which she provides a global context to social movements:

> It's not just what some of us here do, or colleagues in South Africa do, or colleagues in Malaysia do. It's what all of us have to do because the system that we're trying to question and critique and transform is a global system that circulates ideas through a whole range of both obvious and mysterious academic processes. (Linda Tuhiwai Smith, this volume)

Even further, Molefi Asante argues that while these movements draw on postmodernism and decoloniality, they cannot succeed without an assertive 'Afrocentricity' that enables individuals to deal with the powerful 'Pan-European Academy.' Pan-Africanism provides decoloniality with an explanation of how action may be affected, which is a prerequisite if decoloniality as an enterprise is to succeed. Even though Asante does not use the terms Global Norths and Global Souths, he predicates his analysis on Chinweizu Ibekwe's idea of the 'Pan-European Academy' (see, for example, Ibekwe, 1975), which ignores Africa's achievements and the knowledges produced by the rest of the globe. The 'truncated sense of history' (Asante, this volume) in scholarship, dominated by the 'Pan-European Academy,' leads us to not raise any questions about knowledge before Homer and the Greeks. He urges us to ask: If you place Homer around 800 BCE (before the Christian era), then it is reasonable to pose the question of what was happening prior to 800 BCE? Asante argues that the pyramids were completed around 2600 BCE and, thus, go back much further than does Homer's *The Iliad* and *The Odyssey*. This argument highlights that the historical knowledge surrounding Africa and African history go back much further than what is assumed if one only sees African knowledge through European lenses.

While the 'Pan-European Academy' ignores other types of knowledge, such as 'non-Western knowledge,' the latter has had an impact on ways of knowing widely utilized in the Global Norths and has have had beneficial impacts on Western science. For instance, quarantines were widely used by Indigenous peoples to protect themselves from the colonizers who carried diseases (de Sousa Santos, this volume). Local knowledge also enabled the imperial West to accomplish major feats. For example, the pilot who guided Vasco da Gama across the Indian Ocean was of Indian origin (wa Thion'go, this volume). Among other major navigational contributions of the Global Souths to humanity are the African inventions of writing, ink and paper.

African philosophies examined in this volume include *uBuntu* and *Nite*. Ubuntu is a pan-African concept with variants in different languages and geographical regions across the African diaspora, particularly in Brazil (Makoni & Severo, 2017). According to *uBuntu*, an individual cannot be separated from their local context (Souleymane, this volume). The *Nite* philosophy of Wolof (Cornell & Souleymane, this volume) represents the cooperative accomplishments of humanity together. African philosophies, such as *uBuntu* and *Nite*, are relevant not only to Senegal, South Africa or the African diaspora, but globally as well, by providing us with a critical understanding of what it means to be human in local and global contexts.

Recently, as part of its engagement to restore the art looted by colonial troops in Africa and proudly exhibited in the national museums, France has initiated the return of some of the stolen artifacts to Africa. These artifacts reflect the impact of the Global Souths on the Global Norths, and their force was manifested in these museums. Another important aspect of African philosophies relevant to the global world is the opportunity they provide to think differently about our opportunities. This notion of opportunity proved to be necessary in the COVID-19 context, which we globally experienced, albeit quite differently. In other words, rather than focusing on the impotence of individualism in the face of ethnicity, *uBuntu and Nite* are relevant to the contemporary world as they enable us to face contemporary challenges by concentrating. on protecting not only humanity, but all lives on earth.

Afrocentricity, Decoloniality, Southern Theory and Epistemologies of the South

Critical differences exist among 'Afrocentricity,' 'decoloniality,' 'Southern Theory' and 'Epistemologies of the South'. In contradistinction to Epistemologies or Theories of the South that look at the South beyond a specific geographic space, Afrocentricity places Africa at the center of the universe rather than on the margins as is argued in decolonial initiatives. Jean Comaroff's position (this volume) is compatible with that of Molefi Asante's position on rethinking these margins. They both ascribe to the view that Africa is not at the 'old margins,' as these 'old margins' have become the centers of innovation reflecting the complex relations between the North and South. This process where old centers are the new loci of innovation has been going on for some time, but has been rarely acknowledged. According to Comaroff, theory making in Theories of the South is multilateral rather than pluriversal as Walter Mignolo (this volume) suggests. That is, multilateral theories from diverse localities converge.

Afrocentricity re-examines knowledge from the standpoint of Africans as subjects, not as victims on the margins of Europe, on the periphery of China, or on the cusp of 'something else.' In an activist orientation, African people, like other Indigenous peoples, interrogate themselves, their history and their conditions as shaped historically and materially, and they approach this from an agentic point of view. Afrocentric scholars look at African people as agents and not mere spectators to knowledge (Asante, this volume). It is when Africans and other former colonized peoples are framed as agentive, that we begin to appreciate the diversity of the knowledge they produce, knowledge that cannot be captured by Western Frameworks (de Sousa Santos, this volume). Afrocentricity is compatible with Epistemologies of the South because, according to Asante (this volume), Afrocentricity challenges all different forms of racism, oppression and repression and is founded on mutual respect of all people. This is in stark contrast to decoloniality, which is confined to a critique of colonization. Further, Linda Tuhiwai Smith (this volume) would argue that decolonization, like white feminism, does not adequately address issues of race or racism. Yet even when decolonization and white feminism do critique race and racism, Tuhiwai Smith argues that decolonization needs to avoid the weakness of critical approaches which are good at critique (some of which are not generative) but are inadequate in outlining what to do about the problem and enumerating the solutions.

Within this volume, Asante brings together issues of decoloniality and Afrocentricity. He argues that the idea of decoloniality is not sufficient on its own; it requires the notion of Afrocentricity. That decoloniality in Africa requires Afrocentricity makes decoloniality in Africa unique and distinct from other decolonial initiatives across the globe. According to Asante, when European statues, such as the Rhodes statue at the University of Cape Town and other European epistemes, are taken down, it becomes necessary to establish frameworks and epistemes that can be used to analyze African lives in a manner that retains African agency. Understanding the African past in ways that capture African agency is necessary because the intervention of colonialism pre-empted Africans' development of their own ways of understanding, interrogation of their own histories and the advancement of their own epistemes. Some of Africa's intellectual orientation was lost through epistemicide; thus, decolonization in such cases entails revival or reactivation of intellectual and communicational orientations that were suppressed, lost or glossed over by colonization. A revival of these intellectual orientations can, in part, be created using 'non-extractivist methodologies' predicated upon Epistemologies of the South (de Sousa Santos).

According to Boaventura de Sousa Santos, in non-extractivist methodologies the objective is to create subjects and not objects. Participants are treated as historical subjects or protagonists who are holders of knowledge. Ogunnaike (2020) illustrates that even though there was wide-spread epistemicide, traditional of ways of knowing in Sufism and Ife (two West African Intellectual Traditions) have remained vibrant. Comaroff (this volume) argues that some traditions have been retained, so epistemicide has not been as totalizing as one might initially be inclined to believe. It is, however, important to recall that these traditions, such as beliefs in witchcraft, while still retained have been altered by colonization. Similarly, even though Indigenous languages survived colonization, the form, status and functions they took were altered through a process of what Meeuwis (2023) refers to as 'linguistic gentrification'.

While an Afrocentric approach can be adopted even by non-Africans when dealing with non-White contexts, for Tuhiwai Smith, non-Māori cannot adopt a Kaupapa Māori framework. The best that can happen for non-Māori when using Kaupapa Māori is to be non-principal investigators. Unlike non-Māori researchers, Māori researchers have more responsibility when carrying out research among Māori because they cannot walk away from their own communities like white researchers can.

Other contributors of the volume focus their arguments on the impacts of colonization and argue that there is no region, no culture, no nation today that has not been affected by colonialism and its aftermath – 'colonialism is not over, it is all over' (Walter Mignolo, this volume). Indeed, Mignolo argues that modernity could be considered a product of colonialism. According to Ngũgĩ wa Thiongo (this volume), an African Renaissance should or can only take place with African languages at the center. Thus, decolonization needs to involve intellectuals rethinking their own roles, as well as those of the state, in placing a premium on language policies and challenging tendencies toward the hierarchization of languages. Such shifts lend toward the establishment of networks and emphasize the interconnections between languages.

For wa Thiong'o, the critical issue is not whether coloniality, decoloniality or post-coloniality should be used as analytical heuristics; instead, the critical issue is the relationship between decoloniality and the role of language. He argues that African literary production should be carried out in African languages and in his own writing, not only did he switch to writing in Gikuyu, but he also is currently translating some of his earlier novels into Gikuyu. These include *A Grain of Wheat* (1967), *Weep Not, Child* (1964) and *Petals of Blood* (1977), which capture the Land and Freedom Movement struggles (popularly known as *Mau Mau*). Although the arguments made by other contributors in this volume have implications on issues about language, Ngũgĩ wa Thiong'o explicitly addresses issues about language. His work is neo-Whorfian, particularly since Whorf too was driven by the belief that much is lost by ignoring the worldview embodied in languages other than the 'standard Average European' (John Joseph, personal communication May 8, 2023) He does not only argue for the use of African languages in writing, but sees language as constructing memory. Ontologically, even though he argues for the use of African languages, he argues that every language plays a key role as part of an orchestra, with 'each language having its own musicality.'

The nature of colonialism and decolonization

Colonialism was both an aberrant and a violent process (de Sousa Santos, this volume), and Europe remains one of the most violent continents on the planet. In the 20th century, in two European wars, the so-called 'World Wars,' 78 million people were killed. In Mozambique alone, about 250,000 people were killed because of allyship with Portugal against Germany in Tanzania. Fighting occurred in Asia as well including Hiroshima. The Americas were not a battlefront, but the US, Canada and parts of South America provided combatants. Colonialism, as both Mignolo and de Sousa Santos contend, is not a thing of the past. Instead, according to Asante, only 'historical colonialism' is a thing of the past.

Despite its violent nature, decolonization calls for a heightened awareness varies in geospatial and politico-theoretical terms (Comaroff, this volume; Deumert & Makoni, 2023). For example, the debate surrounding decolonization in England is significantly different from the one 'catching fire' in the United States. In the United States, the debate has been linked to issues about social justice, and more recently, issues about reparations. It draws on self-critical discourses 'and embattled universes of campus politics and activism' (Comaroff, this volume).

The nature of decolonization is also complicated by differences depending on the discipline in question. For example, the nature of decolonization in literature, music, classics and physics varies substantially. There is, therefore, no uniform way in which decolonization manifests itself across different disciplines and geopolitical spaces, with some disciplines themselves being products of colonization. Calls for decolonization manifest differently and at times in unexpected ways. For example, Britain's exit from the European Union led to demands for national sovereignty in Scotland. Brexit, therefore, according to Comaroff (this volume), heightened awareness of the nature of 'internal colonization' of Scotland by England.

Despite differences in the ways that decolonization is carried out in diverse disciplines and geopolitical sites, all decolonization calls for heightened awareness of the degree to which Western-academic knowledge, which circulates in universities in the Global Souths and Global Norths, is a product of colonialism (Bhambra & Holmwood, 2021). Further, the calls for decolonization translate into a search for alternative sources of knowledge, alternative ways of knowing, that include knowledge from the Global Souths and minoritized communities (de Sousa Santos, this volume). For Tuhiwai Smith (this volume), the search for alternative frameworks, which she refers to as 'active paradigms of knowing,' or what de Sousa Santos calls 'alternative sources of knowledge,' become important when seeking to carry out research within one's own community, as one cannot escape the potential consequences of the impact of one's research.

The first discipline to be seriously involved in decolonization debates is anthropology is not unexpected, as anthropology is 'a handmaiden of colonialism' (Comaroff, this volume). It is necessary to decolonize anthropology from within 'because the discipline is entrapped in a form of liberal humanism that fuels "ethnographic sentimentalism"' (Jobson, 2020: 261), and fails to address challenges of the current moment – i.e. 'authoritarian rule, racial inequality, pandemic climatic catastrophe' (Comaroff, this volume). Because we are all affected by colonialism, even the formerly colonized cannot escape the impact of colonization in their disciplines. The notion of a discipline itself might be a colonial way of organizing knowledge and needs urgently to be reviewed (Gordon, 2006).

Drawing on these various debates, philosophies and ontologies, the seven chapters comprising this volume consider different dimensions of knowledges born in the struggle, and they serve to plot the contributors within the cartography of activist decolonial scholarship.

Chapter Summaries

In Chapter 2, 'Theory from the South: Thinking Out Loud About Decolonization', Jean Comaroff calls for recognition that what was considered 'old margins' of knowledge production were actually 'new frontiers,' as much critical insight about the world has come from former colonial 'peripheries.' Comaroff argues that as former peripheries become places where new relations between capital and labor work themselves out, the North seems to be lagging behind, taking on many of the features associated with postcolonies. By reflecting on other Southern theorists' work, such as that by Raewyn Connell and Boaventura de Sousa Santos, and exploring how these authors' theories relate to her own, Comaroff draws on personal experiences in South Africa and Kenya to explore crucial questions regarding epistemologies, theories and the necessary rethinking of complex dualities of Northern and Southern relationships.

Boaventura de Sousa Santos, in Chapter 3, 'Epistemologies of the South: Justice Against Epistemicide', discusses two of his books: *Epistemologies of the South: Justice Against Epistemicide* (2014) and *The End of the Cognitive Empire* (2018). Drawing from these texts, he examines epistemological, methodological and pedagogical issues within frameworks of the Global Souths to argue that there is no global social justice without global cognitive justice and that the global understanding of the world far exceeds the Western understanding of the world. Noting that the destruction of knowledge, or 'epistemicide,' takes place in research and writing, he contends that Epistemologies of the South is the third paradigm of knowledge production in recent history and is vital in creating non-extractivist approaches to scholarly practices.

In Chapter 4, 'Upending the Inhuman: Decoloniality, Postmodernism and Afrocentricity', Molefi Asante employs Afrocentricity, an ethic of relations that views social phenomenon from an African perspective and asserts the equal value of a multiplicity of human possibilities and the existence of many centers. Asante argues that (1) the racial ladder must be destroyed as it distorts homo sapiens' reality and (2) that the racial ladder has supported most European constructions of knowledge by ignoring Africa and African achievements. These propositions he finds immensely problematic; he asserts that there is an abundance of productive information that has come, and continues to come, from African perspectives of knowledge and truth. Drawing on these arguments, Asante explores concepts of postmodernism and postcolonialism, and discusses how these concepts both connect to and contradict aspects of Afrocentrism – aspects that are evident in both past and present struggles of gender, race and genocide.

In Chapter 5, 'The Politics of Language, Memory and Knowledge', Ngũgĩ wa Thiong'o focuses on the centrality of language in decolonization and the constraints, as well as the freedoms, that languages provide. By critiquing his own use of English, he pleads for the re-centering multiple languages in literature, such as in his own recent work written in Gikuyu. Further, exploring languages of literature and policies of languages in countries, such as his own country of Kenya, wa Thiong'o advocates not only for the use of African languages, but for all languages, for as he contends, 'Every language has its own unique musicality... No instrument's musicality is less than that of another.' Thus, it is a gross simplification to only frame wa Thiong'o as solely pro-African languages when instead, this quotation highlights a more complex understanding of the relationship between all languages (inclusive of English).

Drucilla Cornell and Souleymane Bachir Diagne look into humanist African approaches of Nite and uBuntu in Chapter 6 of this volume, 'uBuntu, Nite and the Struggle for Global Justice'. They open by examining the Wolof concept of *Nite*, or the process of becoming human. They link this concept with that of *uBuntu* assert the critical need for a politics of humanity, a politics that involves not only protecting human life, and protecting all lives on earth. Connecting their work to the history of South Africa's *uBuntu* Project, and situating the tenants of this project in timely social justice movements such as abortion and the massacre of black men in the US, the authors contend that *uBuntu* and *Nite* provide an understanding of the dynamism of our engagement in bringing new ways of being human into our social reality.

Chapter 7, 'Foundational Concepts and Struggles for Dignity and Life' by Catherine Walsh and Walter Mignolo, reflects on how they came to understand and use the concepts of 'coloniality' and 'decoloniality' in their own work. They connect past and current histories of coloniality to movements such as decolonizing universities, the destruction of the Amazon rainforest and the inequitable global impacts of the COVID-19 pandemic, to ask key questions of how to sow life in these current times of death and how to plant re-existence in these times of de-existence. Further, they use current social justice movements to ask, 'What does decoloniality offer to those who seriously want to engage with it, in body and soul?' Throughout the chapter, the authors argue that while coloniality continues to permeate our existence, decoloniality teaches us how to learn to unlearn in order to relearn.

In the final chapter of this volume, 'Decolonizing Methodologies: Research and Indigenous Peoples', Linda Tuhiwai Smith calls for the continued fight to decolonize methodologies, theory, institutions and society. In her outline of the new 2021 edition of her renowned book, *Decolonizing Methodologies*, she describes the 20 new global projects and new introduction that the updated edition encapsulates. Moreover, she draws on issues such as racism in publishing, feminism in societies such as the Māori in New Zealand, racial inequities further brought to light during the COVID-19 pandemic, and links between religion and colonization, to argue for the continued need to expand on concepts and practices of global decolonization both within and beyond the academy.

Conclusion

Epistemologies of the South and Southern theory can be broadly situated in postcolonial or decolonial studies, and seek to accomplish comparable objectives. However, de Sousa Santos is reluctant to use either term, preferring instead the term *Epistemologies of the South* because he understands that colonialism is not the only matrix of domination in our world. The other two matrixes of domination are capitalism and patriarchy, which may be occluded if you use the term *decoloniality*. Asante (this volume), like de Sousa Santos, expresses reservations about using the terms *postcolonialism* and *decoloniality*. He feels the term *postcolonialism* is inappropriate because, 'We are not "post" to anything yet.' Asante posits that the term *decolonization* is inadequate unless it is complemented by Afrocentricity. Other scholars in this volume, wa Thiong'o and Tuhiwai-Smith, adopt a different perspective than that of Asante and de Sousa Santos and feel that the notions of colonization and decolonization are pertinent to their work. For wa Thiong'o, more so than for Tuhiwai-Smith, language is central to decolonization. The main difference between Tuhiwai-Smith and Comaroff lies in the significance that they attach to indigeneity. For Tuhiwai-Smith, indigeneity is central to the issues she seeks to address and develop, such as the development of Indigenous research methods as part of her strategy to decolonize scholarship. Comaroff warns against the danger of romanticization of indigeneity and explains that indigeneity on its own cannot resolve social problems. She further asserts that the knowledge in the Global North is creolized due to the impact of the South on the North.

As discussed above, this volume offers a unique assemblage of conversations with some of the most prominent scholars and political activists who have been concerned with issues of postcolonialism, decoloniality, Theories of the South and Epistemologies of the South. The readers will notice the thematic overlaps in the approaches of the different contributors to this volume while also noticing the distinct differences in each chapter's arguments. We hope that the careful editorial decisions we made help the readers develop a nuanced understanding of the similarities and differences in perspectives and epistemological imaginaries of the contributors. It is our wish that the contributions in this volume will inspire those engaged in and committed to the development of diverse and inclusive ecologies of knowledges.

References

Bhambra, K. and Holmwood, J. (2021) *Colonialism and Modern Social Theory.* Chichester: Wiley.
de Sousa Santos, B. (2014) *Epistemologies of the South: Justice Against Epistemicide.* New York: Routledge.
de Sousa Santos, B. (2018) *The End of the Cognitive Empire: The Coming of Age of Epistemologies of the South.* Durham, NC: Duke University Press.
Deumert, A. and Makoni, S. (eds) (2023) *From Southern Theory to Decolonizing Sociolinguistics: Voices, Questions and Alternatives.* Bristol: Multilingual Matters.
Gordon, L. (2006) *Disciplinary Decadence: Living Thought in Trying Times.* New York: Routledge.
Ibekwe, C. (1975) *The West and the Rest of Us: White Predators, Black Slavers, and the African Elite.* London: Random House.
Jobson, R. (2020) The case for letting anthropology burn: Sociocultural anthropology in 2019. *American Anthropologists* 122 (2), 259–271.
Lane, P. (2023) From silence to silencing? Contradictions and tensions in language revitalization. *Applied Linguistics 2023: XX/XX: 1–20.* https://doi.org/10.1093/applin/amac075
Makoni, S. and Severo, C. (2017) An Integrationist perspective on African philosophy. In A. Pable (ed.) *Critical Humanist Perspective the Integrational Turn in Philosophy of Language and Communication* (pp. 63–77). New York: Routledge.
Makoni, S., Madany-Saá, M., Antia, B.E. and Gomes, R.L. (eds) (2022) *Decolonial Voices, Language and Race.* Bristol: Multilingual Matters.
Makoni, S., Severo, C., Abdelhay, A., Kaiper-Marquez, A. and Milojičić, V. (2023) *Shades of Decolonial Voices in Linguistics.* Bristol: Multilingual Matters.
Meeuwis, M. (2023) Linguistic gentrification: The Baptist missionary Society and Bobangi (1882–1940). *Afrikanistik Aegyptologie.* See http://nbn-resolving.de/urn:nbn:de:0009-10-56594
Pennycook, A. and Makoni, S. (2021) *Innovations and Challenges to Applied Linguistics from the Global South.* New York: Routledge.
Shilliam, R. (2022) Black bodies. In S. Makoni, M. Madany-Saá, B.E. Antia and R.L. Gomes (eds) *Decolonial Voices, Language and Race* (pp. 68–83). Bristol: Multilingual Matters.

2 Theory from the South: Thinking Out Loud About Decolonization

Jean Comaroff

Jean Comaroff is the Alfred North Whitehead Professor of African and African American Studies and Anthropology at Harvard University, and Honorary Professor at the University of Cape Town. She was educated at the University of Cape Town and the London School of Economics. Until 2012, she was the Bernard E. and Ellen C. Sunny Distinguished Service Professor of Anthropology as well as Director of the Chicago Center for Contemporary Theory. Her research, primarily conducted in southern Africa, has focused on the interplay of capitalism, modernity and colonialism, with emphasis on the politics of knowledge, the task of theorizing the contemporary world from beyond its hegemonies. Her writing has covered a range of more specific topics: religion and ritual, medicine, and magic; politics, law and crime; and democracy and difference. Publications include *Body of Power, Spirit of Resistance: The Culture and History of a South African People* (1985); *Beyond the Politics of Bare Life: AIDS and the Global Order* (2007); with John L. Comaroff, *Of Revelation and Revolution* (vols. l [1991] and ll [1997]); *Ethnography and the Historical Imagination* (1992); *Millennial Capitalism and the Culture of Neoliberalism* (2001); *Law and Disorder in the Postcolony* (2006); *Ethnicity, Inc.* (2009), *Theory from the South, or How Euro-America is Evolving Toward Africa* (2012), *The Truth About Crime: Sovereignty, Knowledge, Social Order* (2016); *The Politics of Custom: Chiefship, Capital, and the State in Contemporary Africa* (2018); and (with George Paul Meiu) *Ethnicity, Commodity, In/Corporation* (2020).

Jean Comaroff

It is interesting to consider debates about decolonization in relation to *Theory from the South* because the latter covers similar ground, and in a similar spirit, but in ways that some people find tellingly different. Much recent mobilization around the question of decolonizing knowledge, the disciplines and the University – at least, in the UK and Europe – was spurred by critical intervention on the part of students from the South. Most immediately, it emerged out of campus protests in South Africa in 2015, out of *Rhodes Must Fall, Fees Must Fall*, a movement that sought actively to determine what it meant to decolonize the university as a key site of social and intellectual reproduction.

One of the conversations sparked by these events took place in the Department of Anthropology at Cambridge; it set out to examine what it might mean, in practical terms, to decolonize a discipline. A special edition of *The Cambridge Journal of Anthropology* (2018) was dedicated to the spirited debates that ensued. It was not coincidental that this critique began in anthropology – long viewed as a special beneficiary of colonial knowledge – but similar anguished arguments soon followed elsewhere: in literature, music, classics, Science, Technology & Society, even physics (see Crease *et al.*, 2019). In their introduction to the Cambridge collection, Mogstad and Tse (2018: 55) cited *Theory from the South,* noting that decolonization should began with the recognition that what had conventionally been seen as 'old margins' of knowledge production were in fact its 'new frontiers'; that much critical insight about the world in general had been coming from former colonial 'peripheries' and had been doing so for a very long time – albeit largely unacknowledged.

The debate in England was significantly different from the one catching fire in America, especially in respect of what colonization meant and how it should be understood in geospatial and politico-theoretical terms. As the Cambridge collection made clear, colonialism was regarded in the UK as a structural as well as a geographical phenomenon. Thus 'Europe' was not necessarily synonymous with the metropole for, as a continent, it had seen internal empires, historic centers and peripheries, its own Norths and Souths; there is actually a publication called *From the European South: Journal of the Postcolonial Humanities*, founded in 2016, on whose advisory board I serve. These imperial dynamics have long been evident in Britain, where empire starts at home, as it were. As was highlighted during Brexit, processes of colonization occur at varying, interconnected scales, one scaffolded on another: exit from Europe, itself pursued in the name of reclaiming national sovereignty, even global imperial stature, set in motion pressures in Scotland and Ireland for *internal* decolonization, for 'dis-uniting' the Kingdom. Similar tensions exist within other nation states in the EU (like Spain and Italy), not to mention between the Union's centers and peripheries, as the crisis over 'Grexit' (the Greek precursor to the Brexit saga) revealed.

The approach adopted here – like the one we develop in *Theory from the South* – treats colonization, and hence its overcoming, as an inextricable politico-economic and cultural-historic process. And while it has been most fully realized, in modern history, in the geographical South, it is not limited to that hemispheric location (just as settler colonialism can be identified not merely in South Africa, Australia, or New Zealand but in North America and Israel). Theories of decolonization that follow from this kind of approach draw on critical thinking from Euro-America's own internal dislocations *and* from its imperial borderlands – often seeking to put such bodies of thought in conversation with each other, thus to 'shift the geography of reason' (see Gordon, 2019). Here we might think of the dialogue fostered, say, between the legacy of Marx, Lenin, Luxemburg, or Gramsci (the last, raised in Sardinia, and often dubbed a 'thinker from the South;' (Conelli, 2019: 234) and subaltern and postcolonial theorists, like Cesaire, Fanon, Said, Chakrabarty or Mbembe. In the effort to understand modern colonialism and dismantle its hegemonic grip on the production and reproduction of social thought, this approach seeks both to relocate received traditions of critical theory-making, treating them as traveling theories, to be repurposed in Southern locations (Salem, 2021; Srivastava & Bhattacharya, 2012) and to 'creolize' them in an engagement with analytical traditions and epistemologies arising on the margins of the imperial outreach of capitalist modernity (Gordon, 2014; de Sousa Santos, 2018).

So, rather than seeking estrangement through confrontation with some form of radical alterity – with radical difference from the outside (Indigenous ontologies, or 'non-modern' discourses, long suppressed (Mignolo, 2012; Viveiros de Castro, 2013)), such approaches work with multiple methods of estrangement and defamiliarization *within* an expanded understanding of Europe, located in the larger force field of empire. This is a task that proceeds, de Sousa Santos (2001: 193) notes, 'by excavating the ruins of the marginalized, suppressed or silenced traditions upon which Eurocentric modernity built its own supremacy' on a worldwide scale.

In the US, as many of us know, the debate has been somewhat different. Here I speak both from anthropology and African Studies, and also more generally. In this context there has been a very much more assertive effort to insert decolonization into the American experience, past and present; to interpret deepening generational and ethno-racial differences as symptoms of histories of enslavement, incarceration and internal colonialism. In anthropology, some younger critics accuse the discipline of being entrapped in a form of a liberal humanism that fuels 'ethnographic sentimentalism' (Jobson, 2020: 261) and an inability to engage the urgencies of the current moment – authoritarian rule, racial inequality, pandemic and climatic catastrophe. Such a world demands new analytical priorities that proceed from a radical humanism – though the shape of the latter remains somewhat under-specified; as do the social and material roots of galloping global inequality, the loss of viable work and the ever more destructive swathe cut across the globe by neocolonial capitalism.

In the US, then, decolonization is widely framed as a domestic matter, focused on self-critical discourses and disciplines, and the embattled universe of campus politics and activism. It should be noted, too, that, within anthropology, this concern is hardly news. Though it has always claimed to estrange Western ways, the discipline has been accused – at least since the 1970s (Asad, 1975; Mafeje, 1976) – of being the handmaid of European empire, of producing scholarly capital by objectifying peoples of the South and of commodifying their knowledge and modes of life. From this perspective, if the discipline is to exist at all, it should become the preserve of the colonized. And this holds good for other, related areas – like non-Western Area Studies, long the project of Northern scholars, for whom Southern knowledge was too precious to be entrusted to Indigenous scholars. While agonistic debate now rages among liberal white scholars about the pressure to hand back fields like African Studies to black colleagues, the Kenyan-based scholar, Mukoma wa Ngũgĩ (2021), has argued that the very existence fields like the 'self-rewarding African Studies Industrial Complex' is anathema, producing 'Africanists (black and white) wearing intellectual black face' – far removed from the conditions of actual life and thought on the continent itself.

Some have also argued that in contexts like North America, where the category of the colonized has been used to refer to descendants of chattel slavery and contemporary carceral populations, 'decolonization' has come to be used as a metaphor for an expanding range of struggles for social justice. Thus, Tuck and Yang (2012) suggest that, especially in settler colonial contexts, the term should be reserved for the repatriation of Indigenous land and life, lest it become an empty signifier, an omnibus synonym for 'emancipation.' The under-specification of the term has also evoked other objections such as for Jia Hui Lee (2021: 126), who writes of Tanzanian rodent scientists, decolonization needs to be distinguished from provincialization. These Tanzanian experts struggle for equity of participation and recognition in the global science project on which they are working and with which they strongly identify. They do not associate themselves with 'African science' as a unique, Indigenous form of knowledge. Rather, they want their own African contribution to general, co-produced modernist science to be accorded the power and access that accrues to the production of universal knowledge. For them, if 'decolonization' is to mean anything, it would involve being able to take charge of scientific knowledge production – not to be associated with a realm of hybrid, alternative or borderland discourse.

That is the field of argument, it seems to me, in light of which *Theory from the South* has to be reread now, ten years after its publication. Depending on how you see it, the book is just another text from people who grew up as white elites – albeit, in Bourdieu's terms, the 'dominated fraction of the dominant class' – on colonized terrain, and who now speak from elite university contexts in the North. From that perspective, the kind of theory-making that it advocates remains concerned with general, if critical approaches, approaches to the making and unmaking of the modern world and to the history of colonial capitalism – is and thus hopelessly universalist, Euro-centric; it has had its day and it needs itself to be decolonized.

To be sure, our position rejects the idea that there are independent 'communal' or Indigenous 'outsides' to capitalist modernity that promise some form of rescue from our common global predicament – although there certainly are margins, resistant local worlds and creolized peripheries that generate friction and critical tension (Comaroff & Comaroff, 2012: 11). In fact, the argument in *Theory from the South* starts from a very similar position to calls for decolonization: that modern hegemonies have always presumed that knowledge production, the nature of truth, the genesis of theory and the means of civilization are located in the North, while the objects or inquiries, experiments and expropriations are to be found in the South. The latter has been the source of data but has not been recognized – by those who speak in the universal voice – as the source of theory-making or knowledge production. But a key difference that we emphasized in *Theory from the South* is that the relationship between North and South is a dialectical, reciprocally transforming one – albeit also unequal in determination. In fact, the very knowledge that emerges as part of the hegemony in and of the North, in its institutions of higher learning and within its disciplines, is often appropriated from the south, plagiarizing or mimicking the insights of its theorists. For the South is still treated simply as a source of extractable raw material – very much in parallel with the workings of the material economy.

In this regard, let me underline something I said above: we do not regard North and South, in the first instance, as literal geophysical locations. We are talking here, above all, of a kind of relationship of oppositions; for linguists, it's a kind of a deictic relationship, a set of structured contrasts that takes shape in use, in relation to a particular positioned speaker. It's a relationship of here and there, center and periphery, not necessarily literally grounded in any one place, although of course, in the construction of the modern world at large, it has an all too grounded colonial history. The contrast between North and South, moreover, occurs at various levels of geopolitical structure: Europe has its South, as does the US or Italy. England has a center and a periphery, its North and South. What we are talking about when we speak of theory from the South is 'ex-centric' knowledge, to use Homi Bhabha's (1994: 6) term; the production of thought, expertise and information from what the North takes to be its margins – by those external to the hegemonic core of the global order, of modernity, of the planetary economy. This includes the worldly understanding of those who look at the center from its outsides, from its constitutive margins –margins also of class, gender, sexuality. That kind of 'ex-centricity' has bred its own sort of critical awareness, what some have called Poor Theory, Theory from Below or Theory from the Margins. It is from here that significant revelatory insight in the contemporary order of things is coming, although that knowledge and insight is often appropriated by metropolitan discourse. We make this argument against the background also of the fact that modernity *itself* has always been a multilateral co-production. The vantage of the colonized world, or the postcolony is not that of a disconnected outside or a resistant Indigenous ontology, but another take on modernity, albeit one shaped by local cultural and material heritage. While it might be experienced as vested in 'tradition' or 'difference,' these are modern, objectifying (deictic) constructs that emerge when local worlds are relativized by the biophysical, symbolic and material forces of a violently expanding, encompassing world that seeks 'only to connect.'

All of us come from places variously situated inside an interconnected modern world that is profoundly hybridizing and creolizing, seeking to translate and commodify, if not erase difference. This process does not do away with the fact that there are always centers and peripheries, albeit shifting ones, the latter being sublimated domains of knowledge and practice that retain distinctive features – as internal others, as it were. The 'modernizing' process aims to colonize Indigenous consciousness with universal truths, and while it hardly erases prior modes of being in the world, it hardy leaves them unaltered. The making of national imaginaries is a similar process that seeks, but never succeeds in supplanting local grounding and commitment. Modernization euphemizes such imperialism as an act of civilizing, inclusion, enrichment, redemption.

In *Theory from the South*, we argue that this civilizing conceit has become increasingly unsustainable, especially in the late modern world. This is not merely because of the ways in which Europe has been provincialized – increasingly outflanked by the development of non-Western centers of economic, cultural and technical innovation. It is also an effect of the radical globalization of capital and the division of labor as markets have freed themselves from state regulation, as production is outsourced beyond national borders, and as supply chains span the planet. Ever more mobile, competitive capital (these days not merely from Euro-America) has sought out minimally regulated zones of operation for itself in former colonies, places where under-employed populations and hunger for investment spur a readiness to host experimental enterprise. New industrial, technological and financial centers have arisen in the East and South, not merely in China, India, Singapore or Korea, but also in Nigeria or Brazil. Meanwhile, the North has experienced rapid deindustrialization, greater reliance on capricious finance capital, austerity and a host of 'third world' problems from authoritarian governance, joblessness and galloping, racially indexed inequality to crime, pandemics, generational conflict and xenophobia. The deregulation of capitalism on a planetary scale and its insatiable drive for new sites of accumulation have turned to older, friction-free sites as objects of profit-maximization.

In many ways, then, as former peripheries become places where new relations between capital and labor work themselves out, the North seems to be lagging behind, taking on many of the features associated with postcolonies: 'America is a Third World country now,' opined McGirt and Jenkins in September 2020, echoing Ariana Huffington (2011); while former UK Minister for Europe, Denis MacShane, has claimed that 'a political Ebola virus' had insinuated itself into every cell of the body politic of 'banana republic Britain' (2021). Of course, this seeming evolutionary reversal is a result of the effects in the West of falling rates of profit of late modern capitalism, and the dismantling, under the sign of neoliberalism, of government economic regulation, labor protections and the so-called social contract underwritten by the welfare state. Western citizens have been reduced, by such means, to the status of colonial subjects – with the attendant risks of precarity, erosion of citizenship and exposure to violence and corruption.

In the face of *these* historic shifts, it follows – and this is key to our argument in *Theory from the South* – that we have to look to former colonial peripheries for insight into the unfolding of the global order at large. Not only do these 'margins' make evident the innovative, experimental edges of our interconnected planetary economy; and here we insist, contra many theorists of decolonization, that these realities are not matters of epistemology and ideology alone. It also follows, because the contradictions of late modern capitalism are more shamelessly visible along these frontiers, it is often there that the most creative thinking emerges, along with new experiments in social organization, redistribution, labor discipline and cultures of politics. But it follows, too, that these new zones of energy, value production and profit-making are also sites of new kinds of exploitation and colonization. If one of the key insights of writers on *decoloniality* is that this itself cannot be reduced to formal decolonization, being a more insidious process of establishing control of the psyches, cultures and material life-worlds of those regarded as other, then colonization remains an ever present, ongoing possibility. Apart from the fact that many children of empire yearn above all for the riches that the metropole promises but fails to deliver (Ferguson, 2006), the languages of critique and emancipation from overrule emerge from within the belly of the beast, as it were; they are the product of its evident contradictions, incoherences and lies. Often these insights emerge out of the perceived contrast between the present and former local life-worlds. Here Boym's (2001) radical reading of nostalgia is on-point: the affective attachment to a vanished past can quicken critique and just intolerance for a degraded present. At the same time, there is no simple return to the *status quo ante;* no way to roll back the effects of destructive colonial histories to recover the lost world that existed before the Midas touch of an avaricious world. More nuanced understandings are needed of how to work from within the insidious entanglements of the global system we share if we are to envision sustainable forms of collective life.

Sinfree Makoni

Jean, thank you very much for this enlightening talk and for the time that you've spent working on these issues about the South. I would like to engage you in a conversation that may help me to clarify a couple of issues.

Other than your work, there's also the body of work that has been written about *Southern Theory* by Raewyn Connell (2007). So when you were talking, what I was interested in is, if you were to compare your work with that of Boaventura de Sousa Santos and Raewyn Connell, what are the similarities and the differences?

Jean Comaroff

I think there is a good deal of similarity, but also some key contrasts. Raewyn Connell and Boaventura de Sousa Santos set out to do slightly different things, both in relation to each other, and to us. Raewyn's work is really about the kind of social thought that comes from the south as a place – the periphery of European empire – and about its geopolitical subservience to the hegemonic center of universal social knowledge, aka 'Northern Theory.' Her project in the book, *Southern Theory,* is to assemble an alternate 'southern' archive of social thought produced in colonial and postcolonial contexts – from the sociology developed in the provincialized Australian academy, to a rich catalogue of sample ideas and theses of various kinds from Islamic, Indian, African and Latin American intellectuals – scholarly and popular, elite or grassroots. Her approach aims to document plurality; as Connell notes, while she speaks of 'southern theory' in the singular, she does not wish to suggest that there is 'only one global-South point of view.' She seeks to foster a new 'world social science' – one that (in the mode of Clifford Geertz on global culture) is inclusive of many voices.

This is a valuable exercise, but what gives form, identity and social–historical grounding to these diverse exemplars? And in what sense do they qualify as contributors 'southern Theory?' Must it engage the Northern hegemon explicitly? What is it that links the texts of late 19th-century Iranian critics of Western materialism or early 20th-century African denunciations of land dispossession to the artwork of contemporary Indigenous Australians? What exactly *is* social theory here, and what kind of more general conceptual discourse might it generate? How might we use Connell's analysis to address the key question raised in *Theory from the South* about the effect of the 'south' on social theory, *tout court* – 'theory' that is neither confined to a geographical periphery, nor judged by the yardstick of 'universalizing' knowledge; theory that is part of a world-wide conversation about the history of long-distance interactions that have made our unevenly interconnected world. Sociology, surely, must examine the kinds of engagements, entanglements and reciprocal understandings that link the distinct parts of the larger world. And that configure the geopolitics of colonial and postcolonial relations which determine its centers and margins, its Norths and Souths in the first place?

In fact, it is arguable that neither Northern nor Southern Theory is as unambiguously discrete a domain as Connell's perspective suggests. What of the impact of *relative* centers and peripheries in each – those pieces of the North in the South, for instance – like Australia, or the privileged preserves of South Africa? Or those bits of the South in the North, like significant parts of the US? Or Northern Ireland? Australia, like South Africa or North America, is one of those microcosms of North-South relations that contains both, locked in close interdependence, structured by racial capitalism and settler colonialism. But Australia is also positioned on the South-East axis of the global geopolitical map. This is significant in light of an epochal shift occurring in the dominant axis of world power, which is ever less North–South than East–West. We are seeing evidence of this shift in the burgeoning relationship between Africa and China, which is eclipsing former neocolonial relations with Europe. Australia is interestingly situated in this regard: its Euro-centric postcolonial identity is being ever more challenged as it is drawn into the economic orbit of China and the Asian world system (its top three trading partners today are China, Japan and Korea). This is a region of complex economic interdependence and political power play, where imperial ambitions are experimenting with new digital and financial means of exerting control. While it has centers and peripheries, it seems to defy simple spatial dichotomies of North and South, or the kinds of borderlands presumed by the project of decoloniality.

Now, when we come to the question of de Sousa Santos, there's a considerable amount that we share – like the fact that he is writing from Portugal, which after all is on Europe's Southern periphery. It is often said that 'Africa starts at the Pyrenees'; that Portugal and Spain are part of it, at least from the point of view of Northern thinking. I think that what we have in common is a sensibility that comes from being decentered, or if you like, displaced elites (South-in-North and North-in-South). One is intimately aware of the fact – as Said (1982) put it – that culture or theory travels. But both are also continually being creolized, in continuous give-and-take with features from beyond their borders, a creolization both intentional and otherwise. In that sense, again, modernity is always being remade. If, as Latour (1993) would have it, modernity demands a purity of form, then neither the North nor the South has ever been modern. Christianity, capitalism, Marxian theory and a lot else besides have all been reconfigured in Africa, India, Asia and Latin America as part of an expansive, global conversation that goes on despite efforts of European 'civilizers' to colonize the consciousness of their 'unenlightened' subjects. In fact, European knowledge – itself never actually free from hybridization across its own internal divides – has been increasingly cross-fertilized in the discourse-and-practice of actually existing empire; this as its putatively universal truths have been rethought and re-engineered in Southern conditions. It is in this historical process that we find the origin of such creolizations as dependency theory, liberation theology, the historical-cultural criticism of the likes of CLR James, or theories of racial capitalism, which traveled from colonial South Africa to post-colonial Britain via figures like Stuart Hall and on to the US through thinkers such as Cedric Robinson. This process resulted, too, in major reform in defining modern institutions, from the social contract and income distribution (like Brazil's *Bolsa Familia*) to the Environmental Justice Movement or the politics of decolonization. With it has also come the defensive dismissal of such 'bastardized' forms by offended metropolitan hegemons.

De Sousa Santos (2018: 7) seems to be expressing a similar sensibility with his concept of 'southern epistemologies.' He speaks of a 'bottom-up subaltern cosmopolitanism' as counter to the 'epistemicide' of Northern universalism, with its unceasing effort to erase the rich variety of other ways of knowing, other languages of self-representation. As I understand it, this cosmopolitanism, for him, is born of the struggle of marginalized peoples everywhere against, capitalism, colonialism and patriarchy – a dynamic that amounts to an unceasing process of intercultural translation in the form of creolization, mestizaje, decolonization (2018: 1–2).

The aim here is less to replace Northern epistemology: the very notion of elite, disembodied knowledge production needs to be overcome, along with the power hierarchies that underpin it, epitomized in the normative dualism that he calls the 'abyssal line' that separates the North from those it dubs 'ethno-culturally and ontologically inferior' (2018: 8). For Santos, that line fundamentally entraps endogenous critics in the North – even the likes of Foucauldian-inspired feminists – who decry Western Universalist claims and insist on the situated, political quality of all knowledge. For these critics show an enduring commitment to the *a priori* value of self-conscious knowledge production as distinct from popular, intuitive insight that is often pragmatic, even non-secular in form. The epistemologies of the South, he maintains, 'reject epistemological or political ghettos and the incommensurabilities they feed on.' Those who would end cognitive empire must find the emancipatory scripts that are being developed beyond the limits of Western-centric politics and knowledge. Some of these are 'foreign' to Northern thinking, others are 'non-Eurocentric renditions' of concepts like 'law, state, or democracy.'

There is a lot to like in this vision, and there is much overlap with what we lay out in *Theory from the South*. At the same time, the position raises some key questions for me. Above all, I am unsure of how to read the status of de Sousa Santos's argument – is it an 'is' or an 'ought?' His position strikes me as admirable in its rejection of nihilism; this is no small virtue; it seems hardly surprising that current conditions foster a mood of ecological doom and Afropessimism that would in fact render decolonization irrelevant or impossible. Like several other exponents of decoloniality, de Sousa Santos (2018: 2) vests his hope in rescue from outside, in the capacity of Southern alternatives to 'occupy' the space of epistemology with its experimental means, thus, to interrupt the hell-bent politics of knowledge from the North that has fostered catastrophic, world-wide social and governmental collapse. To be sure, this is an appealing stance, though it rides on an investment, perhaps a romance, of a redemptive Southern otherness, at once different and separate enough to radically unsettle the axioms of its occidental counterpart. Note, too, that the disruption envisaged here remains at the level of knowledge systems – perpetuating the very fetishism of 'epistemology' that de Sousa Santos identifies in the North, even in the progressive position of Northern feminists. In all fairness, one should note that many feminist writers have argued strongly for the importance of practical modes of knowing, vested in everyday experience, emotional intelligence and so on (Collins, 1986; Smith, 1987) – i.e. they have advocated precisely the perspective that de Sousa Santos sees as a distinctive virtue of Southern epistemologies.

In fact, despite its appeal, I find hard to translate several features of this argument into actual sociohistorical terms – which is necessary if we are to move, as de Sousa Santos seems to want, beyond traffic in philosophical abstractions. Can one really claim that, other than as an aspirational ideal, Southern cosmopolitanism rejects 'epistemological or political ghettos and the incommensurabilities they feed on'? Such statements would appear to reinforce the dualistic – not to mention, universalizing – qualities held to characterize Western, 'abyssal' thinking. Anyone who has grounded experience of the complex, often divisive politics of building anti-colonial struggles within the orbit of empire knows how plural, agonized and often irreconcilable are experiences of dispossession. And can one view Southern epistemologies merely as emerging out of the struggle of the marginalized against, capitalism, colonialism and patriarchy? These are rather sweeping statements about complicated lived realities that do not readily conduce to homogenous abstractions. While there is overwhelming evidence of the enduring repudiation by colonized peoples of their enslavement, dispossession and alienation, defiance has usually taken a host of particular locally inflected forms that have seldom a matter of all-or-none refusal. Anti-colonial resistance has often simultaneously favored local patriarchs, authoritarian traditionalism and new categories of brokers. It has also sought to indigenize the power of ruling discourses and practices, not least, tapping into the energy and charisma of markets. Colonized societies have often responded, too, to the millenarian appeal of Christian salvation, sometimes for emancipation, often to espouse new kinds of universalism and sectarianism. Many subjects of empire, as de Sousa Santos implies, were appealed to by liberal ideas like democracy and or statehood – sometimes to push them in communitarian directions, sometimes also (as Fanon [1963] foresaw) into predatory forms of bourgeois or ethnic nationalism. To be sure, the worlds invaded by European colonialism were often shaped in important respects by the experience of violent overrule that laid bare the conceits and contradictions of Euromodernity. But these worlds were every bit as complex in structure as their metropolitan counterparts. They might have been more accepting of epistemological variation; after all, colonial governance – epitomized by the divisive logic of apartheid – was frequently invested in reinforcing tribal difference. Yet especially in the wake of two world wars, the Southern universe was also voicing ever more unified anti-imperial sentiments of the sort expressed in independence movements, the Bandung Conference and coordinated opposition to colonialism and neocolonialism 'in all of its manifestations.' (Timossi, 2015). This strikes me as an apt instance of de Sousa Santos's 'subaltern cosmopolitanism.' It suggests a worldly, comparative political sensibility, one that is quintessentially modern in its sense of humane entitlement, of unity-in-difference. But the wider world of Southern modernity also has its own demagogues, its new imperialists and its own rampant forms of 'capitalism with Southern characteristics.'

I am less convinced than many by the potential impact of epistemological otherness on 'cognitive empire,' of the capacity of radical difference to break the hold of entrenched hegemonies and destructive beliefs. This idea has appeal at a time of increasingly evident failure of systems all round, when participatory government is challenged across the world and environment and ecological despoliation seem driven by a blind commitment to infinite expansion. Such a moment calls for radical rethinking. 'What is value?' 'What is growth?' 'What really counts?' 'How do we envisage organizing economy, governance and society in ways that more collaboratively sustainable and inclusive in our overheated global ecology?' The values, principles and technologies of other modes of life, past and present, *can* serve as useful injunctions, even if often more rhetorical than pragmatic. But I am more wary than many Southern theorists of the healing romance of indigeneity, more literally understood. Maybe it's because I grew up in South Africa, where colonialization so brutally forced people into a capitalist economy and into its 'civilizing' project. It doesn't mean that indigeneity is not a strategic position from which marginalized or displaced peoples can voice resistance to conversion or appropriation or make powerful claims for the rights and recognition (Almeida & Kumalo, 2018). Claims to indigeneity often offer a compelling indictment of the violence of dispossession. They also speak from a position of outside-inside that encourages the imagining of alternative modes of existence. But as a mode of social life essentially unaffected by the Midas touch of modernity – of that I remain unconvinced. We are much more concerned, in *Theory from the South*, with the ways in which centers and peripheries are configured within modernity, within its world-wide economic and communicative systems, the global electronic commons and so on. Very few of us can plausibly claim to be situated outside these systems or can realistically think of solving the problems of our world without engaging those entanglements in some way. Also, as I have noted, vast numbers of relatively excluded people crave more direct inclusion within the value-creating possibilities of capitalist modernity, as a basis of survival.

Sinfree Makoni

In your book, you ask the following question: 'What if we posit that, in the present moment, it is the Global South that affords privileged insight into the workings of the world at large?' (Comaroff & Comaroff, 2012: 1). The question that I have for you is philosophical as well as methodological.

When I was rereading your book, I kept asking myself the following question: 'If your personal life story and experiences emerged from East Africa, for example, in what way would you talk about the Global South?' There is a sense in which the account that you are giving is strongly influenced by the internal dynamics of the history of South Africa. So, the intelligible interpretation is that it looks like it's an effort to generalize South Africa's history onto the international scene. What if we play the following epistemological game? You leave South Africa and you grow up in, let's say, East Africa or West Africa. Do you think that you would come to the same conclusion? That is, if the surrounding context, the context in which you grew up, which had a formative influence on you, were different, do you think you would come to the same conclusion then?

Jean Comaroff

It's an interesting question and an important one. Of course, all of us come to theoretical questions from somewhere in particular. As Žižek (n.d.) once put it, nobody exists solely in the universal dimension, although mainstream northern writers and thinkers tend as a matter of course to assume the voice of the universal human subject. The first point to make about the argument of this book in this respect is that there is that there's no Archimedean position from which to relate the story of North-and-South. We are *all* provincial; we all talk from one or another vernacular standpoint though we try and roll back the ethnocentrism to the degree that we can. So, *mea culpa*, I start from Africa, but one could have told the story from Latin America, or India, or China. I've just spent half a year teaching in Singapore, and that offers an interesting counterpart to South Africa: another kind of center on the periphery of the former British Empire, with another perspective on the world. One works from where one finds oneself, and treats that location as an exemplary instance, as one vantage on a shared global system-of-systems that we are all simultaneously co-creating and transforming with different degrees of agency – a bit like the idea of blockchain.

South Africa is interesting because it's in many senses a 'First World-Third World' frontier. It has long been one of the most advanced sites of colonial capitalism, and it remains a huge extractive economy. Many of its key resources are still owned by the descendants of imperial elites, who export a sizable proportion of its profits in the financial, mining, manufacturing, transportation and retail sectors. It was among the last formal colonies in the world, and an audacious experiment in illiberal colonial racism, involving a process of 'modernizing racial domination' (Adam, 1971) that extrapolated the general principles of racial capitalism into to a highly elaborate politico-legal order and accompanying segregationist theology. Mahmood Mamdani (1996) has argued that Apartheid was the iconic form of the 'decentralized despotism' of colonial indirect rule. But for all that, it cannot be treated as a token of an ideal type. It was one case along a spectrum of colonial exemplars, interesting both in its generic and its unique features; it makes clear, among other things, the complexities of trying to generalize about 'the South.'

Now, while Kenya was also a notable instance of British settler colonialism – it was said to had 'some of the richest agricultural soils in the world' – it had nothing like the mineral wealth or complex colonial history of South Africa and did not, in the years of overrule, give rise to a significant industrial economy. If South Africa lost its independent black peasantry to the demands of the labor market, Kenya lacked a significant industrial proletariat in colonial times – and also lacked the making of an African working class, unionization and the overt link to international socialist and communist resistance. In both cases, violent land dispossession helped force African agriculturalists into highly extortionist wage work; in Kenya, this was predominantly farm labor. The epic, eight-year Mau Mau Rebellion, for instance, was played out most intensely in the areas of most voracious land dispossession, involving some ethnic groups and not others. It also mobilized local neo-traditional forms like ritual oathing, albeit creolized with modernist guerilla warfare; hence our point about the hybridity of indigeneity and the ongoing historical dialectic of North and South. While the nature of the Mau Mau Rebellion and its impact on the course of decolonization remains controversial, it was one of Britain's costliest imperial wars in both moral and material terms. In my view, it hastened the end of empire by making plain to the metropole that its violent costs were no longer sustainable in a world coming to terms with the inhuman destruction of World War II.

But like in South Africa, Kenya raised important questions both practical and theoretical about the politics of decolonization: in this instance, about the revolutionary potential of peasantries and their 'weapons' (often discounted by the European left); also, about the complicated interplay of ethno-regional, class-based and national alliances in modern state-making. In South Africa, ethnicity has tended to be subservient to issues of race and class – although, in recent times, its salience there has grown. Why? As we argue in *Theory from the South*, the West has seen the rise of ethno-nationalism across the board, and nation-states in the age of neoliberal globalization have everywhere had increasingly to come to terms with difference. In this, as in many things, Northern states have followed postcolonial polities, like Kenya, even down to the increasingly violent rejection by sectarian groups of the outcomes of democratic national elections. This reflects the fact that the ideal of homogenous nationhood is unsustainable if politico-economic and cultural differences within the imagined community become too wide. In this regard, the North is looking ever more unequal and illiberal, ever more like its own caricatures of 'Banana Republics.' The Kenyan journalist Patrick Gathara captures the spirit of our argument perfectly in a brilliant piece about the storming of the US Capitol on January 6, 2021. The piece is entitled 'Papa Don's failed state: the US as seen from Kenya,' it cites quotes a wry Colombian colleague: 'We haven't had any mobs storming the congress here for several decades.'

There are also other dimensions of the argument I could touch in arguing that Kenya can be seen as a harbinger of things to come in the north. Kenya, as postcolony, has faced a catalogue of economic challenges, especially in the wake of structural adjustment. It contrasts quite sharply with South Africa, which, since the late 19th century, has been a hub of global industrial, mining and agrarian capital. But it should be noted that the South African story is telling precisely because it is still a story of *colonial* capitalism; of global investments that profited from the racialization and subjection of African labor and the massive export of profit to the metropole. What is more, our general argument draws not only on South Africa, but on wider observation of the continent, like the fact that old margins have become new frontiers. Precisely because of historic marginalization, former colonies have become attractive sites as ever-hungry capital seeks out sites of cheap manufacture beyond the West. This is the story of the growth of global sweatshops and commodity chains, but it is also a story about local capacities to develop centers of growth by way of the creative appropriation and redeployment of Northern technologies and techniques. Here Kenya provides cogent examples, like it's widely acknowledged

'Mobile Tech Revolution' (Mengistu & Imende, 2013) that has made Nairobi a hotbed of innovation in the domain of mobile money-transfer systems and other types of software and services (for healthcare, for instance) for mobile devices. Already in 2013, 70% of Kenyan adults transferred money to each other via their mobile phones – the highest percentage of any country on earth, reflecting the explosion of mobile phone usage across many developing countries and the rise of new ways of banking for the formerly unbanked. Kenya and the Swahili Coast are part of the Indian Ocean trade system that dates back to the first century. So, these distinctive local qualities have long been tied into transnational systems of exchange. The long-standing Kenyan penchant for managing communications and mobility also has other recent manifestations – like the success of the country's national airline – this against a background of Africa being one the fastest-growing aviation markets in the world – at least, before the pandemic.

So, were we to start this analysis from East Africa, it would begin with distinctive local features. But as one tracks the articulations of each grounded case to the larger context in which it is situated, with which, if you like, it has been dialectically engaged – one very soon comes upon shared, general forces of determination that have the power to translate local difference into trans local currencies, currencies of conversion at once monetary, linguistic, religious, bureaucratic, governmental, legal. Such as been the imperializing force of European hegemony. And of the making real of categories of South and North, periphery and center, Africa and the World. In this respect, whether one starts from Kenya or South Africa, one lands, theoretically, in a similar place.

Sinfree Makoni

Thank you very much. Rafael, let me hand this over to you so that the audience can come in, and then I'll sum up at the end.

Rafael Lomeu Gomes

Great, thank you. In the chat, Jacqueline Lück asks the following question: In our space scholars are arguing that decolonial scholars spend too much time on critiquing northern knowledges and how it has positioned us instead of working with knowledge in southern contexts. What do you think of this argument?

Jean Comaroff

It would help to know which scholars precisely one is talking about here. I think that most of us here would be hard-pressed to see ourselves, definitively, as either Southern or Northern. Most of us are the product of hemispheric crossings of one kind of another. One does not just flip from one to the other as a totalizing life-world or identity. And one doesn't undergo thoroughgoing demystification by crossing a line: 'Okay, now we have reached a point when the North has revealed that its knowledge is colonizing and ultimately counterproductive – because it is now clear that the

North is facing all the problems that we identified in the colony.' It's facing gross inequality, failing states, rising informal economies, an angry planet that we have not served well. It is facing forms of violence and 'tribalism' that used to be projected onto Southern countries. Even if we were to have this insight, we could not simply be to flip the switch, or say 'We must observe what has been done differently in the South: it is forms of Indigenous knowledge will give us the answer.' We can learn a good deal from those at the margins, but alas, the imperial history of the West is that it has not left much of the world to its own devices. It has tried obsessively to turn all difference into sameness, to draw everyone into its own encompassing megalomania. And while such imperialism never succeeds completely, never erases processes of hybridization and resistance, its destructive path is not simply reversible. In many respects, we all share the same problems now because we have become entangled, we reciprocally constitute each other. This is the other thing. We are entailed, North and South, in each other's problems and we use each other to define ourselves. Opting out, or rebooting is not an option. To disentangle from this dangerous embrace requires all parties having to act, being allowed to act. We each have to understand the role we have played in this visceral engagement in order to radically change it.

Many of us are the products of multiple migrations. As I noted above, Edward Said used to talk about the fact that it's the travelers, the nomads of knowledge production, the persons who have to move, who are displaced from one place to another who develop the kind of estrangement and insight into the world that engenders radical critique. They are predisposed to viewing things as comparable and relative, to picking up on the fact that things (like the workings of capitalism, or the politics of race or gender) can be the same in some respects across regions and contrasting in others, rather than being categorically, ontologically, irretrievably 'self' or 'other.'

Those of us who started from politically, economically, culturally 'ex-centric' places become acutely aware, when we move to the metropole, of the discrepancy between hegemonic claims about the nature of things in the world and the way we have found them to be. These include claims about civilization and development, for instance, or the promise of structural adjustment and expanding markets, or faith in infinite growth. The most incisive critiques and interventions that have been made of the development enterprise (late modernity's 'civilizing mission') are travelling theories, emerging out of the circulation of people and ideas between South to North. This was the origin of dependency theory; how it is that, in the name of growth, peripheralized economies are made cripplingly reliant on rich ones. This too was the provenance of innovative projects aimed at rethinking the disastrous effects of radical economic deregulation and economic polarization across the world. And at reimagining the social contract and redistribution through un/conditional monetary transfers, public assistance and basic income grants. But we should note, also, that there are ways of being critical that are constructive and dialectical, and ways of being critical that merely assert a new kind of hegemony. The danger here is to think that redemption lies simply in turning the world upside down, like those old maps that provocatively put the South in the North and the North in the South, resituating London was down-under and Johannesburg and Delhi at the top. The conceit lies in the spurious notion that that if you flip the map, you get a different world.

Theory from the South argues that you can't just flip the map. We are all implicated in a multilateral world where we are conditions of each other's possibility – if in profoundly complex, multiply-mediated, unequal ways. It seems chimerical – indeed, theological – to seek redemption by way of some form of radically different ontology rather than confronting the anomalies or strangeness within a creolized world. It might be fine as a thought experiment, and perhaps that is what it in intended to be, because as a practical enterprise, it presents insurmountable challenges. That is why so much decolonial advocacy remains at the level of rhetorical invocation. What is more, radically distanced ideas and knowledge often do not travel or translate – the subaltern often cannot speak – precisely because, as Spivak and Guha (1988) famously asserted, they remain marginal among the marginalized in an intricate imperial scheme of things. There are no transparent ways, either, to represent them, to speak on their behalf, despite the claims of various emissaries from across the abyssal line.

Rafael Lomeu Gomes

Thank you. We have a question in the chat box from Desmond Odugu: 'southern theory in its various postures appears to have not only an academic interest but also a political one, committed to undoing the structures of power and violence. Since Southern "theories" are largely products of the same intellectual forces of imperialist "modernity" would you consider theory itself as part of that imperial modernizing project? Would the political commitment of "southern theories" become more viable if we abandoned "theory theorization"– viewed here as a totalizing project of setting up cultural hierarchies?'

Jean Comaroff

That's a great question. It's absolutely crucial. 'What is theory?' is one of the things we try to address in that book. Who makes theory? Who are the theory-making classes? Is it a matter of the 'philosopher and his poor' (Rancière, 2004)? Is it those who have the luxury to think because they don't have to work? Is that our vision of theory? Who are the self-appointed theorists who will ventriloquize from 'the other side of the line?' One of the things we argue in *Theory from the South* is that the fetishism of theory is precisely what we need to get away from. I don't know whether it is the same everywhere, but I have found that many scholars have a real anxiety around the question of 'What is theory.' When they write an essay, or a proposal, their immediate concern is 'What goes into the theoretical section?' Theory-work is perceived as set apart from everyday experience and observation. It is as if one has to learn another language to speak the argot of abstraction, the arcane ritual language of accredited experts or oracles. More about form than content, theory-speak often involves a kind of canonical citation practice, one that has rightly become the object of decolonizing efforts. But the latter seems unable to resist seizing the high ground of theory for itself, establishing its own orthodoxy around questions of epistemology, instrumentality, no- homogenization and the like. We would all do much better if we treated this kind of meta-speech as ideology – and I don't mean ideology only in the early Marxian sense of the dominating ideas of the powerful or the ruling class. I mean ideas that are engaged in everyday life and that emerged from practice, whose production is not obscured. Nobody can live in the world without thinking about it, without contemplating and reflecting and speculating. We cannot live without hypothesizing and predicting – i.e. without theorizing. Theory, in short, is grounded thought about the world. Everyone engages in it.

Many of us who've spent time in agrarian communities, have sat with people as they look anxiously at their crops and talk about what's doing well and what isn't. And why. In so doing, they reflect, often metaphysically. This should count as theory. But it usually does not, even when it is objectified and orally systematized. Why not? Because these thinkers – given their location in the world – are not accorded the status of theory makers, or even of organic intellectuals. Scholars from the North, or their accredited Southern counterparts see them as informants rather than theorists. They produce raw materials, but the monopoly on theory and analysis lies elsewhere, usually the metropole, to which their 'added value' accrues. It is a kind of intellectual co-production whose profit is realized in the North. Key ideas, like African theories about the sociosomatic cause of misfortune – as an allegory about the interpersonal psychic and bodily harm (witchcraft) wrought by jealousy, anger, conspiracy and hatred – are a case in point. Popular efforts to understand the emotive crusade of Joe McCarthy, who made unfounded accusations of subversion and treason against would-be Communists in the US in the 1950s, fixed on the image of witch-hunting. But it the usage was predicted by an association made by the African anthropologist Monica Wilson in a pioneering article about African witchcraft and its forensic logic in the *American Journal of Sociology* in 1951. In similar fashion, it is held that the philosopher, T.S. Kuhn (1962) developed some of his ideas about paradigm fixation for the *Structure of Scientific Revolutions* from accounts of the 'logical closure' of witch beliefs in Africa; this by way of the classic account by Evans-Pritchard (1937) via Michael Polanyi's *Tacit Knowledge* (1966).

I find it telling that, in 2009, the South African Ministry of Higher Education actually set up a charter for the social sciences. The argument was that we, as a Southern nation, needed to produce theory and to produce it ourselves – and here we get back to Desmond's original question – so as not be patronized by Northern monopolies. To generate theory for ourselves, from our world. How, without an independent understanding of the global order, and our position in it, are we to talk back to the hegemonic world of power-brokerage, finance, trade and debt regulation. This promotion of theory was especially interesting to me because, at the same time in the North, many scholars were repudiating theory, in the service of a new economic realism, technicism, biologism, empiricism. In Latin America and Africa, by contrast, people realized that home-grown theory was politically essential. So, while I concur that we need to demystify, to de-fetishize theory, I also think that we should not cede the authority to the North. 'Universal' theory draws connections – often deterministic connection – between seeming independent populations and polities in the world, as if on a level playing field, bereft of history and geopolitics. The South should argue back, in its own languages, to the ways in which it is situated on that map, thus to expose how much, for instance, 'development theory' is market ideology, economic colonization, pure and simple. We need to call ideas for what they are; to show how they operate politically, in form and in content, as means to neo-imperil ends.

At the same time, theorists from ex-centric locations should be ready to assert the value of our own ideas: ideas that don't necessarily emerge from the academy, but also from the world of practice. Much theoretical insight in our world now comes from journalism, movies, works of art and aesthetics. Even stand-up comedy. I have gained as much insight about current politics and society in Africa and the US from my fellow South African, Trevor Noah, as from any other thinkers. And if you want to get to the heart of the relationship of labor and race in contemporary America, take a look at Boots Riley's film, *Sorry to Bother You*.

Rafael Lomeu Gomes

The next question is from Kristina M. Douglass: 'Can you unpack how decolonization of knowledge production in African Studies is playing out differently across the sciences (including applied sciences and medicine) and the humanities, particularly considering the differential resources and facilities investments of universities and institutes in the North. I am concerned with extractivist approaches in STEM-oriented African Studies and how these are perhaps receiving greater investment as areas perceived as having great potential to address big challenges like climate change, etc.'

Jean Comaroff

This is very important question. What is happening now with the politics of austerity in universities in both North and South make plain that we cannot take universities, at least as we have known them, for granted. While we live in a very much better endowed educational environment in the North, what we're seeing is a politics of austerity – and it is going to be more so in the wake of the pandemic – that is defunding certain areas of research (the humanities) and teaching and throwing money at others. When we get to the question of African Studies, there are urgent things to consider, especially when we speak of decolonization.

First of all, African Studies in the US and the UK has been in the hands of white northerners, some of them – in the formative years – former colonial employees. In the US, the forms of African Studies produced in Historically Black Universities tended to be seen as 'too political'; there was little dialogue between the latter and elite institutions. There has been something of a renaissance of African Studies in universities in the US with the immigration here of African scholars and the rise of a generation of intellectually powerful black students, many of them energized by the synergy between Black Lives Matter and Rhodes Must Fall. But what's happening now is a new kind of challenge: a shift away from the humanities, not only to urgent issues of sciences of health and poverty, but to towards a concern with utility, with instrumental knowledge, rather than with cultural or philosophical concerns.

Business, tech and economic policy loom large. There is also a focus on health, which is crucially important of course. Yet how that focus is shaped, by and for whom, remains key. There is significant attention paid to pandemic issues, both in research and intervention, at Northern universities. But, as we know from the blatant failure that characterize the US response to AIDS, Ebola and COVID-19, such responses make evident new modalities of colonization a home and abroad, and that serves a range of Northern interests – from technical and pharmaceutical dependency to security emplacements. It's very difficult for African countries, for instance, to decide how to relate to these double-edged aid initiatives, which often entail extraction along with care. Trials of drugs destined for wealthy northern consumers have been carried out on Africans who would never benefit from them. Recently it was revealed that COVID-19 vaccines, produced with cheap South African labor were being exported to Europe at a time when the country itself was desperately short of supplies for its own population.

Rwanda is one nation whose current government is very sensitive to these issues of experimentation and carefully regulates foreign research within its borders. That research is not permitted to be purely extractive or designed largely to benefit populations elsewhere. It has to benefit Rwanda in some way, or to result in the development of local capacity and expertise. In other African countries, authorities are pushing back against the growing quest by US-based contract research organizations to find populations of human subjects to low-income contexts for pharmaceutical trials, that are often conducted on ethically troubling terms (Petryna, 2005). In South Africa, concerted efforts are being made to require global companies that commission such research make investments in the health care of under-resourced communities from which they recruit experimental subjects. This research is frequently driven by corporate biotech interests in partnership with universities in the US; herein lies the industrial–academic complex. Universities also have interests in developing new areas of specialty, like Global Health and Tropical Medicine, brands of expertise controlled in the North. Their relevance to African needs and priorities on the ground is often questionable, and they discount local competence to their own benefit.

More generally, Area Studies programs in the US emerged during the Cold War under the provision of Title Vl. Their purpose was to advance national security by training proficient linguists and experts in 'critical world regions,' such as Africa, the Middle Russia and China. Language and culture were stressed, but so was instrumental knowledge: the world according to US interests. I recall being invited, after 9/11, to apply for a grant to study Religion and Violence. When I spoke of a student who was studying the history of the Lord's Resistance Army, a brutal, putatively Christian movement in Uganda and the Southern Sudan, there was some prevarication. And then they came right out with it: the violent religion they had in mind was Islam. In recent years, STEM and commerce have been muscling out other more humanistic areas of research in African Studies as in the wider academy. There is also a sense, in some elite universities, that Africa should help finance African Studies in the North. Fundraisers from wealthy universities track down rich donors in Nigeria, South Africa, Kenya and elsewhere on the continent to try and raise support the study of Africa in the US – money should, in my view, be going to African scholarship in African universities.

But Northern paternalism in African Studies is being challenged from another quarter. Asia, especially the new axis between Africa and China, is in many ways replacing the old North–South colonial dialectic and opening up a new imperium. There is a lot of Belt and Road infrastructural development going on in Africa, much of it taking over where Euro-America dropped the ball. The implications of this for a new South–South axis of technology, trade, resource transfer, security and political alliance remain to be determined. China is increasingly invested in teaching Chinese and educating Africans and in accumulating knowledge about Africa, opening a crucial new geographic vector of African Studies.

Rafael Lomeu Gomes

And now we have another question.

Teboho Motaboli

I would like to hear Jean address specifically the Chinese incursion into Africa as a new colonial power probably based on technological exploitation and claim that this is equal partnership. It's really not direct like hegemonic Euro-America, which was a clear the kind of exploitation that is straight and makes no excuses. But this is a deceptive China, which has a program to colonize and hugely exploit African resources. It really doesn't necessarily fall within or can clearly be understood by reference to Southern theory, which had so much closer dialogue with Northern hegemony.

Jean Comaroff

Absolutely. We've entered a new moment, in this respect, both in terms of our ability to capture the current world in terms of the North–South dualism, and our knowledge of the multi-dimensional presence of China in Africa. In fact, the Chinese story in Africa goes back a long way. Soon after Sun Yat-Sen took power after World War I, the Republic of China developed official relations with South Africa, where there was already a sizable and prosperous Chinese community. And during the Cold War years, the PRC lent support to African liberation movements, extending interest-fee loans, medical assistance and other forms of infrastructural aid. The end of the Cold War resulted a diminishing interest in Africa on the part of its traditional Western donors and China, having focused on its own internal liberalization, now began to extend itself ever more intensively across the African continent. The rest, as they say, is history – or rather, a great leap forward in 'development with Chinese characteristics.' China has presented itself as an 'all-weather friend,' respectful of the sovereignty and equality of African nations, and – as South-South partner – in pursuit of mutual benefit, without interference in each other's internal affairs. By contrast to Western development in the age of deregulation, China has continued to offer significant state-to-state infrastructural aid, loans, information and communications technology – everything from arms to consumer electronics. It has overtaken the US as Africa's largest trading partner, importing natural resources – especially oil and minerals – from the continent.

But 'China in Africa' is a complicated phenomenon, which operates also at several other, non-state levels. Chinese corporations, whose relationship to the state is murky, engage in semi-independent public-private partnerships in Africa, building hotels, supplying national communication networks, owning mines and marketing pharmaceuticals; but they also enjoy a significant degree of government backing. Huawei and ZTE, for instance, have provisioned states like Ethiopia and Kenya with 5G wireless networks, raising cybersecurity concerns from the US and other national governments, who cite the role of Huawei in the surveillance of minority populations in China. Observers have claimed that equipping African states with such technology, in the name of improving information management and crime control, empowers authoritarian governance and undermines democratic values (Bulelani, 2020). Yet leaders, like South Africa's Cyril Ramaphosa refuse to become victims of a US 'trade war' with China. For them, a company like Huawei offers cheap, reliable equipment and 'attractive financing backed by the Chinese state,' making it 'a central pillar of the continent's growth ambitions' (Prinsloo, 2020). Others have noted that Western suppliers of similar equipment on the continent have not been subject to similar political suspicion, that African statesmen are not merely willing pawns of their Chinese benefactors, and that Chinese companies are responsive to local regulations and modes of governance, both democratic and authoritarian (Xi, 2021).

The jury remains out on this debate. There are accusations that Huawei has worked with Ugandan authorities to infiltrate the WhatsApp messages of a political opponent, but here, as elsewhere, solid data is lacking. One should note, too, that social networking and mass communication providers in the North are hardly politically innocent; such means of communication are *never* free of political entanglement, whether by design, neglect, or willful ignorance of their effects. Those entanglements can be consequential, with or without state-involvement: the effects of trade monopolies, debt and dependence are as dangerous to human freedom as the will of authoritarian governments. And corporations have been active agents of modern colonization; they remain integral to what is sometimes termed informal empire that we erroneously refer to as the 'post-colonial' world. How different are the imperial ambitions of contemporary China? Certainly, we cannot take its manifest ideology of equality, mutual benefit and trade without interference at face value. Claims to an absence of ideology or political motive are politics-by-other-means, often covert means. And the assertion of a shared status with Africa as part of the non-Western is unlikely to mitigate imperial designs or effects. But the advent of China-Africa as an axis of world-making points, as I have noted, to the growing eclipse of an older, paternal North-South axis and push us to rethink the larger, multilateral dynamic configuring the polarities of the global order.

Rafael Lomeu Gomes

There's one more question asked by Sangeeta Bagga-Gupta: 'You argue convincingly in *Theory from the South* that we are all implicated in the modernity project and flipping South–North is not a solution. What do you think about the reflexive need for scholars' positionalities to be transparent – i.e. an epistemic practice of positionalities being made available in the scholarship?'

Jean Comaroff

As I have said, most scholars writing on these topics now are multiply displaced. We come from one place, we are educated in another; and our work often takes us yet further afield. In an age when many seek stable, homogenous identities, a large number of us are actually the product of mixed, not fully reconciled heritages, religious as well as sectarian schooling, and complex patterns of privilege and exclusion. Many of us were shaped, as scholars and thinkers, by life beyond the academy, what in South Africa we used to call the University of the Street. I think it is important to declare these influences and commitments, to the degree that we can. But too much of a concern with reflexivity can be a trap: a lot of what shapes one lies below or beyond the level of consciousness, even as one reflects on the structural context of, and influences on one's work. As Bourdieu (1977: 166–7) once put it, 'It goes without saying...because it comes without saying.' There was a moment in anthropology, in the late 1980s and 1990s, when the discipline went through a pronounced reflexive preoccupation with the conditions of its own production; some even called it epistemological hypochondria. Much of this was long overdue. Anthropology was closely entangled with colonialism from its start, although it was always more than a mere reflex of European hegemony. While it remained, until very recently, a white Euro-centric enterprise, it was also ex-centric within that world, a product often of various social-ethnic margins, of internally displaced elites. And it was unusually self-critical on many of the conceits of Eurocentrism. Much of the concern in its reflexive moment was, in my view, misplaced: it focused more on epistemological anxieties – can we ever be truly objective, what are the limits of textuality, etc.? – and less about the structural conditions of bourgeois knowledge production across the lines of class, race and colonial location. As a result, great effort was placed on rebalancing texts by providing personal data: we began to learn more about the scholars, than we did about those of whom they wrote.

In fact, we are often the creatures of agendas of which we are not aware. That's what's so interesting about colonial knowledge. The missionaries that went to Africa to convert people to Christianity actually carried with them many things they didn't intend. Commodity fetishism was one of them, but so was a certain critical consciousness born of the contradictions of their own project. Their efforts to induct Africans into the Kingdom of God, and to convey the idea of universal truth was blatantly belied by the way they behaved; their own evolutionary beliefs and racism ensured that Africans were never really seen to be equal. They remained in the adolescence of civilization, all of that 'not yet' stuff. What they bequeathed, in the upshot, was an awareness of the discrepancy between the message and the messenger. Their would-be converts soon realized that there is no such thing as universal truth, that those who claimed to be egalitarian kept perpetuating inequalities of gender, race or whatever. And as a result, they read the Bible differently: it spoke to them about the liberation of the oppressed.

So, while I think that it is important to declare certain things about 'where one is coming from' as a scholar – things like why one chooses a particular project, one's intended audience, where one's funding comes from, and so on – one has also to be aware that nobody is ever *fully* conscious of who they are, and what larger interests they might unwittingly be serving. Furthermore – this is a comforting point – one always produces more than one intends and reveals more than one knows. The world expresses its truths in ways that tend to override our prejudices and desires; it uses us and our texts in ways that we can never fully anticipate. We give ourselves away unwittingly. There are things we cannot escape or hide, however much we try to configure ourselves. Also, as the world changes, what one writes and prioritizes changes with it. I would have done *Theory from the South* differently now: I would have certainly brought in a different kind of discussion about the ironies of colonizing and decolonizing.

I think in the end there has to be a balance between reflexivity, self-declaration and so on, and the fact that there are certain things in the world that have an objectivity that exceeds one, and that one really should be talking about and writing about because they're really important. So, it's not only about oneself, but it's about talking about issues out there. I worry that when the concern with auto-critique takes over to the degree that is has it becomes a self-obsession, particularly in the Northern academy. It's now '*Mea culpa*, what have we done?' But we need to get over ourselves and our own importance. There are things out there that we need to do, people we need to join, scholarship we need to support. So, it's the politics and the pragmatics of it, not just the kind of self-cultivation in the academy, that seems to me to be important.

Rafael Lomeu Gomes

We have time for one more question. Ivana Ancic asks: 'Indigenous studies scholars in North America and Australia have demonstrated how Indigenous systems of thought do persist to this day and continue to mediate social relations, provide critical perspectives on incursions of the state and capitalism, etc. So why not think about African systems of thought – for instance, animist ones – in a similar way? They function entirely outside the anthropocentric and Eurocentric theories about subjecthood, development, labor, etc. but that is why they also provide critical insight on how those ideas were developed within colonial capitalist and racializing formations. Are these Indigenous critical genealogies necessarily fetishized?'

Jean Comaroff

The answer to the last question is no. I spent much of my life as a PhD student working on African systems of thought about causality, illness and healing and I was struck by their integrity, radical difference and power. I fully take your point, and I think it's really important. But I would also say, as I noted above, that there are no Indigenous knowledge systems – in Africa or elsewhere – that are completely unaffected by their engagement with the wider world and by the broader contexts in which they exist. This doesn't in any sense diminish the importance of those identified with them, or of we ourselves recognizing them as Indigenous. I understand why people who inhabit local ways of life, at a distance from the hegemonic centers, people who often have been marked as 'others,' might want to reject such labeling and the relativizing it involves. I also understand why they may be fiercely critical of efforts to encompass their world, and to carry it away as a commodity.

Our earlier book, *Ethnicity, Inc.* (Comaroff & Comaroff, 2009), is about how Indigenous cultural knowledge and practices have increasingly become commodified as exotic brands for tourism or consumerism. But this does not necessarily diminish their value to their owners, who are happy to possess them as heritage, heritage whose vitality as 'authentically Indigenous' tradition is – if anything – enhanced by accruing market value. It helps here to keep in mind certain images. For example, the process of Setswana divination that I studied in rural South Africa in the late 1960s, and that was used by healers to diagnose the causes of disease or misfortune, is now offered online. While the procedures seem to have changed in some ways by this mass mediation, the compelling mystique and interpretive logic of the practice – and its rich poetics – have remained identifiably distinctive. Certainly, it has been inside the market economy for some time. Yet for its users, it remains an instance of an authentic archaic technique that complements modern medicine, and that also has adapted itself to the conditions of contemporary life – including the treatment of a range of very contemporary ailments, like depression, or unemployment.

There are many places where both biomedical practice and 'traditional' practice are officially recognized. If we accept that Indigenous knowledge does not actually exist as completely separate, or disengaged from the world, I'm fully on board with you. But the mere fact that it serves to 'mediate social relations' means that is cannot be said to 'function entirely outside the anthropocentric and Eurocentric theories,' whatever its practitioners might claim. The two bodies of knowledge and practice (and surely a lot of hybrids in the space between) exist in a labile relationship that is reciprocally transforming. As Raymond Williams (1973) said of the country and the city, they are conditions of each other's possibility, and both inside of history. There is great critical and strategic advantage in speaking to systems of power and hegemonic knowledge from their margins, even from their outsides. But the idea that the latter is the site of unchanging authenticity is the romance of a world caught up in the terror of constant change and cultural erasure. Many systems that call themselves Indigenous have not until recently become obsessed with questions of authenticity. They just live and do their thing. But in the process of colonization most had little option but to engage the wider, avaricious world, even if only to protect what they came to define as 'their mode of life,' of which they tended to become conscious as never before. Often, they drew on newly empowering means to do so. Folk costume in many parts of the world was made in the 19th century with fabric manufactured in the West and traded on the imperial peripheries, often by agents of the civilizing missions. It enabled styles of dress that blended local and imported elements, styles that came to be recognized as markers of a certain class of people: 'traditional' ethnicized populations on the outskirts of colonial modernity. These signs of indigeneity, then, were themselves creolizations, innovations defined by contrast to Western fashion. While fashion was, by definition, linked to market innovation, folk dress was about differentiation, repetition and reproduction, about a form of cultural authority that was auratic, and vested the past. Tradition *did* change over time, of course; it too was inside history. But it shifted much more slowly, less perceptibly than did fashion. So, with this caveat, I fully agree concur what you're saying. Indigeneity in this sense, is not a fetish. But it can become one if it is invested with false powers and a unique, ahistoric 'aura' in and for itself.

Rafael Lomeu Gomes

Thanks everyone for your very interesting questions and thank you, Jean, for engaging with each of them so comprehensively. Makoni, the floor is yours.

Sinfree Makoni

I'm not going to try to sum up the discussion. I'm just going to try to highlight what I think are the issues that came up, which we may want to think about as we go along. Listening to Jean, and then to the responses to the questions, it became quite clear to me that somehow we need to think of Southern theories at a global level. What do I mean by this? What I mean is that we need to move away from simply thinking of Southern theories in terms of complex relationships between the South and the North. We need to find a way of incorporating, within the constructs of Southern theories that we are building, what Jean was talking about in regard to the internal critique of Chinese imperialism within Africa or globally. So, we need to find a way of including that particular dimension. Once we begin to do that, other possibilities open up.

We then need to find a way of thinking about Southern theories, exploring what sort of relationships may exist between Southern theories and theories that are being produced in the former Soviet republics by scholars who are working in those areas because that is another dimension that we may need to think about. What is it that the post-Soviet republic scholars are working on? And what are their views about issues relating to Southern scholarship? Once we do that, as part of a global project, then we will be able to think about the relevance of, for example, Caribbean thinking and Caribbean philosophy on Southern theories. In other words, what I am arguing for, as I close this session, is a Southern theory that is much more global in its aspiration.

Rafael Lomeu Gomes

Jean, would you like to share your concluding thoughts?

Jean Comaroff

I find Sinfree's remarks extremely interesting. And I am very much in agreement with the spirit of what he is saying. In the first chapter of *Theory from the South,* we ask what it might mean to subvert the developmental telos that casts the 'non-West,' 'the orient,' the 'Global South' as the source of raw data for Northern theory. We suggest that we might look to the South for privileged insight into the working of the world at large – using the South, in the sense underlined above, as an 'ex-centric' location. But the aim in doing this, we argued, was not simply to invert the hierarchy, but to move beyond the binary of north-south itself 'to lay bare the larger dialectical processes that have produced and sustain it' (2012: 2). The North–South dualism is itself a historical–ideological construction, one that configures intersecting planetary forces that have taken various grounded, geopolitical forms in the modern world, a central pivot of which was the imperial interplay of Europe and its others. Though this construction was maintained as a working fiction during the period of Western-dominated colonial modernity and its immediate aftermath, it has long rested on unstable foundations – above all, on the unsteady alliance of industrial capital and the liberal nation-state. This alliance, a marriage of convenience between capitalism and liberalism, was fatally threatened when Northern nations, mired in brutal mercantilist rivalry, lost control of their colonies and, without them, the monopoly on both global extraction and the terms of universal truth. In the process, as we noted, old peripheries became new frontiers, and some older imperial powers (like Russia and China) have sought to reassert themselves. The older North-South geopolitical axis has given ground to a new lateral, East–West polarity. Yet, while China might indeed have become a preeminent super-power, and the workshop of the world, modern history is not simply being written again as a new evolutionary narrative, this time with East Asia as its culmination. While the imperium of Chinese capitalism in its particular, state-led form is of huge significance, it is not a form towards which the rest of the world is evolving. As we have said elsewhere (Comaroff & Comaroff, 2012), China has its own dystopias, global dependencies and contradictions, some of them with distinctive African resonances. In fact, China and Africa are developing a vibrant symbiosis that is very likely to decenter American, European, or Commonwealth dominance. In the view of Keith Hart (2017: 2), Asian manufacturers have already recognized that Africa will be 'the most buoyant sector of world market demand' in the 21st century. On sheer demographic grounds alone, he says, 'humanity's future will be worked out between Asians and Africans.'

Our own privileging of Africa in *Theory from the South* was because this is the place from which we – as scholars and subjects – enter the 'new' global order. In doing so, we also seek to 'dismantle the kind of Hegelian thinking for which Africa long served as the negative pole'; thus permitting us to tell a different kind of story (Comaroff & Comaroff, 2012). It is the story of a multipolar world, in which the argument is not whether Africa *or* China *or* Brazil is *the* vanguard of some future imperfect. Each makes evident a distinct dimension of the ways in which race, economy and polity are intersecting, new currencies of communication are being devised, new sovereignties being extended over biopolitical life. And also, new modalities of critical practice and theory-making being fashioned. For theory-making too, as Sinfree makes plain, must be multilateral; multilateral rather than 'pluriversal,' as in the approach advocated by some divergent visions of decoloniality. Multilateral in that they aim to converge from a range of different, ex-centric locations on the interconnected *lebensraum* – social, material, biological – which together we build, inhabit and strive to make viable.

So thank you all very much. The questions were fascinating, I really appreciated them.

References

Adam, H. (1971) *Modernizing Racial Domination: South Africa's Political Dynamics* (Vol. 2). Berkeley: University of California Press.
Almeida, S. and Kumalo, S. H. (2018) (De) coloniality through indigeneity: Deconstructing calls to decolonise in the South African and Canadian university contexts. *Education as Change* 22 (1), 1–24.
Asad, T. (1975) Anthropological texts and ideological problems: an analysis of Cohen on Arab villages in Israel. *Economy and Society* 4 (3), 251–282.
Bhabha, H.K. (1994) *The Location of Culture*. New York: Routledge.
Bourdieu, P. (1977) *Outline of a Theory of Practice*. Cambridge: Cambridge University Press.
Boym, S. (2001) *The Future of Nostalgia*. New York: Basic Books.
Bulelani, J. (2020) Chinese surveillance tools in Africa. *China, Law, and Development Project of Oxford University*. See https://cld.web.ox.ac.uk/file/678231
Collins, P.H. (1986) Learning from the outsider within: The sociological significance of Black feminist thought. *Social Problems* 33 (6), s14–s32.
Comaroff, J. (1985) *Body of Power, Spirit of Resistance: The Culture and History of a South African People*. Chicago: University of Chicago Press.
Comaroff, J. (2007) Beyond the politics of bare life: AIDS and the global order. *Public Culture* 19 (1), 197–219.
Comaroff, J. and Comaroff, J.L. (1991) *Of Revelation and Revolution, Volume 1: Christianity, Colonialism, and Consciousness in South Africa*. Chicago: University of Chicago Press.
Comaroff, J. and Comaroff, J. (1992) *Ethnography and The Historical Imagination*. New York: Routledge.
Comaroff, J. and Comaroff, J.L. (1997) *Of Revelation and Revolution, Volume 2: Christianity, Colonialism, and Consciousness in South Africa* (Vol. 1). Chicago: University of Chicago Press.
Comaroff, J. and Comaroff, J.L. (eds) (2001) *Millennial Capitalism and The Culture of Neoliberalism*. Durham, NC: Duke University Press.
Comaroff, J. and Comaroff, J.L. (eds) (2006) *Law and Disorder in the Postcolony*. Chicago: University of Chicago Press.
Comaroff, J.L. and Comaroff, J. (2009) *Ethnicity, Inc*. Chicago: University of Chicago Press.
Comaroff, J. and Comaroff, J.L. (2012, July) *Theory from the South: Or, How Euro-America is Evolving Toward Africa*. New York: Routledge.
Comaroff, J. and Comaroff, J.L. (2016) *The Truth About Crime: Sovereignty, Knowledge, Social Order*. Chicago: University of Chicago Press.
Comaroff, J.L. and Comaroff, J. (eds) (2018) *The Politics of Custom: Chiefship, Capital, and The State in Contemporary Africa*. Chicago: University of Chicago Press.
Conelli, C. (2019) Back to the South: Revisiting Gramsci's southern question in the light of subaltern studies. In *Revisiting Gramsci's Notebooks* (pp. 233–247). Leiden: Brill.
Connell, R. (2007) *Southern Theory: The Global Dynamics of Knowledge in Social Science*. New York: Routledge.
Connell, R. (n.d.) *Southern Theory*. Southern Theory. See http://www.raewynconnell.net/p/theory.html
Crease, R.P., Martin, J.D. and Staley, R. (2019) Decolonizing physics: Learning from the periphery. *Physics in Perspective* 21, 91–92.
de Sousa Santos, B. (2001) Nuestra América: Reinventing a subaltern paradigm of recognition and redistribution. *Theory, Culture & Society* 18 (2–3), 185–217.
de Sousa Santos, B. (2018) *The End of The Cognitive Empire: The Coming of Age of Epistemologies of the South*. Durham, NC: Duke University Press.

Evans-Pritchard, E.E. (1937) *Witchcraft, Oracles and Magic among the Azande*. Oxford: Oxford University Press.
Fanon, F. (1963) *The Wretched of the Earth*. New York: Grove Press.
Ferguson, J. (2006) *Global Shadows: Africa in the Neoliberal World Order*. Durham, NC: Duke University Press.
Gathara, P. (2021, January 9) Papa Don's failed state: The US as seen from Kenya. *The Guardian*. See https://www.theguardian.com/us-news/2021/jan/09/capitol-storming-us-failed-state-kenya-patrick-gathara (accessed March 22, 2003).
Gordon, L.R. (2014) Disciplinary decadence and the decolonisation of knowledge. *Africa Development* 39 (1), 81–92.
Gordon, L.R. (2019) Shifting the geography of reason. Interview with Madina Tlostanova, in New Frame. https://www.newframe.com/shifting-geography-reason/
Hart, K. (2017) The West's moral and political crisis. *Anthropology Today* 33 (4), 1–3.
Huffington, A. (2011) *Third World America: How Our Politicians are Abandoning the Middle Class and Betraying the American Dream*. New York: Crown Publishing.
Jobson, R.C. (2020) The case for letting anthropology burn: Sociocultural anthropology in 2019. *American Anthropologist* 122 (2), 259–271.
Kuhn, T.S. (1962) *The Structure of Scientific Revolutions*. Chicago: University of Chicago Press.
Latour, B. (1993) *The Pasteurization of France*. Cambridge, MA: Harvard University Press.
Lee, J.H. (2021) *Rat Tech: Transforming Rodents into Rechnology in Tanzania*. Mount Pleasant, CA: Arcadia.
MacShane, D. (2021, August 11). *Welcome to Banana Republic Britain*. The New European. See https://www.theneweuropean.co.uk/brexit-news-denis-macshane-banana-republic-22374/ (accessed March 22, 2023).
Mafeje, A. (1976) The problem of anthropology in historical perspective: an inquiry into the growth of the social sciences. *Canadian Journal of African Studies/La Revue canadienne des études africaines* 10 (2), 307–333.
Mamdani, M. (1996) Indirect rule, civil society, and ethnicity: The African dilemma. *Social Justice* 23(1/2 (63–64)), 145–150.
McGirt, E. and Jenkins, A. (2020, September 30) *America is a third World Country Now*. Fortune. See https://fortune.com/2020/09/30/America-is-a-third-world-country-now/ (acced March 22, 2023).
Meiu, G.P., Comaroff, J. and Comaroff, J.L. (eds) (2020) *Ethnicity, Commodity, In/Corporation*. Bloomington: Indiana University Press.
Mengistu, A. and Imende, S. (January–February, 2013) Kenya's Mobile Tech Revolution: Nairobi takes its place among the global IT community. *Selamta Magazine* (accessed August 16, 2021).
Mignolo, W. (May 2, 2012) Delinking, decoloniality & dewesternization: Interview with Walter Mignolo, Part 2. *Critical Legal Thinking*. See https://criticallegalthinking.com/2012/05/02/delinking-decoloniality-dewesternization-interview-with-walter-mignolo-part-ii/
Mogstad, H. and Tse, L.S. (2018) Decolonizing anthropology: Reflections from Cambridge. *The Cambridge Journal of Anthropology* 36 (2), 53–72.
Petryna, A. (2005) Ethical variability: Drug development and globalizing clinical trials. *American Ethnologist* 32 (2), 183–197.
Polanyi, M. (1966) *The Tacit Dimension*. Chicago: The University of Chicago Press.
Prinsloo, L. (2020, August 19) *China's Huawei Prospers in Africa Even as Europe, Asia Join Trump's Ban*. Bloomberg.com. See https://www.bloomberg.com/news/articles/2020-08-19/china-s-huawei-prospers-in-africa-even-as-europe-asia-join-trump-s-ban (accessed March 22, 2023).
Rancière, J. (2004) *The Philosopher and his Poor*. Durham, NC: Duke University Press.
Said, E.W. (2014) Traveling theory (1982). *World Literature in Theory*, 114–133.
Salem, S. (2021) Gramsci in the postcolony: Hegemony and anticolonialism in Nasserist Egypt. *Theory, Culture & Society* 38 (1), 79–99.
Smith, D.E. (1987) *The Everyday World as Problematic: A Feminist Sociology*. Toronto: University of Toronto Press.
Spivak, G.C. and Guha, R. (1988) Subaltern studies: Deconstructing historiography. *Deconstruction: Critical Concepts in Literary and Cultural Studies* 4, 220–244.

Srivastava, N. and Bhattacharya, B. (eds) (2012) *The Postcolonial Gramsci*. New York: Routledge.

Timossi, A.J. (2015) Revisiting the 1955 Bandung Asian-African Conference and its Legacy. *South Bulletin* 85, 15.

Tuck, E. and Yang, K.W. (2012) Decolonization is not a metaphor. *Decolonization: Indigenity, Education & Society* 1 (1), 1–40.

Viveiros de Castro, E. (2013) The relative native. *HAU: Journal of Ethnographic Theory* 3 (3), 473–502.

wa Ngũgĩ, M. (2021) White privilege in African Studies: When you are done, please call us. *[en ligne]*, *Brittle Paper* 28.

Williams, R. (1973) *The Country and the City* (Vol. 423). Oxford: Oxford University Press.

Wilson, M.H. (1951) Witch beliefs and social structure. *American Journal of Sociology* 56 (4), 307–313.

Xi, J. (2021, September 21) *Analysts: China Expanding Influence in Africa via Telecom Network Deals*. VOA. See https://www.voanews.com/a/economy-business_analysts-china-expanding-influence-africa-telecom-network-deals/6209516.html (accessed March 22, 2023).

Žižek, S. (n.d.) *Introduction*. Home/symptom10. See https://www.lacan.com/essays/?page_id=454%2C%2520accessed (accessed March 22, 2023).

3 Epistemologies of the South: Justice Against Epistemicide

Boaventura de Sousa Santos

Rafael Lomeu Gomes

Welcome once again, everyone. There are still people joining us, which is really nice. I'm delighted to see many of you here and I welcome all of you and, in particular, Professor Boaventura de Sousa Santos who is Professor Emeritus of Sociology at the University of Coimbra, Portugal, and Distinguished Legal Scholar at the University of Wisconsin-Madison. He is Director Emeritus of the Center for Social Studies at the University of Coimbra and has written and published widely on the issues of globalization, sociology, law and the state, epistemology, social movements and the World Social Forum.

His most recent project, ALICE: Leading Europe to a New Way of Sharing the World Experiences, was funded by an Advanced Grant of the European Research Council, one of the most prestigious and highly competitive international funding institutions for scientific excellence in Europe. He will be discussing his book *Epistemologies of the South: Justice Against Epistemicide* (2014). Welcome once again, Boaventura. The floor is yours.

Boaventura de Sousa Santos

Okay, Rafael. Good afternoon. I speak from Portugal. It's a nice afternoon here today. I'm based now in Portugal. Usually, this time of the year, I wouldn't be here, I would be in Madison-Wisconsin, but because of the pandemic, I am. In fact, I'm in my village. I'm not in Coimbra, but in my village. It's a great pleasure to join you all at The Pennsylvania State University.

Well, thank you very much for inviting me to speak about this book of mine. Actually, if you want to discuss the Epistemologies of the South, we do have to bring in two books. The first one is *Epistemologies of the South: Justice Against Epistemicide* (2014); the second one is *The End of the Cognitive Empire* (2018). The latter book is the full development – not only in epistemological terms, but also in methodological and pedagogical terms – of what I call Epistemologies of the South.

The basic idea of the Epistemologies of the South is that there is no global social justice without global cognitive justice, justice among different ways of knowing. Another important idea is that the understanding of the world by far exceeds the Western understanding of the world. There are many other understandings, and therefore, since understanding is connected with transformation, there are also possibilities of transformation of the world that are not in the script of the Western-centric modernity. The Epistemologies of the South are trying to develop these ideas in epistemological, methodological and pedagogical terms.

Well, how to locate the Epistemologies of the South in the broad spectrum of the theoretical knowledge of the last 200 years or so? I maintain that, so far, we have had two main paradigms of knowledge. The first paradigm is the Hegelian paradigm, which basically states that knowledge must emerge after social struggles, because it's only at that time that Minerva starts thinking, when all the turbulence of social life is over, and we can think and develop our theories in tranquility. So, knowledge after the struggles.

The problem with this paradigm is that, after the struggle, only the knowledge of the winners survives. Where are the knowledges of the vanquished, the losers of the social struggles? They are not there. Of course, our universities have been subservient to this paradigm all along and, therefore, they have been doing research on and disseminating the history of the winners as told by the winners. Therefore, it's really a very biased, structurally biased type of knowledge.

The second paradigm develops with the work of Karl Marx in a famous small text of 1845 entitled *Theses an Feurbach.* In his eleven theses against Ludwig von Feuerbach, Marx wants to develop a science that will help the working class to change the world. The working class is a class in itself, but not for itself. Therefore, it is necessary that the working class get class consciousness. In order for the working class to get class consciousness, it is necessary to develop a science that is an alternative to bourgeois science. Therefore, Marxism is viewed by Marx as a kind of science before the struggle and preparing for the struggle.

Well, this paradigm has a problem with its many unfulfilled promises. The paradigm was very, very influential in my training. My training as a social scientist was originally a Marxist training. The problem is that this paradigm has also been the cause of much frustration. Along the 20th century there were lots of promises based on these ideas, ideas of progressive emancipatory transformation of the world; in many cases, though, they ended up in nightmares, defeats and ugly defeats, and often, even, in authoritarianism.

I think that we need a third paradigm. A third paradigm implies paying attention to knowledges while the struggle is taking place, knowledges born in struggle, so to speak. That's why my most recent book out of this project, a collective book published by Routledge, is *Knowledges Born in Struggle* (de Sousa Santos & Meneses, 2019). That is to say, the idea is to validate knowledges born in struggles, the knowledges of those who have been struggling and fighting against capitalism, colonialism and patriarchy – the three main forms of domination in our societies. Of course, these struggles are conducted on the basis of different ways of knowing. Science is part of this, but never the only knowledge available in struggle. There are many other knowledges: peasant knowledges, feminist knowledges, urban knowledges, Indigenous knowledges, et cetera, et cetera. All of us who have been involved in social movements know that social struggles are carried out by resorting on a cluster of different knowledges.

The third paradigm I call the *Epistemologies of the South* in order to give visibility and to validate the kinds of ways of knowing involved in social struggles against modern capitalist, colonialist and patriarchal domination. A kind of epistemic revolution occurs in our ways of identifying or producing knowledge because not all our knowledge is written knowledge. Sometimes, it's artistic or performative knowledge. Sometimes the authors in question are not known because their kind of knowledge amounts to collective knowledges. They pose challenges to our methodologies, which are basically extractive methodologies based on the idea of the relationship between subject and object.

For the Epistemologies of the South, the problem is not to create objects. It is to create subjects, it is to change subjectivities by, in fact, showing that the people who are historical subjects are all those who fight against injustice throughout history. All of them are historical protagonists. They are holders of knowledge and, therefore, since the dominant Western-centric knowledge negates the validity or even the existence of these knowledges, the Epistemologies of the South are bound to be a counter-current.

Now, I'd like to make three or four points to clarify my ideas. The first point is that the Epistemologies of the South locate themselves in a broad family of postcolonial studies, also known as decolonial studies. There are reasons why I don't speak so much of decolonial or post-colonial. I prefer Epistemologies of the South for several reasons. The major one is that, according to the Epistemologies of the South, colonialism is not the only matrix of domination in our world. It's just one of them. The others are capitalism and patriarchy.

For some kinds of decolonial thinking, it looks as if colonialism were the only matrix of domination in our societies, but I don't believe that. The matrices are three. In the World Social Forum, I have observed, in many movements, these three forms of domination. Indeed, capitalism cannot sustain itself without colonialism and patriarchy because colonialism and patriarchy are about racialized and sexualized bodies, and these racialized and sexualized bodies are the ones that are providing a highly devalued labor and non-paid labor in our society. The free labor of capitalism cannot sustain itself without highly devalued labor, and this labor is produced by people who are ontologically degraded. They are considered sub-humans. There is, therefore, an abyssal line in our societies that divides the sociability of the metropolitan zone, in which the individuals are viewed as fully human beings, from sociability of the colonial sociability on the other side of the line. The latter is the sociability where people are not dealt with as fully human beings. In concrete terms, they are really dealt with as sub-human.

For the last couple of years, 20,000 people drowned in the Mediterranean Sea, refugees from war and famine trying to escape to Europe. Can you imagine what the commotion in the world would be if these 20,000 people were North American or European citizens? It would be a major crisis. But nothing happened because the dead were not really human. They were treated as sub-humans, and the denunciation of this ontological degradation is at the core of the Epistemologies of the South. The problem is that there are three different kinds of domination and they always act in tandem – capitalism, colonialism, patriarchy – whereas resistance is fragmented.

Many anti-capitalist movements have been racist and sexist, many feminist movements have been racist and pro-capitalist, and some anti-racist movements have been sexist and pro-capitalist. I think that as long as domination is connected and resistance is fragmented, we won't go anywhere.

So, the first point is about the three different forms of domination. The second idea is complex; I have to summarize it and, in the debate, we may elaborate on it. The point is that the Epistemologies of the South are not an anti-science movement or proposal. The proposal is rather the following: science is a valid way of knowing, but it's not the only one. There are other kinds of knowledge in the world, but our universities and our institutions of education only teach science, while, in fact, most people run their lives not by science, but by other ways of knowing: other knowledges, other philosophies, other worldviews.

This is very important because, sometimes, in some of our post-colonial studies, the idea is that all science is racist, sexist and capitalist and, therefore, is not valid. I don't think this is adequate and it is leading to a backlash. I get this from two sources. One of them has to do with an individual who fought against Portuguese colonialism in Africa: Amílcar Cabral, one of my gurus, so to speak. He was a great leader of the liberation movement in Guinea-Bissau and was assassinated by the Secret Police in 1973. Amílcar Cabral was very clear on this. Sometimes, he would argue that the science of the colonizer may be useful to us, so you have to use it. We have to select which parts we want since some of them may be useful. The idea is that you must validate science in pragmatist terms; that is to say, science is not altogether racist or capitalist or sexist, and not all together anti-capitalist, anti-racist, anti-sexist. No, we have to be pragmatists and validate which side science is on regarding the struggle. I have been very involved in a struggle against agro-toxics: industrial poisons, insecticides and pesticides in industrial agriculture. Well, in this particular struggle, we take into account, of course, peasant knowledge. But we also must consider the knowledge of the agronomists and biochemists working with us. Of course, not the biochemists that work for Monsanto or for Bayer. Those are not with us. But we do have to heed those that are with us. This is what I call an Ecology of Knowledges. We try to combine scientific and peasant knowledge in the struggle, as well as, in this case, the knowledge of the field workers themselves.

This implies a different understanding of science. After all, science often gets its knowledge and achievements from non-Western knowledges, to start with. For instance, regarding the pandemic, many people today are eager to celebrate science. But we must understand that there are many other ways of defending people that were not invented by modern science; for instance, quarantines. They existed among Indigenous peoples who had to protect themselves from the colonizers. We also realize that some African countries are protecting the lives of their people much better than the United States, just to mention a case. There are different ways the Indigenous people in Latin America are using their herbal medicine to provide immunity to people against the COVID-19. What I mean is that here are a diversity of knowledges, and it's a pity that sometimes we concentrate on only one kind.

These ideas are the main ones. But there is something else: if you want to combine science and other ways of knowing in your research, the way you conduct science is also different. You have to conduct science in a post-abyssal way. You have to develop new methodologies. Most of our methodologies are extractivist methodologies. We extract as much as we can in the fields, mining in the fields. We are also mining people when we interview them. This metaphor of data digging is very prevalent today, for example. That is to say, we extract data, we extract human resources and we extract information because we don't consider that our informants are holders of knowledge. They just provide us with information.

This is part of epistemicide, that is to say, the destruction of knowledge that we very often perform when we are doing our research. So, we must develop methodological collaboration and non-extractivist methodologies to create subjects rather than objects. My best example comes from a great philosopher from Kenya, Henry Odera Oruka, who developed what he called Sage Philosophy (1990). Trained as a philosopher in Western universities, once back in Nairobi, Oruka realized that he was teaching Hegel and Heidegger in his department but paying no attention to the traditional wisdom (or sagacity) of his people, that is to say, to African philosophy. And so Sage Philosophy was born (I understand that Oruka's son is following in his father's footsteps).

I could give you thousands of examples. I've worked with Valentin Mudimbe and with Mogobe Ramose at the University of South Africa (UNISA). We became good friends. We have discussed precisely these other ways of knowing, and not just Western philosophy as opposed to African philosophy or Indigenous philosophy, or Indian philosophy, but also other kinds of knowledge, the knowledges in the fields, in the struggles in which we find ourselves. Doing so, we can develop intercultural forms of knowledge, or what I call Ecology of Knowledges.

These different cultures are not completely transparent to each other. There are zones of incommunicability, of incommensurability, but there are enough zones of interaction that we should maximize. If you really plead for incommensurability, you are trapped in identitarian ghettos. This is something that is plaguing us, and I don't think that we should continue to let that happen. We must broaden our struggle so that the people that are in the struggles against capitalism can join forces with those that are against racism, and team up with those that are against sexism. We have to bring together the struggles; we need to resort to epistemological, methodological and pedagogical strategies that help bring this about. The point is that 'My struggle is not more important than your struggle.' All the struggles are important, though some of them may be more urgent than others.

In the debate, I can elaborate further on a key concept, which is how to distinguish urgent from important struggles. They are different concepts and there is a lot of confusion in the social movements and activism in general, and we should contribute to solve this problem. Thank you very much.

Rafael Lomeu Gomes

Thank you very much, Professor Boaventura. It's been a very enlightening and comprehensive introduction to some of your latest works. I'm sure many of us would like to ask more questions or make some comments. I'd like now to ask Makoni if you'd like to start the discussion.

Sinfree Makoni

Yes. Thank you very much for this very informative exposition of your work. I'd like to begin by focusing on issues about extractivist methodologies. I want to quote you in the last sentence of your paper called 'Epistemologies of the South and the Future' published in 2016. You write: 'the extent to which non-extractive methodologies will be accepted in the future is the only legitimate way of advanced mutually-enriching knowledge is, of course, an open question' (p. 28). This was in 2016. My question is, several years later, what's your view on this question that you yourself raised?

Boaventura de Sousa Santos

Well, it's a very good question. Thank you. Your first name is Sinfree, right?

Sinfree Makoni

My first name is Sinfree, my friends call me Makoni.

Boaventura de Sousa Santos

Well, I'll do the Sinfree.

Sinfree Makoni

Yeah, okay.

Boaventura de Sousa Santos

Well, it's a very good question. You help me to elaborate on something very, very important, which is: are we going through a period of decolonizing or a period of recolonizing? Globally speaking, in the Global North for sure, but even in general, we are in a period of recolonizing. Everywhere I see the extreme right forces emerging. In Europe, it's very clear. We see them also in Africa, we see them in the United States, we see them throughout Latin America, sometimes we even see defenses of colonialism. You probably know of that article by Bruce Gilley (2017) in the *Third World Quarterly* in defense of colonialism.

Sinfree Makoni

Yes, yes.

Boaventura de Sousa Santos

In fact, the argument is that colonialism was not such a bad thing, that, indeed, it was very good. Nicolas Sarkozy, the former president of France, said the same thing and said it in Senegal. He said, 'Well, it's been very good.' I submit that we are in a period of recolonizing. In point of fact, the debate is now raging in France. It's really a very ugly debate because, all of a sudden, in the aftermath of terrorist acts, some started linking terrorism to post-colonial studies. They argue that the promotion of interculturality and diversity of traditions in France was probably one of the causes for all the cases of extremism in France. All of a sudden, dozens of professors at the universities and at CNRS came out saying, 'We have to defend the Western-centric societies and values.'

In a society divided between oppressors and oppressed, to be neutral is to be with the oppressors, basically. These professors are claiming universal ideas and Western values against violence and terrorism, which, quite frankly, is all very hypocritical, because Europe is the most violent continent in the world. In the 20th century, this continent killed 78 million people in two wars, the so-called World Wars. They were European wars, but they were considered world wars because of colonialism. Lots of people in Mozambique, 250,000 people, died because of colonialism, because they were on the Portuguese side against the German side in Tanzania.

We are facing a backlash. Some five years ago, these professors would not be so outspoken. The truth is that some mainstream newspapers in France are now behind these professors, and it amounts really to almost a kind of persecution against post-colonial and decolonial theories and research. Authors of post-colonial works have been under scrutiny and under threat.

This phenomenon also occurs in the US, even at universities considered very progressive. I recently participated in video conferences at Berkeley, in the US, and at Cambridge, in the UK. I had some students and young faculty tell me: 'Professor, now we feel a little bit persecuted in our universities because we are defending some ideas of diversity, of non-Western philosophies and so on. Everything seems to be suspicious.'

The possibilities for collaborative research are there and it's really being followed by many people around the world. Particularly younger people, students and faculty, they are doing this. I could give you lots of examples in different ways in which people are, for instance, writing PhD thesis in co-authorship when they are getting the information from leaders of movements. At the end, they think that the leaders of movements should also be considered co-authors of their theses. There is a movement to make research more open to different people and to engage with different types of knowledge and methodologies, and so on. In Latin America, to give you another example, we have more and more Afro-Latin Americans and Indigenous researchers doing research, empirical research and doing philosophy.

The voices are very much plural now, but I also see the backlash. For instance, in universities in Latin America, previously controlled by white males, there is resentment that numbers of women are rising, but also Afro-Brazilians, Afro-Colombians, Afro-Peruvians, as well as Indigenous people in all these countries.

Seen philosophically, the backlash is espousing extreme rightist ideologies, even in universities that are more progressive in general. I believe we are in a time of confrontation. Thank you for your question because it helps me to be more precise.

Sinfree Makoni

I understand your argument about struggle. I would want to have a more philosophical discussion about what really a struggle is. What I'm interested in is not so much the discussion about whether struggles can be anti-sexist, or racist, et cetera. What I'm interested in is to flip the script and ask the following question: is it possible that some Indigenous ontologies can be sexist and patriarchal?

Boaventura de Sousa Santos

Absolutely. That's a very good question. That is why I have been working on an ecology of knowledges rather than a dialogue of knowledges. It's different. Because if you bring together different ways of knowing, all these ways of knowing or these philosophies or knowledges are going to change. Nothing stays untouched.

The Western-centric scientific knowledge will be transformed. It will be transformed, but it will also transform the Indigenous and the Black and the Afro ideologies and worldviews. No doubt about that. We have seen this happening throughout the world. Look at South Africa, for instance, and the 1996 Constitution. There are traditional laws that are recognized by the Constitution, but then feminist women in South Africa said: these laws do not allow women to have access to land. Is it reasonable? No. Therefore, a constitutional clause was included to the effect that the traditional law would be recognized if it changes and allows for women to have access to land.

It's a big struggle. It is originally very much confined to South Africa, but the issue has become much broader. It shows that when Indigenous movements have the opportunity to be in contact with other knowledges and understand the idea of an ecology of knowledges, they are dynamic and open to change.

One more example: why do we have today a very strong movement of Indigenous feminism that doesn't go along with white middle class feminists? They have a different agenda. For instance, African or Indigenous women always had a very protagonist role in agriculture, in family agriculture. They don't plead to have access to work because they are working already. While Western feminists in the 1970s and 1980s were pleading for access to jobs. African or Indigenous women's problem was the discrimination against them in terms of land tenure, in terms of leadership of the councils in their communities, and so on.

There is an Indigenous feminism that has a different concept of relationship between men and women. For instance, white feminism is based on the idea of equality. The concept the Indigenous feminists use, among the Quechua in Latin America, is called *sachawarmi*. This concept means complementarity. The underlying conception is holistic. It's a way to get equality without opposing the different parts.

They enrich the concept of equality and freedom in a different way. Thank you for your question. No knowledge stays or is left untouched by these intercultural dialogues, because knowledges evolve in the struggle. If you really have a kind of a male chauvinist type of Indigenous people, the women are not going to participate in the struggle – not today – so we have to change the different ways of knowing in this process. That's why I'm against relativism. You have to be aware of which side you are on in the struggle.

Sinfree Makoni

Okay, this is now my last question. In one of your articles, you talk about Portugal having been a semi-informal colony of Britain and then proceed to say that Portugal, in terms of world systems theory, was on the semi-periphery. Now, my question is this: since Portugal subsequently went on to become the colonial force in colonizing Mozambique, Angola, Brazil, et cetera, in what way, for example, did the semi-peripheral position that Portugal occupied as a power in Europe shape the nature of its colonizing tendencies in Brazil, Angola, or Mozambique? How did the fact that Portugal was a semi-colony of Britain shape the nature and character of its colonization of Mozambique, Angola, et cetera?

Boaventura de Sousa Santos

From the 18th century onwards, the treaties that were established between Portugal and England were precisely the same type of treaties that the British will be later imposing in India. For instance, the Portuguese were forbidden to get into the textile industry. The textile industry would be competing with Manchester, so it had to be forbidden. As a compensation for that, Portugal was allowed to produce all the wine that Britain needed. That's why wine and port wine became a major production of Portugal. The same kind of imposition was to happen in India, as well.

Why could the British get away with this? Well, it was possible because during the Napoleonic Wars, Portugal almost succumbed to France, and the British came in support of the Portuguese king. In fact, the Portuguese king fled to Brazil. It was the only colonial power that, for a while, had the capital of the colonial empire in Rio de Janeiro, not in Lisbon, because Lisbon was occupied by the French. So, Britain defended the Portuguese from the French Empire. As a result, the Portuguese Empire and its sovereignty became prey to British domination.

Just think that from the 18th century onwards, most of the gold that came from Brazil did not stay in Portugal. The ships transporting gold were, for a while, in the harbor of Lisbon, but they did not unload the gold. The gold continued its trip to London because it was to pay Portuguese debts to England. Portugal was performing a kind of an intermediation in the world system. That's the concept of semi-periphery, being in between the center and the periphery.

Portugal played its role very well and very consistently. That's why many people find it very strange sometimes that while Britain had to give up on its empire, basically between 1947 and the 1960s, Portugal kept its empire until 1975, the date of the independence of Angola, Mozambique, Cape Verde Islands, Guinea Bissau, et cetera. This was possible because the European core countries were interested in the gold of South Africa, and Portugal was a stronghold against ideas of liberation in that region.

Portuguese colonialism in Angola and Mozambique was absolutely crucial to keep the apartheid system in South Africa and to protect the flow of gold. That was basically the idea and that's why the South African apartheid was so keen trying to kill the independence of Angola. Portuguese colonialism was functional. The battle of Cuito Cuanavale, in Angola, was decisive to defeat Apartheid South Africa. It was won not by the Angolans, but by the Cubans who were helping the Angolan government. The liberation war in Angola and Mozambique lasted from 1961 until 1975. Then, when there was the revolution in Portugal, the democratic revolution of April 1974, the desired independence of the colonies became inevitable. All the countries that emerged from Portuguese colonialism in 1976 went Marxist and socialist. No other European colony – India was a very partial experience when it became independent – went that way. It's a very interesting story.

We know very well the drama of Kwame Nkrumah in Ghana when he wrote his book on neocolonialism (1965). He saw, as Mahatma Gandhi had seen much earlier, that independence, in fact, was political, but it was full of colonial ties and encumbrances. In the Portuguese case, all the former colonies became socialist because the colonial power, Portugal, didn't have colonial power to control these post-colonies. The Portuguese government lacked a strong bourgeoisie to control the fate of these ex-colonies. If you compare the treaties of independence of French colonialism, or British colonialism, with those of the Portuguese colonialism, it's a very different story. The former colonies could go completely autonomous because Portugal was also being liberated from a dictatorship.

Here is a final note for you. When Brazil became independent in 1822, the fear in Portugal was that Brazil could control Portugal. For instance, Brazil could control Angola. Because Angola, up until then, was not a settler colony. The settler colony was Brazil. The fear was that the Brazilians, now independent, in alliance with the British, would destroy Portuguese colonialism and Portuguese influence in Angola. So, Portugal was afraid of reverse-colonialism by Brazil. This shows the structural weakness of a semi-peripheral country in Europe. And that story goes on up until now. We, in Europe, we have internal colonialism. Holland and Germany look to the southern countries as if they were colonies. The Greeks, the Portuguese, the Spaniards are considered by North European as lascivious, lazy, unproductive and so on. There are all kinds of colonial prejudices inside Europe.

My final note, Sinfree, is that all the forms of land tenure in the colonies in Latin America, particularly by the Spaniards, were tried, experimented in Andalusia, in Spain before the colonial expansion. In fact, when the Catholic kings vanquished the Arabs in Al-Andalus, in the southern part of the peninsula, they distributed the land according to *encomiendas,* which was the system that became very popular and dominant in Latin America. So, they did the colonial experiment in Europe before they used these land tenure systems in Latin America. The same thing with the Holocaust, it was in fact tried in Namibia first. The Germans did the holocaust in Namibia before doing it in Europe.

There are entangled stories here of colonial powers that I think continue up until today. Now, you understand why, for me, colonialism is not a thing of the past. What is a thing of the past is historical colonialism, not colonialism in itself.

Sinfree Makoni

Okay, thank you very much. Rafael, I will hand over to you. I'll try to see if we can explore further what the implications are for the linguistics and applied linguistics of Epistemologies of the South. Thank you very much Professor de Santos.

Boaventura de Sousa Santos

Sinfree, if you allow me, let's please keep in touch. I'd like to know more about your research. The question of linguistics and the struggles, linguicide, which is a form of epistemicide, it's all a very promising area for the Epistemologies of the South. Thank you very much.

Sinfree Makoni

Okay, thank you very much.

Rafael Lomeu Gomes

Thank you, Makoni, for initiating the discussion. We do have a couple of questions here in the chat box. Before I ask them, I would like to kindly remind you that it's easier for Bassey and I to chair the discussion if you write in the chat box that either you have a question or a comment to make, or to write the whole thing, and we can read it for you. The first question that I received was from Marian Eda, and the question is, 'Call for non-extractivist research has been explored in qualitative research for quite some time. These callers involved do not use the term Southern Epistemologies, but they reject a top-down Western-centric approach. In other words, not all current research is extractivist, as you seem to imply. Can you speak to this?'

Boaventura de Sousa Santos

Sure, you want me to answer right away?

Rafael Lomeu Gomes

Yes, please.

Boaventura de Sousa Santos

That's an excellent question. Of course, no, not all current research is extractivist. In my book *The End of Cognitive Empire* (2018), I deal with this at length. There is, at present, much collaborative research. I even say that the idea of the Epistemologies of the South is a very old idea; only the name is new. I've given a name to something that has been there all along. Many people have long been working from the perspective of what I call the Epistemologies of the South. This is something that happens frequently in the academy, whether we call it post-colonial, decolonial, or whatever.

Whenever we engage in knowledge separated from other practices, we tend to name things, and sometimes think that we are discovering the things that, in fact, were already there. We come up with new names, nothing else. Of course, there have been lots of new ideas. The problem is that they are very interesting ideas and they have been there for a long time. But the dominant extractivist North-centric type, subject/object type of ideas, epistemological ideas, are still dominant in our academic life, in our universities where there are, of course, differences across the world.

If I'm teaching in Singapore, I know that I have different problems than I have if I'm in Madison, Wisconsin, or in Coimbra, Portugal. You can see that there are lots of people struggling for these new alternatives. What troubles me most is the inertia of dead ideas. That's the reason why I'm following the idea of the Epistemologies of the South as an alternative.

For 20 years, we have been criticizing the Western-centric paradigm, and yet such a paradigm is still dominant. The inertia, the dominance of this paradigm, is not scientific dominance, it is institutional. It's the departments, the journals, or the publishers. All of them conspiring to maintain dead ideas as alive. We have to deal with the inertia of dead ideas, and the only way we have is to produce alternatives. We must move from criticism to alternatives.

Epistemologies of the South (2015) is more on the critique side. *The End of the Cognitive Empire* (2018) is more on the alternative side. I pay attention to the university as well in two chapters. I call for the change from university to pluriversity and subversity. All this amounts to pleading for a pedagogical and epistemological alternative, as Sinfree is trying to do in linguistics. It seems to me that he's trying to do the counter-university inside university. Most recently I published a book titled *Decolonising the University* (2020).

We create tension in our research, and this tension can be created from the outside. For instance, I've been very active in the popular university area. If you go to the page of the popular universities of the social movements (e.g. https://ces.uc.pt/en/formacao-extensao/upms), you can see the hundreds of meetings that we have been conducting in which we bring together social scientists, philosophers and leaders of social movements. We engage in a two-day type of circle of conversation, among different knowledges, to develop new political ideas of renewal. We are going to have a forum of popular universities in Colombia in 2022 if the pandemic allows.

We have to deal with this diversity. One foot inside the university and one foot outside. Sometimes, inside the university, this tension emerges. I agree with you, the name may be new, but the practice is old. We are trying to transform an absence, as I say in my writings, into an emergence. Some things that are not there and aren't considered existent, we are trying to validate them. They only need our validation because we are in a kind of environment in which the Western-centric epistemology of the North still basically dominates our work. Thank you.

Rafael Lomeu Gomes

Thank you. There are a few more questions which are from chats people have been writing to me privately. So everyone has an idea, there is a question from Bassey, from Lynn Mario, from Andre and from Cliff. I will start with the one from Bassey. He asks, 'How would you elaborate on the distinction between urgent struggles and important struggles?'

Boaventura de Sousa Santos

I think that's a very important distinction. Let's take an example. In recent months, all of a sudden, in a city outside São Paulo in Brazil, three or four transgender persons were assassinated. And this created a lot of commotion for the transgender people. And all of a sudden, in that small city, this struggle to protect the lives of the transgender people became absolutely urgent because they were being assassinated almost one transgender per day. Does it mean that the most important struggles in Brazil or in the world are just struggles to protect the lives of transgender people? No. The urgent concept is to be used at the level of conjuncture, of the specific context in this city, in this locale. The concept of importance is the structure level. It's not of the conjuncture. It's a structural level. And at the structural level, that's where I think the work becomes more polemical, but that's because my proposal is polemical. The struggle against capitalism is as important as the struggle against colonialism and it is as important as the struggle against heteropatriarchy.

The three are equally important. I come from a tradition of Marxism that has always told me that the most important struggle is the struggle against capitalism. Now, I say, 'no!' The three struggles are equally important for the simple reason that they sustain each other. But one of them may be more urgent at a given moment. Let's take the Black Lives Matter movement. All of a sudden, this was the most urgent struggle in the United States and an important struggle against colonialism in the form of racism. As this struggle gained protagonism and strength, it brought along the anti-patriarchal and the anti-capitalist dimension of the struggle as well. Anti-capitalism anti-colonialism and anti-patriarchy have to be there as well. We know how women are usually doubly and triply dominated and discriminated against because they are black, because they are workers, because they are poor and because they are women. It's very clear. If you don't do away with capitalism, colonialism and feminism will be there forever. And vice-versa. We may have some victories in terms of feminism, but usually, if there is a victory against patriarchy, there is a defeat against colonialism. It's not mechanical. That is the dynamic. You have to theorize why we have so many feminist gains in a given society, and all of a sudden, a very brutal and violent racism against black people takes place. Why is that? Struggles are interconnected. At the structural level, they are all important. Considering urgency; sometimes some struggles are more urgent than others. And the task of the most urgent struggle, if it gains power and protagonism, is to bring along all the other struggles.

The Black Lives Matter movement, initially an anti-colonialist struggle, became also an anti-capitalist struggle and the anti-heteropatriarchal struggle.

Rafael Lomeu Gomes

Thank you. The next question is from Lynn Mario de Souza. 'You speak of entanglement. For us who deal with language and culture, can you elaborate on navigating between the commensurable and incommensurable without attempting to arrive at convergence?'

Boaventura de Sousa Santos

That's a very complex question, Lynn Mario. Let's take a concept from archaeology, which I think may be useful. In archaeology, we have the concept of the palimpsest. A palimpsest is the sedimentation of rocks, for instance, in which a layer is mixed with the next layer. They are not independent layers. One is upon the other, and we see traces and vestiges of each layer in the previous layers, and sometimes in the following layers. Sometimes, in our society, we are palimpsests. In fact, different temporalities are at stake, not just different knowledges, but different ways of being.

The reason why I speak of entanglement is because we talk about socialists, capitalists, colonialists in patriarchal societies, but this are just theoretical concepts. Societies are much wider and much more than that. They don't consist only of domination. There are other things. For instance, I'm not considering religion here. If I'm in certain societies, if I'm in India, I have to consider religion, because if I'm a Muslim, I'm not a fully Indian, according to Narendra Modi. And if I'm there, I also have to consider the caste system. If I'm a challenged person, disabled or handicapped, I have to speak of a different kind of domination. Society is very, very diverse, and, therefore, sometimes, in order to conceptualize or theorize, we make all these types of distinctions, but everything is entangled. Everything is intertwined, deeply intertwined. But your question goes much further than that.

In order to develop the concept of commensurability and incommensurability, first of all, we need to agree that there are different entities that we can distinguish. That's the first complexity. What happens is that every country has different versions of the same culture. In my work, I have never seen a culture that has just one version – not even Western culture. Regarding the concept of nature, of course, the dominant one is the Cartesian one. I sometimes feel surprised that some people don't know that the person who was really a contemporary of Descartes, Spinoza, had a completely different concept of nature. What we have to explain is why the Cartesian concept prevailed and not the Spinozist one.

Incommensurability is a different question. All different cultures have different versions of things. I usually distinguish in my work two types of versions: the porous or amoeba type of version – the type of version that is open to dialogue, that is open to be confronted with other cultures – and the fortress version. The version that says, 'this is my culture. This is not your culture. There is nothing I can tell you. There is nothing you can tell me. Nothing at all.' Total incommensurability.

These are two versions. I can direct you to concrete examples so that you can see what I have in mind. If you take Odera Oruka's work, you'll note that he distinguishes two kinds of people among the wise people of the communities, the peasant communities. All of them are wise people – the sage, as he calls them – all of them are leaders of the community, but they are of two kinds. Only one of such kinds takes a critical view of the tradition, they are the didactic ones. These kinds of critical sages are the ones who have a critical distance vis-à-vis their own culture, as opposed to those with no critical distance. Oruka favors those that have such a critical distance vis-à-vis their tradition, because they are the ones who move on, who can interact productively with other cultures.

To my mind, what we are talking about is not convergence. Or rather, it's convergence by mutual enrichment, mutual transformation. For me, entanglement is basically mutual transformation. What we have to pay attention to is, 'What are the criteria for this mutuality?' Because mutuality may hide inequalities of power. You have to be very critical about this, because if you take the Eurocentric, Western-centric ways, we do have to ask: what is inclusion? What happens is that we decide what inclusion is and then we allow other people to get in. A truthful intercultural inclusion is that the people that are struggling for inclusion are going to change the criteria of inclusion, only then is inclusion not exclusionary. Our version of inclusion in the Western-centric societies is exclusionary. I think that in these lines we have moved on to the ideas of entanglement. Thank you.

Rafael Lomeu Gomes

Great. The next person who would like the question himself is André Coutinho. André, the floor is yours.

André Coutinho Storto

Thank you. I'm going to try to be brief. Professor, thank you for your talk. I would just like to know, it's something that I feel underlies everything that's been said, so far. You mentioned about the pedagogical, epistemological and methodological dimension of Epistemologies of the South. For me, I'd like to know what you think about the ethical dimension? I think it's also very important, if we consider that capitalism kind of determines all the ethical relationships in societies. We have societies, and more and more, consumers are more powerful than citizens. I would like to know from you, where do you see the role of ethics? To implement an epistemology of different methodologies, we need an ethical shift – paradigm shift as well. I would like to know where you see the role of ethics, and, if there is a role for different kinds of ethics, if it's possible to have an ecology of ethics in this scenario?

Boaventura de Sousa Santos

André Coutinho, thank you very much. Well, it's a hard question. Because if you really distinguish between epistemology and ethics, in Western-centric tradition, ethics are probably more likely to come up with the idea that universalism is fake. If for nothing else, because there are double standards, not just in application, but also in the construction of the standard articles. We can observe this in Hinduism in its different forms, and we see it in Aristotle, as well.

Where do I stand on this? First of all, there are general rules that apply to ethics. The Epistemologies of the South presuppose an abyssal line. The abyssal line is actually the measure of how I understand ethics. My ethics is an abyssal ethics, as opposed to the North-centric ethics. According to the latter, there are human beings, there is humanity, and we apply ethical terms and ethical concepts to humanity. In fact, this idea of ethics considers humanity a reality. For the Epistemologies of the South, in fact, humanity is a project. It's not a reality. Because as long as there is capitalism, colonialism and patriarchy, not everyone can be dealt with and treated as a fully human being. Indeed, you probably know more about this than I, I've been reading some interesting new forms of ethics in some traditions that are really very transgressive, so to speak.

Therefore, if you don't really take into account this idea, the idea of the abyssal line, and apply the ethical standards as if there were no abyssal exclusion of people, it will be very confusing because you are going to apply the instruments of law, of ethics to people who are not considered fully human. If you take the case of George Floyd, we cannot imagine that the policemen would have his knee for eight minutes on the neck of a white person. It is simply impossible to imagine such a thing. But with a Black person, it is possible. Last week in Brazil, a Black guy was killed in the open, in the supermarket, a car supermarket, and there was a woman filming the assassination without intervening. Look at this abyssal line. This woman was making a video, of course, with a very good intention. She could denounce the crime, but she didn't intervene. The protection of life, the ethical value of life, was less important to her than the protagonism of producing a video on that assassination. You can see that our society produces these ethical subversions because of the abyssal line. There are several people in different countries who I am working with on the concept of the abyssal line. As I keep saying – I say it in *The End of the Cognitive Empire* – that this work is in progress. We are still struggling for these new concepts and examining, for instance, the application of the abyssal line to ethics, to art, and to aesthetics.

I'm probably more advanced in dealing with aesthetics than with ethics, because I could deal with people outside academic life who helped me a lot to question the concept of art and the consciousness of it as aesthetics. For example, I work with rappers. You know, music of particularly Black people and Indigenous people now in different continents, from Angola, to Colombia, to Brazil and to Mexico. In ethics, I have had some difficulty. I have worked with Indigenous people and for them, ethics – the values of ethics – are so different from mine that I feel unsettled. For instance, contaminating a river, for me, is a crime against the environment. For them, it is equivalent to a crime against humanity, because the river is sacred, the source of life. It's like killing your mother. I mean, it's qualified as homicide. For me, it's clear that there is no universal ethics. It's clear. I think that we are in a stage in which we have to identify the abyssal line and see the parochiality, the provincializing, and the two sides of the colonial divide Chakrabarty (e.g. 1992) talks about. We have to provincialize ethics and see what we can get from there. And as with our colleague earlier, we don't want to fall into relativism, because we want to develop the struggles against capitalism, colonialism and patriarchy.

We cannot accept the idea that anything goes, that everything is valid for all the purposes. No. How do you construct these criteria? It cannot be abstract and universalist. It has to be constructed from bottom up, through a concept that we have been talking about which is very important: intercultural translation. We have to start from bottom up, from the struggles, and bring in the concept of intercultural translation. The first move for a new concept of ethics, or an ecology of ethical values, starts from an intercultural conception. Let me direct you to a chapter of mine in *Toward a Multicultural Conception of Human Rights* (1997). There is also a small book that I published with Stanford University Press. It's called *If God Were a Human Rights Activist* (2015), where I'm trying to deal with liberation theology, intercultural theologies and so on. I know it's impossible to give you a full response, but that's my response. Thank you very much, André.

André Coutinho Storto

Thank you. Thank you very much.

Rafael Lomeu Gomes

Okay. We still have 10 more minutes left for this general discussion, and I have a couple more questions that people have written in the chat. The next one is from Cliff Ndlangamandla. He writes, 'Please comment on knowledges born in struggles of marginalized African languages in South Africa. Should Indigenous people demand protest and use these languages forcefully so that the English status quo can be dismantled?'

Boaventura de Sousa Santos

Cliff is the name of the person, right?

Rafael Lomeu Gomes

Yes.

Boaventura de Sousa Santos

If we really follow seriously the Epistemologies of the South, we don't have general recipes. We don't have norms or measures that are universally valid, because, by nature, norms or measures have to be born in struggle. We have to contextualize things. What is a struggle, an important struggle and an urgent struggle? From what I've experienced in South Africa, and I was reading recently a paper by Julius Nyerere, the leader of Tanzania whose three-volume work just came out. Nyerere wrote in the 1960s, long before Ngũgĩ wa Thiong'o, about Indigenous languages in

Africa. He was really concerned that education would not move forward if people were not able to speak and to learn in their own language, meaning, not English. And, as you know, wa Thiong'o developed this idea much further.

As far as I know, the struggle is going on. I understand lots of people are doing research about those Indigenous languages. What we need is intercultural translation among different languages. The problem is that we cannot translate everything, because there is no absolute transparency between cultures, nor is it desirable. We are in between two extremes of total transparency and total incommensurability and there is the danger of falling closer to one or closer to the other. You have to know the contexts very well and pay attention to transformation: 'Why do I have to go on thinking that English is the language of Britain?,' asked Chinua Achebe. 'Language is being reinvented all the time. Our language is our language. It's my own language I have to take over.'

I don't know the case of South Africa, but I know the case of Mozambique. Samora Michel, from the very beginning said, 'Portuguese is our vehicular language.' It's a national language because it's the language that allows us to understand each other, because the north speaks Makhuwa, Xitsonga – not everyone speaks Xitsonga – the different languages. We need a kind of a vehicular language. At the time, there was an idea that all the other languages would also be taught at university and schools. This is the part that has been neglected ever since. I think that probably, people in South Africa will find a way of having a kind of a general, vehicular language for certain purposes, and probably another language for other purposes, as they already have an official law for certain purposes. For instance, for commerce, and then for family issues, they have the traditional law. They have different laws.

Rafael Lomeu Gomes

Okay. We have time for one final question before Makoni makes some final comments, and this is from Cristine Severo. She asks, 'thanks for this inspiring and challenging discussion. My question is related to the challenges faced by us in creating a more solidary and dialogical knowledge-making and disseminating processes. What do you understand by solidarity?'

Boaventura de Sousa Santos

Solidarity means taking risks, basically. Taking risks is to take part in the struggle against domination, and you can't do that if you are only at the university. I think that the death sentence for the Epistemologies of the South is when it will become a good name for a department or for a course. The Epistemologies of the South have to prosper outside the university and in the struggles. Of course, the university is also a site of struggle. We have to do that. Please, don't get me wrong. The other struggles are outside, so you have to fight outside, and I have dedicated my life to this for already 20 years. 50% of my time is with the university, 50% is with social movements. It's the only way not to be corrupted, because the generative ideas in my theorizing come from practice. I don't invent them. I've been working now very deeply in a theoretical issue: the criteria to distinguish important struggles from urgent struggles. Where do they come from? They come from needs of struggles that I'm confronted with. That I'm in those struggles and with people – what are you going to do? And all of a sudden, 'this is urgent. We have to focus on these.' But are we going to invest in this for our lives? No; there are many other struggles, but this one is the most urgent one.

The process is like that. If you are doing solidarity, you take risks. Just to give you an example, it's a privileged example. I almost hesitate in giving it to you. If I'm an author, I'd like to have my books read and so on; everyone that writes would like that. Books have a good readership. Because I'm very involved in criticizing the current genocidal president of Brazil, Jair Bolsonaro, some public institutes have ceased to recommend my books and indeed have blacklisted them. That's the risk that we have to run into. I'm very glad to be on that list, because the people that are in my company are Karl Marx, Michel Foucault and Paulo Freire. Can you imagine? Paulo Freire! I think that this risk is a very small risk if you are out there. The pandemic is affecting our struggles immensely because our struggles have to be done outside and now, it's confinement. And it's difficult. The extreme right is going out to the streets, not the left, because the left is really concerned about the pandemic, the extreme right ignores that. They are taking over the streets in many, many places. We have to be aware of that, and also to deal with that critically. For an academic person engaged in his or her work and career, solidarity with social struggles entails risks.

If you are in academic life, you have to take care of your promotion. I'm always in favor of helping young scholars and young faculty. Don't take too many risks, don't take them individually. You should take them always collectively. Organize yourselves, because, individually, you get very easily neutralized. If there is an association of progressive or intercultural, decolonial scholars, then you are better protected. You must do that collectively, so that you are better protected. But then, there are other struggles. In the other struggles – one interesting thing for you, Cristine, is that once you are outside, your knowledge is of very little value for you. It may help you in certain things, but then you see that you are as fragile as many other people, that you are as afraid of the police as they are, and you want to protect yourself as they want to protect themselves. It's a sense of humility that you have, once we are outside our comfort zone. Thank you.

Rafael Lomeu Gomes

Thank you, Boaventura, for taking risks and for inspiring us to take risks. And thanks, everyone, for your comments and questions. It's been great. I thank, in particular, Mari (Haneda), Bassey, Lynn Mario, André, Cliff and Cristine, and thank you, Boaventura, for engaging with the questions. It's a very insightful discussion. Makoni, would you like to have some final words?

Sinfree Makoni

Yes. Again, thank you to everybody. What we are going to try to do now is to give an account of my own intellectual career in a way that I have never done or said in public. My PhD was in psycholinguistics of second language acquisition, the acquisition of English by Shona speakers. But when I got into South Africa, I quickly realized that it was totally irrelevant, and the only article I have written in that area is one article which was published in the journal in the University of Edinburgh. The question then is, has the psycholinguistics of second language acquisition changed since I did my PhD in Edinburgh? My answer is no. One of the reasons why second language acquisition studies or some types of applied linguistics in Africa, in the Global South are unsuccessful, is because I think they run counter to all the various principles of what we are calling here the Epistemologies of the South. Second language acquisition, for example, sociolinguistically lacks any sense of the nature of the politics of language learning, focusing largely on an epistemology that is free of politics and struggle.

It also tends to give the impression that knowledge is about language taking place in a planet which is free from struggle, and I couldn't find a way of linking up or associating myself with it, so that's why, possibly, I think I never managed to write anything useful in that area. The second aspect of it, I think, is that second language acquisition, in some aspects of applied linguistics from the perspectives of Epistemologies of the South, is very colonial. Let me explain. If you are in a continent in which you have more people who are multilingual in different African languages, but the main thrust of the research focuses on the acquisition of English, if you situate those studies in a historical framework, what you are doing unintentionally is that you're celebrating the nature of knowledge that is validated by colonialism. And then the other thing which is there is that I think second language acquisition needs to develop a sense of a decolonized imagination. What would these studies of language acquisition look like if you pushed aside English for the time being, and tried to explore how Africans learn other languages, et cetera.

In other words, if you centered Africa in second language acquisition, the body of research that you will generate will be completely different, and I'm sure you'll come up with a much more energized second language acquisition. I would be hard pressed at the moment to come up with names of five or more serious African scholars in the psycholinguistics of any language in Africa. That is not by mistake. The absences, to borrow from Professor de Sousa Santos, is quite telling. Why is it not a fruitful line of study? Why is it that people just sidestep it? The reason, I would argue, is that it fundamentally violates some of the key issues that we're talking about in terms of Epistemologies of the South. What is important, I think, is to try to begin imagining a world of scholarship in which African sociolinguistics is at the center of the global universe. For example, Dr. Santos talks about cases where with his students will tell him that some of the problems that North America or Europe are faced with have already been solved in Tanzania, Bangladesh, et cetera.

In other words, my argument is that the strategies of language learning, which are used in an African context, may provide much sharper insight into the nature of language learning. Not only in Africa, but in the Global North as well. In other words, what I'm arguing for is a form of scholarship that moves towards Africa, rather than tries to drag Africa towards Europe and North America. That's my concluding aspect about this. This is the basic argument that I've been working with

Bassey Antia on as we're trying to develop the Epistemologies of the South. I'm now trying to narrow that down to certain segments within Applied Linguistics.

Ofelia García

I just want to say a word, Boaventura, because I think I was introduced to your work very late by Lynn Mario de Souza, and of course, Sinfree Makoni. You have transformed the way that I think about language and language education. It's always very interesting when you learn from just another perspective, so thank you, first of all. I just want to follow up with this question of the ecology of knowledges, because it's always an aspiration. It's not a reality. Even in the situations that you described today. There were people who wanted to enter into the dialogue, and I always think of Gabriela Veronelli's work (e.g. 2015) on the decolonial, which again, Lynn Mario introduced me to. Her ideas surround the fact that there is no dialogue possible when people are considered less than human, which is still the way in which many racialized language learners are looked at today. I wanted you to talk about the ecology of knowledges in those situations of such unequal ways in which we look at each other, that the communication is impossible. Thank you.

Boaventura de Sousa Santos

Ofelia, this is really a million dollar-worth question at the end of our conversation today. Well, it's a very important question because sometimes we have this anthropocentric type of idea that we solve the problems of the world, and it is obvious today, in our lifetimes, that history has a much larger patience than we do. If you enter a situation of extreme discrimination and extremely drastic and violent hierarchy, in such a situation in which some humans with whom you are trying to have an interaction are generally considered as sub-humans and, therefore, have no equal partners for a conversation, this is very challenging. It's challenging for both parties, in fact. I have to tell you, that's why I came up with the idea of the popular university of social movements (see www. universidadepopulardosmovimentossociais.org). I encourage you to try to organize this, because this project of popular education is important, in my view. We organize two-days workshops. Staying for two days in residence where the 1/3 intellectuals, academics, and 2/3 leaders from different movements – women, ecology, peasants and urban, and so on – and no more than 40 people. Then, we work and we live in residence. We're in the same place, not a university place, of course. And we have our meals, and so on, for two days. In our circles of conversation, nobody should speak for more than five minutes. It's an amazing transformative experience, particularly for academics. Just to give you an anecdotal type of information, but it's real, in the first day of conversation, usually leaders, particularly Indigenous leaders or peasant leaders or activists, are relatively silent. If not silent, they don't speak much, while the academic people are used to speaking. It's really difficult to keep the intellectuals to three to five minutes. But the leaders, usually the activists, don't even take that time. Then, we go out at the end of the sessions, we stay there because we are in residence, and we go for lunch. After dinner, we're just dancing or chanting, and sometimes drinking some alcohol (if we are not in a Muslim country). The transformation is the following. Often intellectuals/academics don't know how to dance, while activists dance very well, in general. All of a sudden you see the intellectual in a corner, trying to go on with the discussion on the topics of the day, just because they are very uncomfortable. They don't know how to dance. They feel very uncomfortable, and the activists, they dance and sing and so on and they – it is almost, you know, playful revenge. The second day, the activists are speaking. They gain their place and their location – speaking location – and they speak more confidently, and so on. And people start to learn. This is just an anecdote that tells you that all knowledge systems are contextual and are systems of ignorance. It's to say, whenever we teach something and learn something, we tend to produce ignorance on some other things. Therefore, that's why we are very good at theories, but very bad at dancing. Therefore, you have to create situations in which you are outside of your comfort zone. And when you are outside of your comfort zone, you become much humbler. On the following day, we pay much more attention to what other people are saying. They're sometimes confronting you. We pay them our attention, because in a sense, they have grown up out of this inequality, because there was an opportunity for them to show capabilities that you don't have.

This is what the society does not allow us to do, so you have to go by experiments, to try to train more people, young scholars, young people and activists, because our knowledge is very useful for activists. Don't get me wrong, they sometimes need it badly. Another anecdote: some years ago, I was in a meeting of Indigenous leaders in Bolivia. There were women, there were activists, it was the time of Evo Morales. And the women were insulting each other, saying 'You are a neoliberal! You are a neoliberal! You have done that...' and so on, and they were going on for an hour, and I was a little bit taken aback. 'What is this? These women have been in social movements all their lives.' By the middle of the conversation, the leader of one of the women groups addressed me, 'Professor Boaventura, could you explain to us what neoliberalism is?' After these insults for an hour, I tried to explain what neoliberalism was. At that point, my explanation calmed down people: none of them was neoliberal. They have different views on politics, but neoliberalism was an insult. Sometimes in a highly polarized situation, you tend to insult instead of arguing.

Our knowledge is useful and it's very important in the struggles, and we should develop that. But fairly, it's a process of co-creation of humanity. This attempt to interact with people is to co-create humanity. Humanity is not a given. It's an aspiration, as you very well said. Thank you.

Ashraf Abdelhay

Hello. Thank you so much. I need to ask a question, and before that, I need to make a comment about the word 'dialogue.' First, I need to thank you for the very insightful presentation. The way the word 'dialogue' is used in political discourse – a serious form of political discourse – if you look at the word 'dialogue,' the way it's used, for example, in the Israel-Palestinian conflict, it is used as a strategy of containment, a strategy of control. The word 'dialogue' is misleading. It serves the interests of the person, not the word 'dialogue' in the way that can transform both sides. My point is, don't you think that we need to differentiate the way we use 'dialogue' in a more critical way? The second question is about intercultural translation among languages. How do we do the cultural translation for social justice if some languages themselves are treated as sub-languages, and of course, human themselves? How can that be done, similar to Ofelia's question?

Boaventura de Sousa Santos

Could you explain a little bit more on the second one?

Ashraf Abdelhay

To have intercultural communication among different languages, to achieve social justice or equality or something, we need to at least assume that all languages, or at least those languages, are validated as languages, as fully respected languages, at least. But if some languages are degraded or invalidated, how can they be part of that process for achieving social justice? I mean, the intercultural transfer itself again can be misused, can be abused, see what I mean? The last point is about colonialism. I like your distinction between historical colonialism and other forms of colonialism because this can allow us to bring on board other modern, non-Western colonialisms which are performed by – as were conceived from the Western perspective – peripheral countries. Let me give concrete examples; look at Yemen. There's a war in Yemen. That war actually is launched by another country, a neighboring Arab country. The Yemeni people are now seeing that war as a kind of colonialism, it's a form of colonialism. Saudi Arabia is colonizing that country, and Emirates is corrupt, see what I mean? Of course, the West is included as colluding with those powers, but there are other forms of colonialism, outside the second, see what I mean? I think that distinction which you've made that the historical colonialism and other forms of colonialism can address those issues. How do you react to this? Thank you.

Boaventura de Sousa Santos

Thank you very much. What is your first name?

Ashraf Abdelhay

Ashraf.

Boaventura de Sousa Santos

Ashraf, That's a very good point. The first one on dialogue, yes, we have to start from the assumption that these concepts are either used in good faith or not in good faith. But what does it mean to be in good faith? In my work, I'm more concerned with creating inter-knowledge to strengthen struggles among the oppressed than between the oppressor and the oppressed. What I have found in my work is that often the articulation among social movements is difficult: Indigenous people don't go along with women, women don't go along with trade unions, trade unions don't go along with the ecological movements, and so on and so forth. There is a problem, because we need to unite struggles against domination, to avoid the fragmentation of resistance. Many progressive people think that after independence, there is no colonialism. But we have to say that there is colonialism. It has been argued, for instance, that Apartheid South Africa was not colonialist because it was an independent country. But we have come to know that in post-apartheid Africa, there is still a lot of colonialism. It is enough to look at the land question (think of Steve Biko). Very little redistribution, and, should we say, redistribution or devolution. Think of 1913 laws.

Our concepts must be posted on these two registers. If we were dealing with inter-knowledge among oppressed groups, these contradictions and these differences would have to be dealt with through dialogue in good faith. Sometimes – maybe not – but you have to develop the common interests against oppression, out of which you can develop a sense that we can grow together and grow better if you are in interaction, if you are not alone in the struggle and isolated from the others. The dialogue here is empowering, to the extent that we strengthen our struggle against domination. But what is the dialogue between an oppressor and the oppressed? When power differences are so striking, there is no dialogue possible, at least in good faith, because dialogue is sharing, but a reciprocal sharing that has nothing to do with unilateral philanthropic sharing. Our focus should be on self-empowerment.

Again, examples. For instance, we have a tradition in which social movements don't interact with parties and parties with social movements in many countries. I looked at the municipal elections in Brazil in 2021. At that time, 200 Indigenous people became members of the local government; also, all of a sudden, 47 black women that came from the social Black movement were elected to the government through a leftist party. How did this happen? These women had never been heard of before. They were invisible before they organized a movement. They organized a movement, they became visible, and all of a sudden, they rose to the position of inter-dialogue with a party to change the priorities of the party. There are things that we have to do through non-dialogue to become a partner in a dialogue. That's something the liberal dominant ideology does not allow, because they think that everything can be dealt with through dialogue. Habermas represents the most accomplished liberal consciousness, and I respect this philosopher, but he is an abyssal philosopher, because he presupposes that we are a humanity in argumentation. We are not. What kind of a dialogue is happening between Europeans or North Americans and the immigrants from Africa trying to enter in their countries? All the dialogue is trying to do is to convince them to go back to their countries, to deport them.

It's bad faith. It's not dialogue. That will be my position on that concept, and I thank you, Ashraf, for that question. The second is concerning intercultural translation. You can never have this romantic, liberal idea that interest in intercultural translation means that both parties are on an equal footing to enter into a conversation. Now, a progressive intercultural translation is a device for developing interknowledge among groups that starts from inequality and moves toward reducing that inequality. It's always like this, it starts from the assumption of unequal power and tries to rise to a more equal power position. More equal power means changing the terms of the dialogue and even the topics of the conversation.

The third one is a very easy question. Of course, colonialism existed before capitalism. Then capitalism reconfigured it to produce highly devalued labor like slave labor, and then it became a Western thing, but as we know, some of the slaves were already slaves in Africa. Today, there are many other forms of colonialism, well, China, for instance, produces colonialism inside China. See the situation of Rohingya people in Myanmar. They are victims of colonialism by the Buddhist monks. It is true there are many non-Western forms of colonialism, because, I think, they have learned the lesson from the West. The West has been very good at teaching colonialism in one place, and some people that were formerly colonized are now producing colonialism among themselves. Saudi Arabia is a very good example, because it's a creation of the Western power to grant access to the oil.

Okay, I'm running out of my time, you go on with the after-party, but unfortunately, I must attend to my students here. Thank you very much for the session. Goodbye. Thank you, all of you. Thank you.

References

Chakrabarty, D. (1992) Provincializing Europe: Postcoloniality and the critique of history. *Cultural Studies* 6 (3), 337–357.
de Sousa Santos, B. (1997) Toward a multicultural conception of human rights. *Zeitschrift für Rechtssoziologie* 18 (1), 1–15.
de Sousa Santos, B. (2014) *Epistemologies of the South: Justice Against Epistemicide*. New York: Routledge.
de Sousa Santos, B. (2015) *If God were a Human Rights Activist*. Stanford: Stanford University Press.
de Sousa Santos, B. (2016) Epistemologies of the South and the future. *From the European South: A Transdisciplinary Journal of Postcolonial Humanities* (1), 17–29.
de Sousa Santos, B. (2018) *The End of the Cognitive Empire: The Coming of Age of Epistemologies of the South*. Durham, NC: Duke University Press.
de Sousa Santos, B. (2020) *Decolonising the University: The Challenge of Deep Cognitive Justice*. Newcastle: Cambridge Scholars Publishing.
de Sousa Santos, B. and Meneses, M.P. (eds) (2019) *Knowledges Born in the Struggle: Constructing the Epistemologies of the Global South*. New York: Routledge.
Gilley, B. (2017) The case for colonialism. *Third World Quarterly*. https://doi.org/10.1080/01436597.2017.1369037
Oruka, H.O. (ed.) (1990) *Sage Philosophy: Indigenous Thinkers and Modern Debate on African Philosophy* (Vol. 4). Leiden: Brill.
Nkrumah, K. (1965) *Neo-colonialism: The Last Stage of Imperialism*. Nashville: Thomas Nelson & Sons, Ltd.
Veronelli, G.A. (2015) The coloniality of language: race, expressivity, power, and the darker side of modernity. *Wagadu: A Journal of Transnational Women's & Gender Studies* 13.

4 Upending the Inhuman: Decoloniality, Postmodernism and Afrocentricity

Molefi Kete Asante

Chanel Van der Merwe

Molefi Kete Asante is Professor and Chair, Department of Africology and African American Studies at Temple University in Philadelphia. He also serves as international organizer for Afrocentricity International, and is President of the Molefi Kete Asante Institute for Afrocentric Studies. Asante is a guest professor at Zhejiang University, Hangzhou, China, and Professor Extraordinaire at the University of South Africa. Thank you so much for being with us here today, Professor Asante. The floor is yours.

Molefi Kete Asante

Thank you very much. I am extremely delighted to speak with you in this forum. And I understand that you have been going for maybe several years. It's a wonderful thing and I'm delighted. On behalf of myself, but also my department at Temple University, which is the first university to have a PhD in Africology and African American Studies, we are truly, truly happy that we always get a chance to at least raise questions that sometimes are rarely raised.

There are two propositions that I start with today, and I want to share those with you as we speak. The first one is that the racial ladder must be destroyed because it distorts Homo sapiens' reality. That is the first proposition. The second proposition is that the racial ladder has supported most European constructions of knowledge by ignoring Africa or Africa's achievements. This has also absolutely been the case with the Pan-European academy as defined by Chinweizu (Ibekwe), who has argued that in the West, what we have is a Pan-European academy with its own international guardians, deans, guardrails, protocols and regulations that substantially emphasizes a white cultural and racial supremacy and ignores Africa and the rest of the world. It has also been the case not just within the West. I mean, Marxism had that problem very early on, and Lenin especially expressed it. And many African Americans who had early on joined the Communist Party in the early part of the 20th century felt a need to express their alienation around the questions of nation and the question of culture.

These issues that are situated by the two propositions I have mentioned have been problematic, and they're problematic not just for African cultural spaces, but they are problematic in assuming that so-called 'developmental stages' of Europe represent a universal pattern of development. This is not just in terms of material development, but also in terms of epistemological development. Some people have taken the false idea that there is a lack of productive information from African culture as a part of their worldview. I assert that we need a new ethic of relations, and I also assert that the ideas that have been offered – whether postmodernism or decoloniality for example – have offered us routes to establishing new relations, but without an assertive Afrocentricity. These have gone nowhere in terms of dealing with the Pan-European Academy.

A few years ago, I was invited to a conference in Penang, Malaysia, where we discussed the decolonizing of the universities. In that conference, I explored the idea of human knowledge being derived very early on by Homo sapiens who originated on the continent of Africa and spent three-fourths of the time of Homo sapiens on the Earth inside Africa. In other words, not until 70,000 years ago did Homo sapiens migrate out of Africa. Of course, all Homo sapiens didn't migrate out of Africa but the migration to the rest of the world began about 70,000 years ago, even though we know that Homo sapiens have been around about 300,000 years. The question becomes, certainly to those of us who think about it, what happened to Homo sapiens during the 230,000 years that Homo sapiens lived on the continent of Africa? I mean, what were people thinking about? What did they do? How did they form societies and relationships? Who established ideas of kinship? Who looked at the stars and named them? Who domesticated the cow? Who first decided how to forge a stream and to go across a river?

I mean, all these things had to be worked out, including how humans lived with each other, how humans spoke with each other and how humans had interactions with each other. These things had to be worked out before the migration out of Africa. It would seem to me that that is possible. Part of what has happened to us as modern scholars, or people who are investigating knowledge and information, is that we have a truncated sense of human knowledge. This notion of human knowledge, beginning with Homer, for example, with the Greeks, has devastated human thinking and has created corruption in almost every theory, almost any episteme that you think about in terms of the Western field of knowledge. This has rarely been questioned. It seems to me that Afrocentricity, which emerged in the 1980s and was, of course, hotly contested by those who felt threatened by the questions that were raised by it, really has been, in my judgment, the only episteme that has challenged the cocoon that has become the Pan-European Academy. This is a profound problem in knowledge, and in not just knowledge production but in our understanding of ourselves as Homo sapiens.

I'm raising this question this way because for me, the problem with this condition that we find ourselves in as intellectuals is that we are running around in the same arena over and over again thinking that when we see something that is a little different, then perhaps we have finally found a way out of this arena that we are stuck in, and we have not. Now, I want to talk probably a little bit about postmodernism and then a little bit about postcoloniality, and then offer some Afrocentric ways of adjustment to this. Maybe I should start with postmodernism, because I think as a graduate student at the University of California, for me, I grew up in the era when postmodernism was extremely popular. This is, of course, what we all were engaged in, to some degree. I was also engaged quite heavily in the anti-apartheid movement and the civil rights movement during that era as well. But all these things sort of converged, in the work of, and certainly the writings of, Frantz Fanon. We also saw them, of course, as I will point out, in other writers as well. Amílcar Cabral, for example, and so on.

Postmodernism, as we all probably know, is considered a response to modernism. It thrusts us into, what I call, the discourses of uncertainty, of fluidity. That is why one of the Portuguese Afrocentrists, the late Ana Monteiro-Ferreira, has been able to critique postmodernism with Afrocentricity in her book, *The Demise of the Inhuman* (2014). Using Lyotard's concept of the inhuman, she takes time to demonstrate that we can only bring about the demise of the inhuman through engagement with the truth of human reality. And this truth of human reality is really something that has escaped the Western academy, only because the Western academy was defined – or defines itself in relationship to Europe being sort of the universal pattern, the universal model. If you accept that Europe is a universal model and you are prescribed by that, then there's almost nothing outside of it. In fact, you do not even have to raise questions about China or India or any other culture or civilization. Certainly, you do not raise any questions about knowledge before Homer and the Greeks. And, if you give Homer a date around 800 BCE, before the Christian era, then as an African scholar and an Afrocentrist, you ask the question: what happened before 800 BCE? I mean, the Pyramids were completed around 2600 BCE, and that's much further back than Homer's Iliad and the Odyssey.

If anything is the magnet for our understanding of knowledge in the ancient world and antiquity, particularly in terms of what we have as written information, then the Pyramids would be the central document of antiquity. If the Pyramids are the central document of antiquity – whether you're talking geometry or astronomy or chemistry or physiology or writing – if that's the truth of the matter, and it seems historically that that is certainly the case in relationship to the Greeks, then we have been led down a false path. Not only have we been led down a false path, our path has been made much too short. Of course, that means that is a problem for our knowledge because, after all, Imhotep, who was the Black founder and creator and developer and architect for the first Pyramid, is a name that is far more significant in terms of human knowledge than Homer.

I raise this because these are – people say they are contentious, but they are not contentious. They are just enlightened or endarkened information. It is information that you do not normally get, whether you are in school in the United Kingdom or the United States or even in South Africa. I mention South Africa too because I'm in South Africa quite frequently and two years ago, before COVID, I flew to Mpumalanga to visit the Place of the Stones. This is where you have, of course, the oldest human construction that we probably have on the Earth in *Inzalo Y'langa*, 'Place of the Rising Sun.' And it's suspected that it's over 100,000 years old. You ask yourself a question when you see it, as I did – I just made a special trip there with my friend Simphiwe Sesanti – to ask myself the question, where is this in the record of human knowledge and information, construction, architecture? Who has done this? I mean, who has looked at this, and so forth?

You have to ask these questions only to get at an engagement with the truth of human reality. Otherwise you are locked into this box, this cocoon that we all are debating about and we get engaged in, and then we find out we cannot get out of it. Perhaps we have forgotten the lessons that being human – I mean, the lessons that have always been given to us by the experiences of humanity. And in fact, we have often, I think, violated the very basis of our humanity. Hence, we are today, in some senses, as far away as we were 100 years ago in this country, in the United States, with the Red Summer of 1919 which saw the epitome of the lynching of Black people in this country. We are not so far away from 200 years ago when, at 1821, Africans in the United States were being so badly dealt with that those Africans who were free, who were not enslaved, decided they wanted to move to Liberia.

What are we engaged in? I think the suspicion betrayed by two movements, by the postmodern one and the postcolonial one, is that we are held hostage by an imaginary construction, a mental imprisonment that is being now breached by many of the people that you could refer to – and I am one of them – as prisoners. Take postmodernism again, for example, because it achieved its height, during the time that I was a student at UCLA at '60s and '70s with European authors such as Foucault, Lyotard, Derrida, Althusser. There was something valuable in the movement, and I recognized that as a young person. I was sort of happy, in a way, about some of it because it seemed to me, at that time with a young mind, that they were in fact really going to take down this whole regime of white racial hegemony that had dominated education. Of course, alas, I was disappointed.

The Afrocentrist, Monteiro-Ferreira, discussed this situation in a wonderful way. She said the conceptual rigidity of a hegemonic European sense of truth and history, whose super ordained structure not even the Marxist revolution could disrupt, was in fact shaken by the radically emancipating activities of the feminist agenda, civil rights movement, and so forth. We felt that, perhaps for the first time, women would at least bring us some new venture that would challenge the very structure that had created the oppressive hierarchy, the patriarchy that they were living under. Again, we were disappointed that the white women, certainly in the Western world, did not see that reality as a part of what they were engaged in. They, in turn, adopted that structure that had already been established.

The postmodernists have generally taken, what we have called, an 'anti-modern stance.' That is a good thing because they are against, as we know, the grand narrative, the Western grand narrative which has always emphasized, when you look back at it, the supremacy of reason, universal truth, and perhaps the coming of human happiness and progress by virtue of reason and truth. Of course, the definitions of reason and truth by Europe have always been self-interested. I have always taught my students, and I always believe, I really do quite strongly, that postmodernism in the West is nothing more than an extension of the totalizing ideas of Western modernity with a new face because, in the '60s and '70s, we thought we were getting something new. They called it the 'New World Order.' Sometimes they would even say the 'New World Information Order.' But this New World Order, is passing now, in a sense, because what people discovered was it was simply the extension of the old world order.

So how to get from postmodernism to anti-modernism reminds me of the coming debate that we – or the debate that we are having now all over Africa – I mean I was at UNISA maybe three years ago and was asked to speak to the entire faculty of UNISA about Afrocentricity. It was one of the most powerful intellectual experiences I have ever had because I spoke to every faculty – the Faculty of Law, the Social Sciences, Agriculture, et cetera, et cetera. Each day I would go to a different faculty and we would spend two or three hours talking about how to actually re-examine the knowledge from the standpoint of African people as being subjects and not victims. Not on the margins of Europe, not on the periphery of China, not on the cusp of something else, but African people interrogating themselves, interrogating their own history, our condition historically, our condition materially, and what we have seen, and approach it from an agency point of view, African people as agents and not mere spectators to knowledge. After all, Homo sapiens arise in Africa and after all, the first civilizations are Africans.

If Homo sapiens rose in Africa and the first civilizations are out of Africa, the question has to be: What then were the form and ideas of those people, those societies? We normally say in Western tradition that these were prehistoric of times. When you say prehistoric, that means, 'Well, let's not even go there. We do not have writing as defined by the West.' But I've been in many of the caves and under the ledges in South Africa and Zimbabwe where I lived for a time, and I've walked up in Domboshawa and seen the writing of African people, the people on the continent many thousands of years ago, long before the Pyramids. When you do this, you ask yourself the question: how do we get the idea that there is not writing; that human beings have not communicated with each other; that they are not entertaining themselves through signs and symbols? I mean, who made this separation and why? These are the questions that have to be raised and they have only been raised, it seems to me, by the Afrocentrists. I am very happy that Dr Nah Dove is here because her book, *Afrikan Mothers* (1998), for example, was one of the very earliest books to emphasize the role of the African woman at the very beginning and the very heart of understanding how human societies are put together.

The other contribution that she has given is the idea of Maaticity, based on the ancient concept of Maat, that was at the heart of what African people understood by how you lived together with people. How do we live together without killing each other? I mean, there had to be a miracle to that – not a miracle, but there had to be a human achievement. There had to be a great achievement to live together because if, as we say and as we know, that early human beings on the continent of Africa had to establish certain protocols of life so that we could live with each other and share with each other, then we had to understand that that had to be based on something. What was it based on? The farthest back we can go is the concept that truth, righteousness, justice, order, harmony, balance and reciprocity would provide you with this. But not only that, African people knew even on – when I say African people, I mean the early Homo sapiens in Africa knew – I mean, even if you take the question of difference, which is very big in the conversation today, the question of difference, I mean Africans knew that human beings came in all forms and shapes. Some were lighter than others, some were darker than others. Some were tall, some were short. But Africa – never, never in antiquity is there a place where Africa saw difference in terms of the ranking of human beings. Think about that. That, as far as we know, for at least the time that African people were living solely only in one continent, human beings were living on one continent, what was at work was Maaticity. That is the search for order, balance, harmony, justice, truth, righteousness and reciprocity. It had to be a search for how we live with each other. But it was the imposition of ranking on humans, and rating of humans by imposing one's imagination – this imaginary racial ladder that I have spoken of earlier – that becomes the biggest, biggest problem.

The modernists posited liberty and equality as something that was real, but the postmodernists saw that these things were not grounded in human conditions as we knew it. I mean, you can talk about liberty and equality and these ideals, and we may think of them as worthy ideals and worthy objectives, but they are, nevertheless, ideals. This, I think, is a contribution of postmodernism to point that out, although from an Afrocentric point of view, we see that postmodernism is elusive itself as a concept. I mean, postmodernists say that equality and reason, these things are elusive, and liberty, this is elusive, but postmodernism as a concept is elusive. One could say that we knew where the modernists were, but the ambiguity and the fluidity and uncertainty of postmodernism often appears to me like a fleeting feeling in the brain. Yeah, I see it, yeah, I don't. Yes, I see it, no, I don't. But it prevailed in our thinking with the breaking down of the totalitarian regime of modernism. I am happy about that, and I am happy about its demise, its collapse, but it remains in many guises.

So that's the one thing that postmodernism – I may come back to that, but let me just say this a little bit about postcolonialism and also probably a little bit about decoloniality. Postcolonialism refers to the effects of colonization on culture and society, and decolonization refers to the taking down of all forms of colonial power, but they are often considered different from decoloniality. I know this is a big issue right now in South Africa and in some universities. There is a whole debate over decoloniality and Afrocentricity. I think that there are certain ways in which these ideas may certainly converge and that there are certain kinds of things that they are trying to get at. I probably would not use decolonial for reasons that I will explain later. But, I do understand what is attempted here.

I often say, however, that when you have a big debate or discussion, as they had in Cape Town in South Africa over the statue of Rhodes, that it is good to tear down the statue of Rhodes. Of course, he was one of the biggest racists of all time. But the question is then, if you want to represent something, then what do you do next? That is a real question, and that is where Afrocentricity has often come in because Afrocentrists say, 'Okay, well, you can take down Europe materially, you can even take down the epistemes that have been developed by Europe, but what do you have that you can use to understand your own life?' That is where the assertion of agency on the part of Africans come from. But the only way that Africans can get this kind of assertion is to interrogate the African past. The interrogation of the African past has been delayed because what intervened was the European way of thinking that came in and stopped Africans from even inquiring into their life in the village in a contemporary sense.

One of my students from Nigeria came to me and said, 'After listening to you, I'm going to go home and talk to my mother about the sacred places in our village because as we were educated, we were educated away from our own history and our own ancestors. So listening to you, I think I want to ask her these questions.' She went on and told her mother this and said, 'Mother, I want you to take me to the strides. I want you to tell me what the history of our people is. How did we come up with these things, with Agriculture and Metallurgy? Tell me about this.' The mother broke down and cried and said, 'My daughter, who's gone to school in Switzerland and in Ohio, has now come back to Nigeria and asked me the questions that I knew she would never ask me being educated in the West.' I saw the same thing in South Africa, at UNISA. People said, 'Well, I teach Agriculture, and to teach Agriculture, I have to learn from the Western scholars who write about Agriculture.' I said, 'Wait a minute. Where are you from? How long have Africans lived in this place? Didn't Africans plant? Didn't they harvest? Have you ever interrogated that?' 'No, I haven't.' So what has Europe done? Europe has imposed its own way as universal on everybody. Of course, the Chinese now are competing for this with the Confucius institutes all over Africa, because they see it as a contest of ideas. In all of this scramble for the African mind and for the minds of the world, the real question is do we interrogate ourselves and our own history and culture to add to knowledge?

Postcolonialism, I understand what people mean by it, and I understand what people mean by decolonial. I have a big problem with it. I think postcolonial studies tried early on to interpret the impact of the inherited relationships that have come from the imperial regime of Europe. They have tried to explain contemporary political situations by looking back and saying, 'Well, when the British or the French or the Portuguese were here, these were the things that were left.' If you take the works by Grosfoguel, Mignolo, Sabelo Ndlovu-Gatsheni, they have added to our understanding of the structures of power which have been often masked in the terms of gender or race or class or religion by nation-state relationships. They have pointed out, I believe, that there are indeed bad guys and good guys. There are those who seek to eliminate competition, to deny human rights, to dominate the different, especially women, and to murder the lovers of truth. In that sense, they are different from those who aim to enlighten the ignorant or to cause justice to flourish, elevate the poor, for example, or to preserve the environment.

Postcolonialism, from its beginning, was meant to evoke a narrative, a discursive narrative about the historical role of imperialism in establishing today's power relationships. My issue with postcolonial is two-part. One part is that we are not postcolonial in the first place. We have not gone beyond – we have not gone there. We are not post anything. It is still the same system, the same hegemony. We have decolonized in many respects, but colonialism still exists. Secondly, we should not use colonialism – now I am talking specifically about Africa. We should not use colonialism as a tag for periodizing African history. It was an intrusion. It was an invasion, an imperial enterprise of about 150 years, even though the influence was longer than that, 500 years later. But the actual – for most of Africa, except for perhaps South Africa, it was less than 150 years of being in Zimbabwe, or being in Ghana, Nigeria. This intrusion, this invasion, this imperial enterprise in Africa really is small when you compare it to Africa's long history, the longest history in the world. It is unwise to speak of postcolonial in reference to Africa. What has passed is what has passed, what has been overcome is the European political occupation of the continent. That political occupation of the continent was, of course, something that we can look back at now and say that it was not only aberrant, but it was something that certainly did not help African people in terms of appreciating the possibilities that were inherent in the original structure of African society.

What we want to know Afrocentricists, as even the so-called postcolonialists, is how to unravel the state of the world. This is a worthy thing. But, I think that neither postmodernism, nor postcolonialism, can do this alone or with each other. Something more is needed, and that something more has been provided by the Afrocentrists who have been maligned because the ideas did not originate with Europe. Afrocentricity is not a white idea. That is the main reason as to why you have not only white critics of it, but Black critics of it. And you have Black critics of it because Black people also have been affected and victimized by the episteme of Europe. Part of that episteme, as you will see, comes from, what I call, 'the racial ladder.' As African ideas, or an African idea, Afrocentrists have challenged the imaginary structure of the racial ladder. Forms of oppression and forms of repression are glued to the European project.

As an Afrocentrist, I offer several observations. First as to postmodernism, it challenges the hierarchical order of the Western enterprise. Afrocentricity is a holistic theory of knowledge, a relocation of African cosmological and ontological thought of the most ancient civilizations. I seek in my work a paradigmatic demise of the Euro-centric monolithic racialist perspective of the world that establishes Europe as a universal model of the world. I also seek an end to the race paradigm which fuels the contemporary structure of the power relationships of the world. This is seen really clearly in the United States of America. Kyle Rittenhouse's acquittal was met, as you would expect, in unison by most African Americans, as an indication that a white teenager who shot and killed two people and injured a third with an AR-15 long gun would have a hard time being convicted for killing whites who demonstrated against the killing of an unarmed Black man, Jacob Blake. We saw that and we were like, 'Oh, what is this about?' It's not about law. Law is a part of it. That is the protocol. What it is about is a racial ladder. A 17-year-old Black man with a long gun shooting protestors and killing two of them could never make a defense that he was defending himself, and that he was using his gun in self-defense. That is a crazy thing to most Black people. We would say, 'Wait a minute.' Why is it crazy? It is crazy because it only happens with white people. It is a Zimmerman situation with Trayvon Martin who can get away with killing Black people. Or, killing white people who are thought to, in the vernacular of the American society, love Black people. Those white people also are considered trash in the minds of the white people who are white supremacists.

This is a contemporary issue. This is an epistemological issue. The jury's verdict in this case would never have gone that way for any young Black teenager because of the convergence of the European hegemony and the race paradigm itself. Afrocentricity does not deny a center – we accept the notion of centeredness, but this – and it's unlike postmodernism in that regard because Afrocentricity asserts the equal value of a multiplicity of human possibilities, of many human centers. Afrocentricity is an assault on every form of racism, patriarchy, oppression, repression, and is based on mutual respect of all people. That is a problem for a white racial, cultural, hegemonic, imperialistic, dominating ideology. That is why Afrocentricity is a problem. It is grounded in two facts – the African origin of humanity and the African origin of civilization. I have told you that before but, I want to just explain now this racial ladder and I will be finished.

The racial ladder has been constructed, it seems to me, over time, by religions, by saints, sages, priests of all imperial religions. You take an imperial religion, you can definitely see the ranking of people by race. You can see the racial ladder. It is so clear in history that the people who have been lighter consider themselves at the top rank, the people who are darkest at the bottom. The Black woman is at the very bottom of it. She is even below the Black man. That is the way this ranking goes. White man at the top and, in between, all these variations of color. That is an imaginary ladder. It does not exist in reality, except in the minds of the people who are practicing it. That is the key here. We have argued in social sciences that the real issue is that race is not a biological fact, so we have to get rid of race. But, the reason we cannot get rid of racism is not so much in the word 'race' itself that something is – that it is not biologically a fact. The reason is because even if you got rid of the term 'race,' what you have in the West is this conception of a racial ladder that is in the mind of almost every white person, and almost every Black person, and every Indian and every Chinese in the world largely affected by the European spread of white domination. I am not saying that the Chinese and the Indians are not affected, because they are. I mean, you can just look the Varna system. Indians see definitely that they are affected by it as well.

This notion of ranking of human beings, which also leads us into this whole question of dealing with intersectionality from critical race theory, these are all systems that are designed to obliterate the idea that we are all human beings. Being human being. If you walk through my door into my office, I do not have to ask you what your gender is, or what your sexuality is, or what your class is. If I accept human beingness, then to me, that is all that matters. That is the way it was in the beginning, and so should it be now. That is our problem. If we get rid of this, we condemn the race paradigm, we condemn the racial ladder that we have written about, Dove and I, and being human beings, transforming the race discourse. Not just for asserting the idea of race, but a cultural construct with no biological base but for constructing the racial ladder itself, the imaginary idea that keeps generating what we call 'racialist decisions.' That is our problem – something that in Europe we have dealt with for several centuries, beginning with the Germans and the English. Von Humboldt and Darwin, for example, were key actors. We all remember that Darwin's book, On *the Origin of Species* (1859), had a subtitle, *The Preservation of the Favoured Races* – whites at the top and Blacks at the bottom.

I just want to stop here and just say that I am open for any conversation. Thank you very much.

Chanel Van der Merwe

Thank you so much for that, Professor Asante. I echo Visnja in the chat that this was a very insightful and inspiring talk. Thank you so much. I will now give it over to Dr Makoni to start the conversation.

Sinfree Makoni

Yes. Thank you very much, Professor Asante. I wanted to explore a couple of ideas with you and then we can see where we go from there. Am I correct in reading your work, and reading Ana Monteiro-Ferreira's book, that you are saying that Afrocentricity is, to some extent, *Homo sapien*-centric? Would you agree with such an interpretation of Afrocentricity?

Molefi Kete Asante

Well, I would think that, if I understand you correctly, that it is definitely centered on the idea that comes from Cheikh Anta Diop who argues in his book, *The African Origin of Civilization* (1974), and also his book, *Civilization or Barbarism* (1991), that the earliest notions of how human beings have existed and lived on the Earth was found with the woman. That the notion of not just matrilineality, but matriarchy, was itself at the very beginning. It is interesting for us to explore not just woman-centeredness but the whole idea of how the transfer came in human knowledge to patriarchy. Matriarchy should not be understood as a counterpart to patriarchy, but rather, as a complementary system, but this is a different thing from what came into existence.

I would agree with you that what came into existence as a patriarchy was hierarchical and was oppressive and repressive. The system we have inherited and that has been maintained by the West was not an African system. It does not exist. It only exists in Africa after the coming of the Arabs and the coming of the Europeans. It is not an African system. The women are at the center of the African system, and if we began as Afrocentrists to probe that, we can see exactly how this came into being.

Sinfree Makoni

On page 15 of *The Demise of the Inhuman*, Monteiro-Ferreira writes – and I think this is quite consistent with your argument – 'Based on the Ma'atian ethics, an Afrocentric field of knowledge embraces a conception of a shared world of plural perspectives without hegemony.' Can you just elaborate a little bit on that?

Molefi Kete Asante

I would be very happy to. She (Monteiro-Ferreira) learned very well from one of my earlier books about the idea of pluralism without hierarchy. Essentially, what the

Afrocentric position takes is one that says that we all as human beings, regardless of what your culture is, has a cultural issue. It's not a biological issue or a racial issue. It is a cultural issue. You can have a person who may look biologically one way – I mean, if you think about how people look, people look all kinds of ways. But let me make it more concrete. Clarence Thomas, who is a Supreme Court judge in the United States, is considered a Black man. But, by all cultural indicators, he's a white man. If you look at him, you see a Black man. But culturally, he is not Black. What does that mean? You can also find white people who are culturally Indian, or you can find Indians who are culturally European. It is a cultural issue. For me, I accept all human beings without hierarchy. That is the essential notion. But what Europe imposed and many of the religions imposed was this notion of hierarchy. Hierarchy is problematic anywhere. In human beings there are 99.9% similarities. We are all human being, but our cultures can certainly be different.

Sinfree Makoni

Yes. Let me continue with this. From your past experience through your exposition of Afrocentricity, are there any studies by white students in which they are using Afrocentricity to analyze white or European behavior? Are there some students who have said, for example, 'Let's go and study how the Scottish behave using Afrocentricity?'

Molefi Kete Asante

Wow. That is a very powerful thought. I'm going to suggest that to one of my students next week. I have a white student now, Christopher Viscuso. Chris is actually studying Black culture, but the study of the white culture I think would be a really profound work. I mean, no, we do not have that yet. But I'm sure it will come. That's a powerful idea. I appreciate that.

Nah Dove

Ana Monteiro-Ferreira is an example. You were reading her work.

Sinfree Makoni

Yes.

Nah Dove

She's an example and a role model for the students who will come because they are getting it – we have white students getting into the discipline and understanding the freedom that it gives them to step outside the race paradigm. And she (Monteiro-Ferreira) offers leadership that way.

Molefi Kete Asante

Thank you. Yes, that is what Ana did. She made that path, and she was, of course, schooled originally in Europe and she was grounded in postmodernism. She came to Afrocentricity and she saw for the first time an idea that she thought should be more widely known. Had it not been for me calling it Afrocentricity, if I had called it something else, it would have been a different idea. You see what I'm saying?

Sinfree Makoni

Yes, I see what you mean. Yes.

Molefi Kete Asante

The idea was that it was based on the fact that *Homo sapiens* originated in Africa and that was the first civilization, so that is why I call it 'Afrocentricity.' But if I had said 'centricity' or something else, maybe I would have had many more people not to attack me. But the attack on Afrocentricity is a part of the racial ladder itself because can Black people theorize? Can Black people come up with theories that white people don't know anything about? That is a whole different story – so they (white people) say, no, they're (Black people) at the bottom of the ladder. There is no way it is possible that Black theorization could be a legitimate idea.

Sinfree Makoni

Yes, that's true. But even in the American academy, the Black professors only just practice. They cannot theorize. They cannot come up with new ideas which we can learn from. No, that is not possible.

Molefi Kete Asante

Yes, that's right.

Makoni

In Black Linguistics, the argument will be, 'they are just practitioners. They cannot theorize.'

Molefi Kete Asante

You precisely understand my point.

Sinfree Makoni

Yes. Yes. They just do those minor things. Anyway, then another thing that is interesting about Afrocentricity, for example, is when you talk about the dialogical methodology.

On page 32 of Ana Monteiro-Ferreira's book, she writes – this is very interesting – 'until lions can tell their tale, the story of the hunt will always glorify the hunter.'

Molefi Kete Asante

Well, she's quoting from an old African proverb.

Sinfree Makoni

Yes. Yes. But until they can – I mean, until lions can tell their own tale, the story of the hunt will always glorify the hunter. You will never get to know how the other animals were dodging or running around in circles.

Molefi Kete Asante

That's right.

Sinfree Makoni

Then she proceeds in a very interesting and concrete way. She then argues that methodologically, for example, Afrocentricity is centered in terms of location, time, place, and stance at the point of reference from which a cultural, philosophical, and historical analysis can be conducted. What I like about this is that she gets into a big philosophical discussion, but then she is very concrete about how you could proceed if you were trying to do this.

Molefi Kete Asante

Yes, it is a method. Absolutely. And we argue that – now, one of the points, Professor Makoni, that I didn't go into deeply, and it was a few years ago now, maybe 15 or 20 years ago. I was in a debate with my friend Cornel West in Dayton, Ohio. I think it was at United Theological Seminary and they had us having a debate. He (West) said, 'Molefi is interested in place, and he's interested in centeredness. But coming from the postmodern view, I am interested in fluidity.' When I had to respond, I said to him and to the audience, 'I don't have a problem with fluidity, but everything comes from somewhere. So, you have some posture and then you can be fluid.' In our lives there are many uncertainties. We cannot take a modernist position that everything is based on structure and reason and that 'it' is what it is – day is day and night is night. We must understand, though, that you must have a point of beginning. From that point, you are open to all possibilities. I think that's the same thing that Monteiro-Ferreira would say.

Sinfree Makoni

Yes. And that's why also your discussion about Afrocentricity and the issue about holism being an African conception all tie together. What postmodernism does intentionally or unintentionally is to fragment everything.

Molefi Kete Asante

Yes, of course.

Sinfree Makoni

And the impulse of Afrocentricity seems to be to go the other way around, like to go to the other extent and say 'No, look here, you need to look at these things in terms of how they are interwoven and interconnected to become a bigger whole, so to speak..'

Molefi Kete Asante

Well, that is correct, Professor Makoni, because what I am examining often is this – how we put things together again. Because Europe has many talents and many skills, Europe has done many wonderful things, and one of the things that probably helped advance European science to some degree was this notion of classification. Europeans are experts at the idea of classification and in the 16th, 17th and 18th centuries, they tried to classify everything. That is one of the talents of Europe. But the problem with that for Africa is that in many ways, in African society, you cannot separate, for example, agriculture from religion. You cannot make these separations because they are all a part of the same process and the same thing. If you made these discrete separations, you would not understand anything because everything is a part of everything. We are a part of everything. Human beings, all human beings are part of everything. Even the trees are a part of everything.

In Ghana, where I have done work, you would have drummers who would go out to the forest and before they cut a tree down, they would give a praise song to the tree to say, 'I know you are living, you are living thing, I am a part of you, but I just need you to be in another form, and I am going to cut you down to make you strong.' That is a whole different response to ecology and to environment than we would get in the West. They would say, well, trees are totally separate from us. They do not have anything to do with us.

Sinfree Makoni

Yes, thank you very much. Let me give the conversation over to Chanel and then she can invite everyone else to the conversation.

Chanel Van der Merwe

Thank you so much. Teboho Motaboli has a question.

Teboho Motaboli

Thank you to Professor Asante and thank you to organizers and attendants. I highly appreciate Professor Asante's clarification of his position and his appreciation of both forces – that it was the force of hegemony and oppression, and the possibility of Afrocentrism and empowering people who have been oppressed and whose knowledge has been overlooked or even suppressed. My perception is that the biggest problem at the moment is racism. Yes, it has historical roots, but the way I see the solution to racism is to enhance the power of Afrocentrism together with all the other south that is oppressed, and that this unity should fight in the manner of both intellectual change, psychological change, and legal change such as Martin Luther King's civil rights movement. I am a Pan-Africanist but I'm also an American, so I would like to live in a society which is fair and has equality. I see that as the biggest problem. I refer to the past only to find out which forces can help to transform these Euro-American perceptions – racism and oppression – to change them to accept equality of people from both Africa and the south altogether. Thus, I want Professor Asante to try to speak to what is a future solution to this problem as I see it myself. I see it as the problem of changing the mentality of the powers that be in Euro-America, and their perception to understand equality and accept it, and therefore after that we can live happily ever after.

Molefi Kete Asante

Teboho, thank you so much. I appreciate your comment and your question. For me, of course, for many years I asked the same question that you asked. That is why I think I kept working to come to what I consider to be a way to deal with it. If you live in a racist society, all institutions are touched by racism. If you live in the United States of America or in the United Kingdom, for example, all institutions are touched by it. I mean, they are touched by this thing. So, you want to know as a scholar, how do we resolve this issue? How can we deal with this issue? I wrote a book many years ago, 20 years ago now, called *Erasing Racism: The Survival of the American Nation* (2003). It was a very popular book at the time. But I've come so far away from that idea because that idea was based, I think, on the predicate here in your question. That idea was based on the idea that you can transform human beings by somehow teaching them that we are all equal, and that you should not look at race, and so forth.

But I have come to see that this is not the way that it works. The way I believe it works, Teboho, is something like this: The way it works is that in a society that establishes itself as our American society on somebody else's territory, first of all, the Indigenous people, you come and you set up a polity on the land of the people who are already there, and you create rules, and regulations, and laws and a constitution and say that we are now the new people who have come here. We represent a new polity and the old polity – Cherokee, and Seminole, and Muscogee, and Wabanaki and other people – they don't matter. In fact, not only do they not matter, but we will also kill you, we will eliminate you in order to advance our particular polity. And in fact, that is why so many have been eliminated.

At one time, there were only about 400,000 or 500,000 of the Indigenous people still left in the United States. Fortunately, they have grown back to over 3–4 million now. But they were just wiped out. There were campaigns to kill them – if you killed a Native American and brought their scalp, you could get acres of land for that. That was one of the patterns in New England. In Florida, near where I was born in South Georgia, Andrew Jackson set it up so that if a white person killed a Seminole and brought back the ears of the Seminole, then they could get 160 acres of land. That is how the white settled Florida. In Texas, the idea was when the whites came and took over Texas, which was part of Mexico's territory, they wanted to bring in slavery. In 1829, Mexico's first Black president, Vicente Guerrero, outlawed slavery in Mexico. The Americans then brought slavery into Mexico, and then there was the big Battle of the Alamo where the whites wanted to protect slavery and the Mexican government in Mexico City said, 'No, this is Mexico. You can't bring what you had in Louisiana over here into Texas. This is a totally different thing.' Of course, the ultimate result of this was that the whites won in the end and took half of Mexico's territory, including California and Colorado and so forth.

I'm giving you this background to say that how you deal with this issue, how you deal with race and biological issues of race and so on, is that you have to destroy the imaginary racial ladder that gives white people a sense that any and every event – whether it is an event at Penn State or at Temple or at University of Lagos, wherever it is – that white people, because they are white, by virtue of their whiteness, are at the top of the ladder. You have to destroy that. You do not have to destroy the white person. You just have to destroy the imagination in the white person's mind, and in the Black person's mind, and in the Asian person's mind that this is real as it is total rubbish. That is why, in the African American community, we are insisting that Black people confront all examples of the racial ladder. This is why Kyle Rittenhouse shows you clearly another example: the assumption that a white man who kills white people who is protesting because a Black man had been killed by the police, an unarmed Black man. That is why those protestors were out there, and those protestors were shot while running. They were people who had, in a sense, decided that culturally they were for a more progressive society, and that is what we must do. So, I don't think that talking about equality, for example, is a good issue, and there will be people who will keep those battles going, but the real battle would be every instance where you see an example of the racial ladder. It has to be attacked.

I just saw a beautiful documentary two days ago that Ava DuVernay made on (Colin) Kaepernick's life growing up. You see it very clearly that this young Black man adopted and raised by a white family is involved in situations that the family does not even understand. They do not understand why he is angry and upset. They do not see the racism against him. They do not see that a white person, a young teenager, can go and get an apple from a basket and no one says anything, and if he (Kaepernick) gets an apple from a basket, he is put out of the place. It is a whole construction, and that construction is a thing that, to me, has to be dealt with most.

Chanel Van der Merwe

Thanks so much, Professor Asante. Professor Mufwene?

Salikoko Mufwene

Yes. Thank you very much Professor Asante for presenting a clear and concise picture of Afrocentricity. And the point of the message, if I get it, is that we all must fight against Eurocentrism. And that is a fight that is more global than Africa.

Molefi Kete Asante

Yes.

Salikoko Mufwene

And in a way, Asians have been engaged in it, especially the Chinese, regarding, for instance, the evolution of mankind and the position of East Asia in this. And that is really all welcome and I'm glad that in your presentation you reflected how you have been paying attention to all these evolutions in this light. I'm very grateful that you have carried on in the tradition of Cheikh Anta Diop and reminding us of where we should go in order to reposition Africa in the history of mankind. One thing that I particularly appreciated this morning is you questioning postcolonialism. I have had this question and have discussed this question with my wife who is in the audience too. About a month ago, we were having a conversation and I said 'there is something wrong with postcolonialism, especially when it comes from North America. Because the United States, in particular, is still colonial. The people who invaded North America set a world order that belongs to them, and people think of the United States mostly as a white country and not as a Native American country, a Native American territory. And so, if people have to speak of postcolonialism, they wouldn't have to look outside the Americas. If you go to Africa, you have a certain semblance of postcolonialism in reality because the white rulers have left.' But you have also made clear that you do not need a white ruler to maintain colonialism.

Molefi Kete Asante

Absolutely.

Salikoko Mufwene

That has continued in some other ways in Africa, and intellectually we are all trapped in there. We have to start by emancipating ourselves as intellectuals in proposing alternatives. About three years ago, somebody invited me to contribute to a volume titled '*Decolonial Linguistics*.' My first reaction in reading the papers was, 'My gosh, for the past 30 years, I have been engaged in decolonial linguistics without knowing it.' It sounds like *Jourdain* in *Le Bourgeois Gentilhomme* saying 'I have been speaking prose all my life and I didn't know it.'

On the other hand, I think every approach like yours that questions the received doctrine needs refining. What I find confusing is the way in which you keep referring to Africa. To me, it is not clear if Africa before the exodus of *Homo sapiens* out of

Africa was the same or similar to Africa today in terms of people and in terms of cultures. How are we expected to think of the exodus Africa? Did that Africa not have ancestors of the same people that left Africa and the people that later on returned to Africa, and so forth? I think we need a clearer picture of that. I think during the presentation, you did not mention Black. But in answering some of the questions, Africa became confused with Black Africa. That is something that, to me, needs clarifying. At some point, you spoke, for instance, of Africans domesticating the cow. I think the domestication of the cow comes with the invention of agriculture. You did refer to African practices in agriculture and so forth, and it is all welcome. But that is the Africa post-exodus, not the Africa pre-exodus. So, we have a problem with the organization there.

I think that you would gain a lot of mileage in developing Afrocentricity in clarifying the way in which you refer to Africa. For me, born in Africa, raised in Africa, Africa is diverse even among the Blacks. That is not really against your approach because your approach is very open to diversity, to variation, but also points attention to respect of the other, and points attention to some sort of egalitarianism. That is all welcome, but it would really help if you could unpack 'Africa' and point out specifically the kinds of things that we should pay attention to and situate in the right periods of history. That is my reaction.

Molefi Kete Asante

Well, I really appreciate that, Professor Salikoko. I'm familiar with your work and certainly I appreciate all the work that you have done in your field. I appreciate your comments as well. I would like to just take up a couple of them, ones that I can remember, and see where we are. First of all, Afrocentricity is not a counterpart to Eurocentricity. Eurocentrism, as I see it, is an ethnocentric position of the hegemony of the white race. But, it doesn't have to be that. It is possible that people can be Eurocentric and, at the same time, not hegemonic. I mean, there is nothing wrong with a Eurocentric culture. If you're born in Europe and you have European traditions and values and so forth, that should not be a problem. The problem is the European attempt to dominate other cultures and other ways of life. So, if Europe, for example, took itself as itself, there's no problem with that. But then if you say, for example, that ballet is classical dance and that there is no Akan classical dance, then you have a problem with me because ballet is a European classical dance, but the *Kete* in Kumasi (Ghana) is a royal classical dance as well.

The idea that Europe imposes itself as if it is universal, that is Europe's problem. That is why we say Afrocentricity does not impose itself as if the culture of Africa, as it is interpreted today, should be imposed on everybody. We say that the values that the early African people had on the continent, that those values that we see early on in African civilization, are values that did not have the ranking of people by difference. It's the ranking of people by difference that allows Europeans to create this imaginary racial ladder in their brains and to put that in the brains of other people so that when people walk around, if they see a Black person, they have a particular view of that person. Or a young Black teenager walking the streets of a city creates a different reaction than a young white person walking the same streets. That is because there is this notion of the ranking of people on the basis of their biology. I mean, the black person may be a Clarence Thomas walking the street. So you cannot go by that. You cannot go by biology. That is what we have to confront all the time.

Now, the question of Africa – you have raised a very good question. There are 7 billion people on the Earth today. According to biology, all of them are Africans. That is, everybody on the face of the Earth today has DNA that comes from the earliest African woman that they could discover. She has given all of us her DNA. So, in that sense, the world is populated by Africans – by DNA that comes from the earliest *Homo sapiens* who are African. When people left Africa, their DNA was still African. It was still from the continent of Africa. We get the rise of humanity in East Africa and humanity spread throughout Africa first. It spread throughout the continent of Africa and then left the continent of Africa. The DNA, though, is the same. So that is why we do not deal necessarily with biology, but with culture. But what happens is that our cultures are different, and our cultures are often different by our environment.

For example, I was always fascinated as a young person to see that – and please, this is just my own personal thing – I know a lot of people love dogs, right? Well, I grew up in South Georgia. I had a dog, but the dog was outside. The dog did not sleep in my bed. The dog did not stay in my house. The dog was outside. But Europe had a special relationship with dogs – I never understood the special relationship with the dog until I heard someone say that in a cold climate, in Europe, perhaps what the people would do at the entrance to a cave is they would build a fire and they would have the dog there to protect the fire so someone could not steal the fire or put the fire out. The dog became known as man's best friend. We do not have that experience in Africa. That is a whole different kind of relationship to a dog, you see. So, environment matters. If you live on an island, it's different from if you live, perhaps, on a massive mainland.

I hear you about clarifying this notion of Africa, but I do not use the term Black Africa. My mentor, Cheikh Anta Diop, used that term, Black Africa. He used it as an emphasis. It was emphatic for him to use it to say that the ancient Egyptians were Black Africans. He had to say that in his words because otherwise, Europeans would think that the ancient Egyptians were Arabs. He said, no, they were Black African just like the Senegalese, just like the Guineans, just like the Ghanaians. These were Black Africans. I do not use the term Black Africa because we do not say white Europe. We do not necessarily say yellow Asia or brown Asian. I think that Africa, in terms of the population, in terms of the complexion of Africa, is very diverse. It is probably the most diverse continent on the face of the Earth. That is part of why the DNA of Africa is everywhere. It is very, very diverse and there are all kinds of people. I've been all over the continent, and there are all kinds of people in Africa, all kinds of languages in Africa. So, this notion of Blackness, I think we have to be careful about Blackness in that sense because the movement out of Africa obviously brought about more differentiation in how humans look. But, it is the cultural part that is much more important than anything else.

Salikoko Mufwene

Thank you.

Molefi Kete Asante

Thank you. Thank you, sir.

Chanel Van der Merwe

Professor Dove, did you want to say something?

Nah Dove

I just wanted to add a little bit to Dr Asante's work and ideas to bring in the cultural piece. I noticed that Dr Mufwene had touched upon the concept of evolution and that there is a certain evolutionist 'European way' and 'Arabic way' of looking at African people. There is an area and time when African people were supposed to be primitive. There is the idea that people leaving Africa became more civilized. But there are thousands of years where, in our discoveries, we found that African scientists, who could plot the movements of the planets and so on and so forth, had been looked at as primitive people who knew nothing, did nothing, and just barely survived, when actually, they were scientists. Among many skills that they had, and they have, they laid the groundwork for today's scientists. We must re-evaluate what we are saying when we are looking at Africa from a primitive European perspective.

The other thing I wanted to add is that, of course, there are many people in Africa, but many of them are conquerors who have imposed their cultural beliefs and values upon African people. Within Africology, we look at cultural differences and cultural similarities and we have found those things that enable us to use Diopian ideas of culture from that perspective – not the anthropological perspective, but from Diop's perspective of using culture as a tool of analysis so that we can step outside the race paradigm and re-evaluate what is actually going on in Africa. Who are the people who understand the ancient traditions or the source of ideas that can be used in today's politics? Who are the people that are there to take from Africa its wealth, and undermine the people who are there, and use the people who are there to regain this type of wealth? There are cultural differences in Africa through enemies of Africa. We have to be careful to analyze these cultural differences. I just wanted to add that, not to make it complex but to add to what has been said.

Chanel Van der Merwe

Thank you, Professor Dove. Professor Mufwene?

Salikoko Mufwene

Yes. I really appreciate your contribution, Professor Dove. For the rest of the audience, I invite you to do an exercise. Google 'the evolution of mankind' and look at the images. The representation goes from darker complexion to lighter complexion, from an image that is closer to chimps to an image that is more and more Caucasian. I have often started public presentations with that image and invited people to tell me if they saw anything wrong in the presentation. My audience is generally predominantly white in North America. Nobody ever notices that until I point it out to them. The other thing I asked them is: 'Is there anything else that you can notice?' They don't notice anything. And I say, 'It's all male.' That is very interesting. You will find several things that carry on precedence since the 19th century.

Molefi Kete Asante

Excellent.

Salikoko Mufwene

Thank you.

Chanel Van der Merwe

Thanks, Professor Mufwene. I will now take a question by Ashraf Abdelhay. He writes (in the chat): 'thanks for the useful presentation. Is there any difference between your conception of Afrocentricity and Pan-Africanism as a political movement? And also, how do you relate Afrocentricity to Southern theory?'

Molefi Kete Asante

The question of Afrocentricity and Pan-Africanism is almost like a vehicle and an engine. I think Pan-Africanism without Afrocentricity is a vehicle. It may even be very much a slogan, but it does not have a core. The core of it – and if you're talking about Pan-Africanism as a movement for the unity of African people and for bringing into existence the United States of Africa, or for bringing into existence some sort of common African project – the only way that can happen is when African people who are engaged this are on the same page. If they are not on the same page in terms of historical sensibilities and episteme, then you will not have a Pan-Africanism that functions. The core of Pan-Africanism was set by African intellectuals who were socialists. The original idea was that it should be a socialist Pan-Africanism or a socialist Africa. It was George Padmore who was a leading intellectual in this idea. I wrote a book on this last year called *An Afrocentric Pan Africanist Vision* (2020).

Chanel Van der Merwe

Thanks, Professor Asante. There's a discussion going on in the chat. It was initiated by Sangeeta (Bagga-Gupta) who says that she is wondering whether spinoff discussions are taking place in terms of Asiacentrism, South American-centrism and so forth. And a very interesting discussion between her and Lynn Mario de Souza and Cecile Vigoroux is taking place. I will now ask Professor Makoni to just summarize for us.

Sinfree Makoni

I would like to thank everybody for finding time on a Saturday to attend this worthwhile forum. I think Professor Asante and the conversation with Salikoko highlight some of the issues that we've been trying to grapple with. The one that I think is quite interesting, which we need to continuously think about, is about the United States as a settler colony. Once you begin to think about the United States as a settler colony, then the issues about decoloniality and postcoloniality will assume a very different shape. One quickly realizes that if they are in North America, particularly in the United States, they are still within a very strong settler colony. Then you begin to see connections, let us say, between different parts of the world. For example, when Ian Smith in Rhodesia was trying to set up the unilateral declaration of Zimbabwe, or of Rhodesia at that time, the United States was his model. He wanted to take over a country belonging to other people as the white Americans have done here in the United States. It is those connections that I think we need to keep making. I also think the argument that Professor Asante has been making between the connections between ideas in decoloniality and Afrocentricity is important for us to keep thinking about. We must work out where we think there are compatibilities and where we think there are differences, because I think this is a very important project to expand on. Thank you very much, Professor Asante. Thank you very much.

References

Asante, M.K. (2003) *Erasing Racism: The Survival of the American Nation*. Buffalo: Prometheus Books.
Asante, M.K. (2020) *An Afrocentric Pan Africanist Vision: Afrocentric Essays*. Lanham: Rowman & Littlefield.
Darwin, C. (1859) *The Origin of Species: Or the Preservation of the Favoured Races in the Struggle for Life*. London: John Murray.
Diop, C.A. (1974) *The African Origin of Civilization: Myth or Reality*. New York: Mercer Cook.
Diop, C.A. (1991) *Civilization or Barbarism*. Presence Africaine.
Dove, N. (1998) *Afrikan Mothers: Bearers of Cultures, Makers of Social Change*. Albany: State University of New York Press.
Monteiro-Ferreira, A. (2014) *The Demise of the Inhuman: Afrocentricty, Modernism, and Postmodernism*. Albany: SUNY Press.

5 The Politics of Language, Memory and Knowledge

Ngũgĩ wa Thiong'o

Sinfree Makoni

I'd like to welcome all of you from wherever you are in the world. I'm going to get engaged in our conversation with Professor Ngũgĩ in which I will pose a couple of questions and after that, we will open up the discussion to everybody. I want to begin with a Swahili proverb, which he cites in his book *Globalectics* (2012) that is on the celebration of his 70th birthday at Irvine. He says '*ni mebwaga chumvi nyingi*,' which means 'I've eaten a lot of salt.' He then proceeds to say it means, 'I have earned the right to go back and tell tales of the past.' Now, my first question to you, Professor Ngũgĩ: What are the two key stories of the past that you would like to share with the audience?

Ngũgĩ wa Thiong'o

Yes. And by the way, this is not only in Kiswahili but also in the language of the community I come from, Gikuyu. We talk of age as the right to tell stories and little wisdoms. But I don't have much wisdom. But I can share some things. When I look back, generally, I keep on coming back to the language matters in my own life especially. When I look back, in my beginning as a writer, my first novels were *The River Between* (1965), *Weep Not, Child* (1964), *A Grain of Wheat* (1967) and even *Petals of Blood* (1977), which are talking intimately about the post-colonial condition in Kenya in my village, in my town. They are often talking about people who lost their lives fighting for our independence. And yet, what puzzles me when I look back is how I could have accepted in my mind so easily the talking about the exploits of freedom fighters in Kenya, who obviously spoke African languages, who organized in African languages, how I could take their story and package it in a language they did not actually use. So, do I use one language to organize, or several languages for that matter to organize? But of all the many African languages in Kenya, I chose to package that struggle, if you like, that vision of the moral, I choose to do it in English, which was the language of the very settler system against which we were fighting. The more I think of it, the more disturbed I become in a sense of saying; how could this have happened? How could it have been so normal for me to think that if I go for baptism, an English name is holy? So, as I get on with age, so to speak, those are the kind of things that bother me a lot.

Sinfree Makoni

If I continue with that line, you talk about the relationship between your creative imagination and language. Can you elaborate a bit on that? How is your creative imagination constrained by English, and how was it liberated through your use of either Gikuyu or other African languages?

Ngũgĩ wa Thiong'o

I would say it is not necessarily constrained by English. For example, if you take African writers as a whole, they have produced really great works, so I cannot think of Achebe writing *Things Fall Apart* (1958) and having been constrained as such. Or for that matter, if you take another example, I cannot think of, say, James Joyce, abandoning his Irish for English. He doesn't seem to have been very much constrained. So, it's not really so much the quality of English language, it's – let me put it another way – every language has its own unique musicality.

In that sense, language is like a musical instrument, if you like. We have a piano for instance, we have a guitar, we have a violin. Many instruments, some tiny, big instruments, but each of those instruments, whatever their size, whatever shape, has its unique musicality. They can play the same melody, but you can tell more, is the texture of the piano or the sound texture of a guitar. But we don't ever say that we ban all other instruments or suppress them and have the piano only. Or the guitar only. We don't say that other instruments with all their musicality are lesser than. But if you had a colonial process, it tells you that when it comes to language as organized sound, in the same way as music has organized sound, they tell you, 'No, there are some languages whose musicality is more musical, if you like than others.' They say, 'No, let's suppress these other instruments, and have only the one that comes from imperial centers.'

Now, I can go back to the image of a musical instrument. Musical instruments can come together, they can connect. And when they play together, then you get orchestras, or quartets, or duets, or any other combination of instruments. Languages are really the same. English has its unique musicality different from French, or Japanese. When you hear them speaking, you can hear the sounds are different. African languages also have their unique musicality. And we do not want to lose that musicality plus everything else that language carries. The knowledge systems, the memories languages carry, the science the languages carry. Why do you want to lose that? Why do you want to say only English can carry all the memories? Can English carry all the sciences? Every language has a knowledge system that arises from its environment where that language developed. It has vocabulary and knowledge about the ecosystem in the area. Every language has that because if you grow up around some plants, you know more about them than someone who is far from those, who grew up witnessing other types of plants. We lose all that because the very musicality of the languages is different, but no language is any more musical than any other. 'But why then should I,' I asked myself, abandon that language with all its musicality, with all its memories, with all its knowledge systems, for another particular musicality from imperial centers?'

What I'm saying is there are writers who have written in other people's languages, and they've written masterpieces. Joseph Conrad, who I really admire, he was Polish. In fact, he learned English at around the age of 19 or 20. Before that, he spoke French fluently, and of course his Polish language, and probably Russian, though I'm not quite sure. But he wrote in English, good books, but in writing in English, he was not contributing to Polish literature. No. He was taking from Polish culture and depositing it into English, so to speak. James Joyce is another. I talk about him a lot. What did he do for the Irish language? He did a lot for English literature. He's all over the world, you know, as one of the leading figures in English literature. But, what about Irish? Where is he in Irish literature?

Sinfree Makoni

Let me take your memory back to the 60s and 70s. I want to revisit one of the important documents that is now been associated with your career. That is the document entitled 'On the Abolition of the English Department' (1972) when you were at the University of Nairobi. Could you revisit that document and try to provide us with an ideological, epistemological analysis and pedagogical implications of what you were trying to say in that document, which became quite controversial?

Ngũgĩ wa Thiong'o

I think one can easily argue that that document became a kind of foundational thinking of postcolonial theories and other things, because before that document, a lot of departments of literature in Africa were actually English departments. They taught literature from Shakespeare to T.S. Eliot, or some people, in Nigeria, say from Spencer from Spender. In other words, they were English departments teaching English national literature. They weren't even teaching literature in English from different parts of the world. They were teaching English literature literally from the types of Shakespeare to T.S. Eliot, or 20th century, and now 21st century. And then I remember, there came another proposal about reorganizing the department of English so that, in future, it might admit African literature in English, as a subsidiary, or kind of token. And some of us said, me among them, 'We're in Africa. Should literature really start with what is produced in Africa? What is produced in African related societies like the Caribbean writers, African American writers, related to Asian and Latin American literature, because we are products of the same colonial and anti-colonial structures and so on. And then from there, you can study English, or French, or Russian literature, or any other literature available through English as the common language.' That was the kind of thinking we had then when there were three of us, Lo Liyong, Owuor Anyumba, and myself.

I'll never forget that because it gave rise to a lot of thinking and rethinking about the departments in many parts of Africa and Caribbean. One thing we were very clear about was that we were not calling for the abolition of English literature. We were talking about the organization for Africa, what should be the center? Just as in Europe, what should be the center? In America, what should be the center? In Asia, what should be the center? So we were really after raising fairly fundamental questions. Now I'm looking back about the cognitive process, the system. How do we acquire knowledge, how do we come to know? And the colonial system tended to always argue that to know anything, you must go to Europe first. That you must start with Europe to know anything. It's like traveling – you start from Johannesburg to go to Kenya. But they say, you can't get to Kenya from Johannesburg. It is easier for you to come to London, and then connect to wherever you want to go. So actually, although the focus is on the English department, I think we were raising fairly fundamental questions which went against the colonial process itself. Because the colonial process was always everywhere, whether in Africa or the Caribbean, and always assumed that the imperial centers were the centers of the world. Their knowledge system was the center of all knowledges. Their languages were always the center. Now looking back, I realize we were raising fundamental questions about the knowledge systems.

Sinfree Makoni

In one of your recent articles, you say that what imperialism has done is that it has also made us blind to seeing the connections between Africa, between Kenya and Asia, for example, because the tendency has been to look at the relationship between, for example, Kenya and the UK. What is the impact of India on Kenya and what is the impact of Africa on Asia?

Ngũgĩ wa Thiong'o

Take Kenya, or East African ports: Malindi or Mombasa. Prior to Portuguese coming to Kenya via South Africa, those city civilizations were always connected through trade. They were connected to India. When Vasco de Gama arrived in Kenya, the one the pilot who showed him the way across the Indian Ocean, so to speak, was of Indian origins. There are connections between the Kenyan coasts. You can talk about the Indian Ocean civilizations, because obviously in those days, the waterways were easier; they were better at connecting places, because of means of transport. It was easier to connect Mombasa in Kenya to Mumbai or other coastal towns of Asia. If somebody started a journey from Mombasa – one coming inland, one going to India – the one going to India might arrive there first, before the other one walked, or rode a donkey, or a cow, over the mountains of Kenya. You can see the impact on languages, on the food and cultures and so on. So, there was trade, I think, between the Kenyan coast and China, for example. There's a way in which the Indian Ocean brought all those city and states together while there.

But after the arrival of the Portuguese and then the British colonial settlers, there were many Indian people who were then brought to Kenya as what they call 'indentured laborers.' Indians were taken from India to East Africa, the Caribbean, and so on. So, even that makes connections. But most important connection is the fact that they were all struggling against one or two imperial centers. And many of the legal systems developed by the British in India became the legal systems in colonial Kenya. Even the language thing, the language issue, again it was India where Macaulay, one of the ministers in Indian education, talked about abolishing, or sidelining Persian and Sanskrit, and other languages in education, and having English as the language of education. And he was very clear as to what he wanted. He wanted to use a class or Indians, Indians in skin color, in clothes, even in religion, but most importantly with an English mind. And again, he was clear why he wanted that class of Indians with an English mind was to make them become like a buffer zone between their ruling English, or the East India Company at the time, and the people he governed. You get a class that becomes a buffer to help in further exploiting India.

Now some of those outlooks were later transported to Africa. They became the way of doing things in Africa, in the Caribbean, and other places. Of course, we can go even earlier, and think of Ireland, where some of these things were tried in Ireland, in the same way. There were patterns. From Ireland to India, India to Africa, there were patterns of imperial, colonial systems, being tried first in Ireland, by the English. Then on to India, then more refinement into Africa and other places. There are a lot of connections. But their impact is also there, food cultures in the Caribbean and Africa, some of the cooking was very much impacted by Indian cuisine.

Sinfree Makoni

Thank you very much. What I'm going to do now is hand this over to Rafael and Magda, and Bassey, and they are going to coordinate the questions coming from the audience. I'll come back later to try to sum up the discussions.

Ngũgĩ wa Thiong'o

Before that, let me show you a book. My latest book is called, in English translation, *The Perfect Nine* (2018), but it came out in Kenya two years ago as *Kenda Mũiyũru*. This the English translation *The Perfect Nine*. The reason I mention it is because, first, of course, I wrote it in Gikuyu language. But most important for me, it's about the myth of origins of the Gikuyu people, my own interpretation of that myth of origin. It means that I'm writing in Gikuyu about the origins of the Gikuyu people in the Gikuyu language. In fact, in this book, there is no, except by implication, there is no colonial, so I'm going back before the colonial. I'm connecting myself through the Gikuyu language to my origins, so to speak. It would have been terrible if I had written about Gikuyu people – me, talking about the founding father and mother of Gikuyu people – writing it in English. But in translation, that's ok because languages can connect, and they do connect through translation. And there's absolutely nothing wrong with that. We can even talk about liberating Shakespeare from English prison and liberate many other writers from the prison houses of their languages, of their language nationalists. Let them be free. But I'm very proud to, at long last, have connected, or drew from my origins, and wrote about it in Gikuyu language. And the book has been out for the last two years in Kenya in Gikuyu. The English translation came out two years later. And that is the order I prefer – from African languages to English to French and so on. But even more importantly, from African languages to *other* African languages and Asian languages. We can open a new world altogether when the languages can talk to each other fairly freely through translations and other things.

Sinfree Makoni

And you are convinced that the world is a better place when it learns from Africa than when we learn from English?

Ngũgĩ wa Thiong'o

No. We learn from each other. That's the whole point. It's from where, where do we start? What's my base? That's the key. The connection is important. We have a lot to learn from English writers, from French writers, from Zulu writers, from Indian writers, from Chinese writers and so on. And hopefully, they also have a lot to learn from African language writers. It's the connection, from where does knowledge start? If you like to think about it, I don't want to give a lecture here, but knowledge starts from our own bodies, from our hands. A child growing up, they know about their own body, but also the mother's body, they know about the bodies closest to them. Then they go adding that to other experiences. And the previous experiences enable them to appreciate difference between what they knew and what they are adding to what they knew. Normal cognitive processes – remember what we do normally is going from wherever you are to other places, and then you learn from that. The more you know about other places, the more it helps to know more about where you come from. I'll make very clear that the English language, French language, etc., have a lot of treasuries of beauty and other things, but equally so, has also Indian languages; equally so, African languages; equally so Native American languages. It is the colonial process which is a negation of normality. The modern world is built on this structure of abnormality, which has been a normalized abnormality and a kind of foundation of what they call modern societies.

Sinfree Makoni

Let me just quote you, then I will hand over the conversation again to my colleagues. In one of your books, you say that languages, cultures, and literatures constitutes a network. This is similar to the argument you're making here, akin, but not identical, to Deleuze and Guattari's 'rhizome' (see Deleuze & Guattari, 1986). The key word there is what you're calling here the 'network,' which captures this complex relationship of cultures, languages, and network.

Ngũgĩ wa Thiong'o

In that book, for instance, I was also talking about memory, in a way. If you look at what happens with the naming system as a system of planting memories. For example, take New York. Before New York, it was occupied by the Dutch people, and it was called 'New Amsterdam.' But before New York and New Amsterdam, there were other names which were used by the native people to that area. So the new naming plants a new memory on the place that already had its own memories. What happens to memories, previously connoted by the names given to that area we call New York by the native people who lived there? It's the replacement of one memory or a burial of one memory by an imperial memory. Or an occupation of memory. All those memories of place and their history are buried, and you bring another memory, restarting memory of that place. And it's not true. Mumbai was Bombay, and it went to become normalized until India had enough, and said it is Mumbai not Bombay. And other names as well, you know.

Rafael Lomeu Gomes

I was wondering Professor Thiong'o, if you could perhaps make a comment on this discussion that's taking place in the (Zoom) chat box. It starts like this: 'I support 30% of identity preservation of ethnic groups in a nation. But 70% allegiance to the national identity. Cultural identities of ethnic groups compete for sovereignty. They threaten national existence. How can we retain both without suppressing/sacrificing one or the other?' And then Unyierie responded to this question in the following way: 'How does one measure or define 30% of identity preservation of ethnic groups and 70% allegiance to the nationality identity? 'How can we retain both without suppressing/sacrificing one or other?' you ask. Well, the 30%/70% division does exactly that – sacrifice/suppress one in favor of the other.' So, professor, could you please comment on this discussion in the chat?

Ngũgĩ wa Thiong'o

There is an American writer who said, 'I contain multitudes.' Walt Whitman. In other words, who can say that even those of us who are on a screen can say they are just one identity? Like now I live in California. If I had taken up an American citizenship, I would say, 'I'm Californian. I live in California.' But I'm also Kenyan. I think of myself as a global citizen. Wherever I go, I feel I belong. We have many things. I can call myself a Kenyan, for instance, but who's Kenyan? Kenyan is a people in that country, it's a people who's got languages. They have got knowledge systems. Kenyan is not an abstract thing or being. A Kenyan is at the same time a person who speaks Gikuyu, a person who speaks Luhya, a person who speaks Kiswahili, even Gujarati because we now have many Kenyans of Indian origins, and so on, and also some who speak English. So, we're not just one thing.

But let's discuss how we use language to – any language, but English in this case - how we use each language to really distort realities of people. Like the use of word 'tribe,' for example. I know we do not use it in this forum today, thank God. But 'tribe' and 'ethnic,' you know, we use those terms all the time. 'Ethnic' is not so bad, but 'tribe' is meant to be the opposite of what 'civilized' was, or whatever it is. And in Africa we happily use it. It is seeing it as something great to say, 'I'm so and so, this tribe.' When we talk about the English, we need to make a distinction between the *English*, or the *English people*. The *French* or the *French people*. When it comes to Africa or the formerly colonized, the word 'people' is removed out of it, even in English, and it becomes 'tribesmen,' 'Giyuku tribesmen' or 'Zulu tribesmen.' Even with the Prime Minister or President of a country, and they not only say that he is president but also mention that he is a tribesman. So already this is using language in such a way that lessens some people and elevates other people.

For the English? 'People.' For Africa? 'tribes.' Iceland has 300,000 people. But we don't talk about Icelandic tribesmen, right? Denmark is, I think, 4 million people. But the Yoruba of Nigeria are 40 million people. How come the Danish are somehow called a 'nation,' or whatever terms we use, and 40 million Yoruba are somehow called 'tribes' and 'tribesmen'? So, you see, naming itself is used to condition people to look at that community in a certain way. The people who come to use a term in relation to themselves also use a colonial outlook on themselves to define themselves. We deny the colonized, the notion of people – in English, at least. They're not people, they're tribesmen. An African comes to adopt that as a way of defining themselves. 'Oh, I'm a Zulu tribesman. I'm Zulu by tribe.' It's so irritating. So, we end up, ourselves – as African people, African intellectuals – we end up defining ourselves by the way we were defined by the English colonial system.

Rafael Lomeu Gomes

Thank you. I think your response touched on so many other questions that I feel tempted to try to pass some of them to in front of the order that they appear, but just to make sure that everybody gets a chance to have their questions asked, I'll follow the order. That means that now I'm moving on to Busi's question: 'reading Mazrui's history of English in Africa, it seems that African nationalist leaders supported the use of English as a language of instruction in former British colonies. As these colonies were preparing for independence, the same African nationalist leaders were entering into agreements with the British government to utilize the British council about training teachers for teaching English etc. With this in mind, would it be correct then to conclude that African nationalist leaders have been complicit in the underdevelopment of African languages?'

Ngũgĩ wa Thiong'o

Yes, we have. I mean, I would not suggest that to African leadership, the African intellectual community, so I don't take myself out of that anomalous situation. I remember in the conference we had, I talked about it in *Decolonising the Mind* (1986) and said that the new African writers of the post-colonial era met in Makerere in 1962 under the title 'African Writers of English Expression.' There was not a single invitation to any African writer who was then writing, who had been writing in African languages. There was not even any attempt to see whether there were any who had written in African languages, you know. No. It was assumed African writers were writers in English. And this was a conference of *African* writers on the *African* continent. I mentioned it because I was part of it. I was a participant in that grand deception. We could have paid a little homage even to African languages, one way or another, by inviting a few participants who had been writing in African languages. So, it's not only African governments, is the entitling community.

But governments do matter because they create policies. And it's true that after independence, we in Kenya, in Africa, opted to continue with imperialism at the center of our being. I'm not saying we should have abolished imperial languages, but we made them the center of our being. Let me give you the example of Kenya. After 1952 in Kenya, there were thriving newspapers in African languages. There were thriving schools, where African languages were not banned or despised and so on. In 1952, we established a state of emergency in Kenya, because of a liberation war fought by what the British called 'Mau Mau,' but what we called 'Kenya Land and Freedom Army.' They thought the entire education system or knowledge system championed by African-run schools, African-run newspapers, and African languages were somehow antithetical to colonization. In 1952, all schools run by Africans were abolished. All newspapers in African languages were abolished. Some of the editors were put in prison, and others had run away into exile. Thereafter, English language borrowed from the policy in India. Then the governor of Kenya at the time said English must now be the language instilled in the school system and so on. Between 1952 and 1963, when Kenya got dependence, there was a complete shift in language matters. African language education and African press were all abolished. The few left were run by either missionaries or colonial bureaus, and so on, where political content in publications was tuned out.

When we regained our independence in 1963, something happened. There was a commission on education run by Africans. You know what they did? They said, now, where before in the colonial era at least African languages were taught up to three to five years of primary education, they said, 'No. Abolish African languages in school systems.' They said you must start learning English as early as preschool – nurseries. That did a lot of damage to the psyche of the Kenyans in terms of how they look at their languages, and how they look at one another, and so on. That, in a way, helped more in terms of making people look at each other through English eyes, so to speak, in how they define themselves. So policies by government are very important. I would like to see in every African country, whether Kenya or South Africa, wherever, that people or intellectuals actually insist that it is child abuse – child abuse to humiliate a child for speaking their mother tongue. Corporal punishment, even today, is admitted to children all over Africa because they're caught speaking of their mother's tongue. So we bring up children, and you shape how they look at themselves with shame and pain, and being beaten, and being laughed at. The same symbols of shame and humiliation that were used in the colonial era – we use them ourselves. We've nationalized them. We say we are true Africans by abusing Africans, you know. Or we appear modern, we don't need all this Africanity to interfere with modernity. Or we are now a nation, why? Because we don't speak other languages. We are now a nation, we speak English. Or French – we are a French-speaking nation.

You know, languages can communicate with each other. There is translation. If we had policies that put African languages as primary, there's nothing wrong in other languages, even English, being a language that enables communication across the different language communities, or different languages. There are things that can be done differently, and it needs to come from government and from pressure from intellectuals. Otherwise, there is now an economy built on rejection of African languages. Globality has come to mean some vague thing, like people who speak English or French. (Laughs.) Sorry, I find it, while it's also tragic, it can be laughable. That's why, for instance, my book is now available in English, but it's already available in Gikuyu language. Being Gikuyu does not prevent it from being available in English. But it could be available also in French, in Kiswahili, there is a Kiswahili translation going on. It could be available in many African languages and that'd be a good thing, not a bad thing. And I'm not just talking about my book alone. I'm talking about books written in Yoruba being available in Zulu, or Gikuyu, or Luo, or Luganda, and so on.

But government policies have to change. We don't want an education system that creates a class of Africans. Africans in skin color, but with an imperial, colonial system in their minds. Often, in Kenya for instance, we've got Kiswahili. It's an African language. It's spoken across Kenya by many people, even beyond Kenya, in Tanzania, East Africa, Congo, and so on. Have you ever seen or heard an African leader from East Africa addressing an international community in Kiswahili, which is spoken by people in those countries? Or even addressing national audiences on important national days in Kiswahili? And it's available as an African language. Macron goes to the United Nations; he does not speak in Dutch or English. He speaks in French. And he's translated. And Kiswahili, you can't say we don't have an African language that is spoken across the many peoples of Kenya and East Africa. We see this reflected in, say, a prime minister or president on a national day, who speaks to Kenyan people in Kiswahili, for instance. And then getting the speech translated into English for the public diplomats and so on. But now, even if there is one diplomat, when he's addressing thousands of people, he'd rather speak in English for the benefit of that one diplomat who's sitting there than speak to the entire nation in a language that is generally well known or understood in the whole community. Why? That's a question maybe we should ask. And not of only the leadership, but of the African intellectuals.

Look, you look at history – intellectuals were always some of the first to break through. Dante is a good example, Tuscan. You know, everyone was writing in Latin at the time. Someone was telling him, 'dante, if you write in your language, you'll be lost to mortality.' And Dante replied in a poem, but in perfect Latin, 'No.' Then somebody wrote to him, and he replied in a poem, but in perfect Latin. He compared his language to a sheep with, in Kiswahili you say 'matiti,' who's full of milk. And he said, 'No, no. Okay you guys continue in Latin, but me, I'll continue milking this ewe who is full of milk.' But among those who were writing, who were telling him that he'll be lost in mortality, it is Dante who is still very much alive. It is Dante who is copied. Dante is very much alive today. But in those days, he was the one who was being told, 'Oh, poor Dante, he'll not be remembered. He's lost Latin.' The English, by the way that they murdered the first English person to translate the Bible into English from Latin, they later killed him. I don't know if they killed him because of the language issue, but it's very interesting that they would end up murdering the first translator of the Bible into English because even they then thought English was a barbaric language at the time. But when we say becoming a sense of a nation and imperializing and so on, that's when English begins to become this great language, which it is, just like German is a good language, just like French, just like Gikuyu, just like Kiswahili, just like Zulu.

Rafael Lomeu Gomes

The next question is from Rosemary Jolly: 'Would you consider South Africa an exception, in the sense that the apartheid government's funding of Nguni/Tswana language groups was aimed at a divide and conquer approach to 'non-White' groups? This, along with the instruction of Blacks in Afrikaans, rendered English the written language of anti-apartheid texts. I am not contesting the notion of 'English as a foreign anguish'; but local instantiations of the language in postcolonial communities differ.'

Ngũgĩ wa Thiong'o

Now, South Africa, of course, is a very interesting case where, you know, language policy is very, very interesting. Even within Kenya. There was a time, in fact, when white settlers in Kenya didn't want Africans to learn English. So it's a bit more complex in reality, and South Africa is a case where there is a case in point where the Afrikaner governments especially retained African languages, but so as to control the content in those languages. Africans fought for English, and said 'No, no, we want access to many other things, which are available in English' and so on. But the Afrikaners wanted Africans to not have access to English, but to African languages only. And then control the content. The books published in those languages and so on.

Rosemary Jolly

And radio, in particular, Ngũgĩ.

Ngũgĩ wa Thiong'o

Radio as well. You can see the same thing, the content was progressive, like the songs you know sung by African masses in South Africa. Remember when you had, in Johannesburg or other places, when there was singing. Oh my god. In Africa, you felt the earth tremble. It's how you use some of these languages. The irony, then, is that African languages – the irony was not intended by the Afrikaner government – African languages in South Africa are fairly – I don't live there, so I don't know – but African languages there are fairly thriving, or they're there. And I like the current South African policy of recognizing nine other African languages in South Africa, without necessarily also saying that English does not matter. But note. What about resource allocation? It's one thing to say, 'we have Kiswahili,' but what if you don't at the same time put resources into Kiswahili? All the resources in Kenya, I think, resources devoted to languages, probably go to English. There must be a change in how we look at languages.

Let me just give you one thought I have. If you look at the language question and the language relationship at present, it assumes that languages can only relate in terms of hierarchy. Hierarchy is very dangerous. It's an imperial thing that some languages are inherently higher, inherently higher than other languages - are inherently more of languages than other languages. Hierarchy becomes a problem, essentially, so that if today you had to say Gikuyu or any other language, suppressing others, it will be recreating hierarchy as a basis of language relationship. No. Language can also relate in terms of a network of equal give and take. There's nothing that says that to be English, you must suppress other languages. Or to be Yoruba you must suppress other languages. Or to have an African language you must suppress other African languages.

Rosemary Jolly

I love the idea. I just have one comment, which is that I have a friend from – and a student of mine, but she's also a friend – from Zimbabwe. When she speaks English, because she's Zimbabwean, when she speaks English on the taxi in Johannesburg, she gets attacked by everybody else because they identify English as a hierarchical language. And why are you not speaking an African language? So English still carries that implication of a hierarchy in sub-Saharan Africa in the wake of the anti-apartheid struggle. It's like if you speak it as a black person on the bus, it's like, why aren't you speaking your own language? In fact, you get kicked off the bus. Because they were speaking in English, which implies that you're a snob, that you're a colonial snob, that you're a sellout to…

Ngũgĩ wa Thiong'o

Oh, they say 'don't speak English, speak an African language?' Oh, that's a good one for a change. But what I'm saying is languages don't have to relate in terms of hierarchy. There is absolutely nothing wrong with English as a language. There's nothing wrong with French as a language. But there's something wrong in a hierarchical relationship between French and African languages, where African languages are suppressed in favor of the existence of French. It's not the French language itself. It's when it's put hierarchically higher than all the other African languages, other languages, that is a problem. And of course, like France, they have economic value of having a French language community. You know when you want to negotiate armaments and so on, you might find it easier to go to to a country whose language – when you talk, you seem to understand each other. Even when you're negotiating your own exploitation. You can never say it in French. I want to repeat: languages, all languages, have their unique musicality. That's the key. English, French, Mandarin, Gujarati, Hindi, Gikuyu, Zulu and Native American languages. But if they relate in terms of hierarchy – if I say Kiswahili should be the national language in Kenya, or East Africa but we must therefore suppress Yoruba and Igbo and Zulu, then I say no. We should end up with the same problem.

We can find a way where a language helps in communication across the different language communities, while also respecting and giving resources to community languages. It's not a contradiction. And in real life we do this all the time. I know I talk about Russian literature. I'm quoting Tolstoy all the time, and Dostoevsky and so on. But I never read them in Russian. I access them through translation. I'm quite happy, but you won't become a specialist in Russian literature without having to learn Russian. But for parts of ordinary knowledge, Russian literature, and so on, I'm quite happy that I can access it in English. I'll be happier if I could easily access it in Kiswahili, through translation to Kiswahili, or into Gikuyu, and so on. So, we mustn't confuse language as hierarchy. Hierarchy is exploitative, it's an abnormal system, and we are normalizing abnormality.

To give you an example – today even an English person wants to go and study French to become a French teacher. She is not required give up English to acquire French. But in old colonial systems or post-colonial systems, to become national or whatever it is, to know English, you must be humiliated in connection to your own languages. In Kenya today or across Africa, children are still beaten, punished, for speaking their mother tongue in school ground. Why would anybody in their senses, so to speak, humiliate a child for speaking their mother tongue? It doesn't make sense. But we do this, it continues, the colonial system. Native American kids were beaten, thrashed, when they spoke Native American languages in school in America. Māori people were thrashed the same way, beaten until blood came out of their butts. Australia, the same thing. It's the system. It has nothing to do with languages. It has everything to do with power, or unequal power between the Imperializing culture and the minorized cultures, nothing to do with the languages. It's a question of power. And we continue humiliating African children. Some parents are even punishing their children because they are speaking their mother tongue in their presence instead of speaking the language they don't understand. And they're very proud that, 'Yes, my kids are now speaking English, although we don't understand it, it's very wonderful, our kids have arrived.' This continues in Africa, even today. The other day I accepted an international award from Catalonia, Spain, and I spoke in the Gikuyu language, and there were subtitles. It was televised in Catalonia, there were subtitles in Catalan, I believe, and it was freely available in English. But some Kenyans, intellectuals, not many, but they thought this was very shameful. 'He's an embarrassment to the country.' If I had spoken in Japanese, they would have said, 'Oh my god, this guy, he knows languages! He can even speak Japanese! Or French.' It's a mental mix-up, we are mixed up. And only intellectuals can lead the way. Dante is a good example. There are many others who are good examples of what they were able to do for their languages.

Rafael Lomeu Gomes

I'll try to bundle the three last comments and questions in the session. A quick comment from Hosea Malik says: 'the statements you made about the instrumentality of different languages is very well agreed with in Gloria Anzaldua's *Borderlands/ La Frontera* (1987) who uses both the Chicano and English languages in her text.' And then two more interventions, one question from John Joseph and one question from Lynn Mario. The question from John Joseph is: 'I've always wondered whether other Gikuyu speakers consider Prof Ngũgĩ wa Thiongo's Gikuyu to be … how to put it? … affected by his other languages. Does he feel that he can really connect with how he spoke before learning English?' And the final question then from Lynn Mario who would like to ask the question himself.

Lynn Mário de Souza

Professor Ngũgĩ, it's a pleasure listening to you. You mentioned already the damage to the African psyche and knowledge system, and I think when our focus goes on to language, we tend to forget other aspects which are related to language that are equally prejudicial to our psyches. Here, I'm talking about one of the effects of colonization, which was literacy. What literacy has done is that it has led to an almost complete devaluation of the oral tradition. Now what we see, and when I say 'oral tradition,' I'm not just talking about knowledge that is not written. I'm talking about different onto-epistemologies, different knowledge systems, looking at different beings who are capable of being knowledge producers. When we simply think that we can translate from knowledges of our native languages into English, what we have seen in colonization is this has been left out. It's either called 'tribal' – all these traditional knowledges, which are very much in the oral tradition because they have a whole system of guardians of these knowledges, and who are capable of repeating and producing them, which runs parallel to the literary tradition. All of this is very much jeopardized. I'd like to know what your thoughts are on this.

Ngũgĩ wa Thiong'o

First of all, historically, in Kenya, when we came up with the idea, or with a policy of abolishing the English department and having Africa in the center, oral literature, or what we now call 'oral literature,' was actually introduced in the department. We were cognizant of that very fact that before there was a written, there was oral. And written essentially tries to imitate, if you like, the spoken. Spoken words were there before words written. Oral literature, generally, as a whole system of knowledge production in African language is very, very, very important. Or any language whatsoever, it's not just African languages. When it comes to oral literature, we can think of English oral literatures, Native American oral literatures, Maui oral literatures, and so on. These are all very, very, very important. But in Africa, oral literature is very, very much alive, you know. And take it this way: a language that develops in a particular area, no matter the extent that people grow food and they had to look at the weather, and the rain system and other things, we have obviously developed our vocabulary for those systems. They have different vocabularies for plants in that area. And there's nothing like global trees. There's nothing like a global tree or global plant because different plants grow and thrive in different ecosystems and so on. So, the language that grows in a particular area is sometimes best placed to tell you a lot about the ecology of that area, including what plants are good for medicines or whatever. There's a whole knowledge system contained in languages as a whole. Right. By banning African languages, we also cut access to those knowledge systems. Oral literature is very, very important in African reality. Some of them, people who are now 80 years old, or older than me, let's say 100 years old, they know a lot of what happened, more than 100 years. They may not write, but they can talk about it. Writing is not what is original to human beings. The original is the sound. Language, like music, organized sound. And whenever there's been language, there's been organized sound. The organized sound tells us something. For those who are Christians, in the beginning was the world and the world became God, or whatever. Or the one, the sound. And come to think of it, you look at sound, at least on our globe anyway, everything has a sound, and there's no soundless. Even a dead body has sound, rocks have sound, thunder has sound. So the sound is actually very important to our being in a way.

Rafael Lomeu Gomes

Thank you. I think, we've reached the end of the session. And I'd like to ask Makoni if you'd like to make the final comments before we move on to the much awaited after party.

Sinfree Makoni

Thank you very much to professor Ngũgĩ wa Thiong'o and to everybody. I thought the way to sum up this discussion is by citing a couple of lines from some of your own work (*Something Torn and New: An African Renaissance*, 2009) which I think neatly capture the essence of what we're talking about here. Let me start off with a quotation that I think provides a powerful argument for the rationale for decolonization of scholarship. And you write, 'there is no region, no culture, no nation today, that has not been affected by colonialism and its aftermath. Indeed modernity can be considered a product of colonialism. This book speaks to the decolonization of modernity' (p. xi). And in the same book, you proceed to say, which I think is very interesting, you are talking about the role of the African intellectuals in decolonization, and you ask this rhetorical question, 'How does one begin to explain this attitude of the African bourgeoisie towards the languages of their cultures?' (p. 55). You then proceed to say to the intelligentsia is as it should be. There can be no renaissance that can come out of state legislation and admonitions. In other words, if you are going to have any form of African renaissance, then there must be some form of writing in African languages. The other issue that in is important for us to bear in mind is that in this discussion, it became quite clear that any decolonization will have to include, to some extent, the intellectuals rethinking their role, the role of the state, some emphasis and premium on language policies, and then we will have to challenge the tendencies towards a hierarchicalization of languages to try to shift towards establishing something like a network and interconnections between languages. And then you make, I think, a very powerful argument that the writing in African languages, for example, goes way back, even to the work published in Timbuktu, in Ethiopia, etc. So the tradition of writing in African languages is not a new one at all. So it's quite surprising when you have got a lot of academic resistance to that tendency, because there is a long tradition, like you effectively point out, of people writing in African languages.

Ngũgĩ wa Thiong'o

Even Egypt. Don't forget Egypt is an African country.

Sinfree Makoni

Yes. Thank you. Thank you very much.

Ngũgĩ wa Thiong'o

Thank you for inviting me to this forum. It was very interesting.

References

Achebe, C. (1958) *Things Fall Apart*. London Heinemann.
Anzaldúa, G. (1987) *Borderlands/La frontera: The New Mestiza*. San Francisco: Aunt Lute Books.
Deleuze, G. and Guattari, F. (1986) *Kafka: Toward a Minor Literature* (Vol. 30). Minneapolis: University of Minnesota Press.
wa Thiong'o, N. (1964) *Weep Not, Child*. The Hague: Heinemann.
wa Thiong'o, N. (1965) *The River Between*. The Hague: Heinemann.
wa Thiong'o, N. (1967) *A Grain of Wheat*. The Hague: Heinemann.
wa Thiong'o, N. (1977) *Petals of Blood*. The Hague: Heinemann.
wa Thiong'o, N. (1986) *Decolonising the Mind: The Politics of Language in African Literature*. Nairobi: East African Education Publishers.
wa Thiong'o, N. (2009) *Something Torn and New: An African Renaissance*. New York: Basic Civitas Books.
wa Thiong'o, N. (2012) *Globalectics: Theory and the Politics of Knowing*. New York: Columbia University Press.
wa Thiong'o, N. (2018) *The Perfect Nine: The Epic of Gikuyu and Mumbi*. New York: The New Press.
wa Thiong'o, N., Owuor-Anyumba, H. and lo Liyong, T. (1972) On the abolition of the English Department. *Homecoming: Essays on African and Caribbean Literature, Culture and Politics*, 1972–145.

6 uBuntu, Nite and the Struggle for Global Justice

Drucilla Cornell and Souleymane Bachir Diagne

Souleymane Bachir Diagne

Thank you very much for having me. I'm assuming that the text I sent ('UBuntu and Nite Pioneers of African Philosophy,' 2022) has been circulated, so I'm going to present a slightly different and shorter version before my good friend, Drucilla, jumps in. Let me first say that the text I sent you was a response to a call by late philosopher Charles Mills. I wanted to mention that to pay tribute to his memory before I start.

Now, in this version of my text that I assume was circulated, I am going to start with a Wolof concept, not the uBuntu concept, but a Wolof concept – the Wolof concept of *Nite*. I will start with a proverb, 'Nit, nitay garabam,' meaning that the human is the remedy for the human. Of course, this is a proverb, nothing more than an example of the wisdom of nations to be found in all societies and which always, everywhere, is full of maxims that say everything and their opposite. So, we should not be making much of proverbs except when as philosophers we examine what a proverb tells us about the meaning of humanism.

This was done, for example, by Léopold Sédar Senghor, the First President of the Republic of Senegal, philosopher and poet. In many passages of his philosophical work, he quoted and analyzed the proverb at length, in particular in a speech he gave in 1978 at the International Congress of Jurists in Dakar organized around the theme of development and human rights. The purpose of that meeting was to advance the cause of African states adopting a continental charter of human rights. Senghor pushed in that direction in his speech on the philosophical foundation of human rights. What he was saying then, in substance, was that far from being something foreign to the cultures and traditions of Africa, the charter of human rights – individual human rights – would, on the contrary, be a modern translation of the meaning given to humanism by this maxim: the maxim is: Man is the remedy for man.

First, why the word *remedy*? What malady is being cured here? The answer is: the malady of not being human enough yet. The malady of still being short of where we have to be as human. To say 'the human is the remedy of human' is to say that humanity is not a state, but a becoming and a task, and that my neighbor is someone who helps me to accomplish precisely that. One is not born, but rather becomes human, to paraphrase a famous saying. Moreover, the Wolof people clearly manifest this sense of 'becoming human' when playing with words. They sometimes formulated the same proverb as not 'Nit nitay garabam' but 'Nit niteey garabam.' So here I hope that I made you hear that I changed one vowel in the proverb and turned *Nitay* into *Niteey*. And this makes the sentence mean this: 'the remedy for humans IS to become humans.'

Here we should point out that, unlike the stereotype of African societies being essentially collectivist totalities where the individual is absolutely nothing and only has duties toward the group, which is the sole bearer of rights, what the humanism of 'nit nitay garabam' says is that the function of the group is to accompany and to aid the individual in becoming a person, becoming human. That is, *Nite*. This corresponds to what Drucilla, in her wonderful text on *uBuntu* and feminism, presented in this phrase, The person is individuated through the support of others. Saying that, she was defining *uBuntu*. This is the rapprochement I am making between *Nite* that I just presented and *uBuntu* as I have learned from it, obviously from the fact that *uBuntu* has become now a global concept, but mainly from reading Drucilla and discussing with her. So that is how I started thinking about *uBuntu* coming from *Nite* in my own work.

As I understand it, the semantic field of this word, *uBuntu* as *Nite* is very rich. Linguists teach us that it means humanity in general, the fact of showing humanity in particular; that it translates belief in a universal bond, but also respect, human dignity, compassion, solidarity, loyalty and even consensus. We know that the use of a word is actually what determines its particular meaning and makes it a concept. There is not such a thing as philosophical concepts being immediately given in languages. Languages are made up of words. Philosophical construction of a word into a concept is precisely that: a construction. It doesn't make sense to say that *uBuntu* was the bearer of some pre-existing philosophy that we just have to dig out. This is not true. It was constructed as a philosophical concept from being a word through its modern history, in particular by Mandela, Desmond Tutu and the UBuntu Project of which Drucilla is also a philosopher.

This is precisely the role it played in the new South Africa when it became a concept for law, a concept of transitional justice and a philosophical concept. It is as such that Barack Obama, when he gave his beautiful eulogy for Mandela, mentioned that it (*uBuntu*) was the gift of Mandela, not just to South Africa, but to humanity. What does that mean? That *uBuntu*, from being just another Bantu word, became – when it was constructed as a concept – became a gift, not just to South Africa, but to humanity itself. This is what is of interest to me. So, before I look at it in that sense, let me say that one doesn't have to be naive about *uBuntu*. We know that South African youth, in particular today, are very impatient when you talk about *uBuntu*. They consider it some kind of lyrical illusion because they are looking at what it meant when it was formulated and encapsulated in a South African Preamble of their Constitution in comparison to what the situation is now.

These youth get the sense, which corresponds to the reality of the situation they are experiencing, that the injustice of Apartheid based on racism gave way to the injustice of economic inequality and the inequality of opportunity that generally maintain the same distribution of positions among whites and blacks of South Africa. This keeps them apart, even though Apartheid laws have disappeared. But then, shall we say that *uBuntu* failed to fulfill its promise? No. Instead, it has yet to come. The new Apartheid – we should recall its first meaning, 'separate development' – is now economic and social inequality. This means we don't need less *uBuntu*, but we need more. This falls under the definition of *uBuntu* as it is about repairing the tear in the social fabric that eases the widening of inequalities; thus, it needs to be pushed forward.

It was urgent that the end of Apartheid not be translated into a cycle of vengeance and violence in the community, but into a way of a new world to be built together. The ethical theological *uBuntu* of Desmond Tutu, and the political *uBuntu* of Nelson Mandela, responded to this urgency and offered guidance. But *uBuntu* is a movement that must now be continued to fight against inequalities and promote social justice – not just in South Africa, but beyond the borders of South Africa. To paraphrase Jürgen Habermas here, we should be speaking of the unfinished project of *uBuntu*. Drucilla says this well when she writes, 'there is always more work to do together in shaping our future.' I believe that this would be *uBuntu* as indicating a direction, rather than *uBuntu* as a state of being. This is how Drucilla would consider that the *UBuntu* Project should also become this project of defining feminism differently (as she has written in her paper that she is presenting today).

I would like to push this in another direction addressing the pandemic that we are experiencing now. I want to show the ethical and social-political meaning of *uBuntu* and the Wolof *Nite* in this context. This extraordinary period of the pandemic that we are experiencing shows us that humanity is united before an invisible enemy that no wall will stop. It reveals to us, if we did not know already, how small our earth is and how finite our world is. It also reminds us how vulnerable we are and how, after the first phase of self-isolation and boundaries, we need to envision a future of solidarity around human safety and the value of life. This is what I call a politics of humanity, of *Nite* or *uBuntu*.

The life that it is a matter of protecting is not only human life, but all lives on earth. The life that it is a matter of protecting is not only human life but all lives on earth because the cosmology in which *uBuntu* draws its meaning is a cosmology of the continuity of the living. One has to break it down, down to the radical, the root 'ntu,' the vital principle of all existing and of life. The vital principle, 'ntu,' runs through the chain of all beings – from the force of forces to the mineral. In such a cosmology, nothing is inert. In a universe in which all living, from God to the pebble, as Senghor said, are in solidarity. Before being translated, then, into person-to-person relation, *uBuntu* is inscribed in the philosophy of life itself. It requires always strengthening the universal, vital principle. This is why the humanism of *Nite* and the humanism of *uBuntu* are not just about the human, but about life in general. One might call it a 'vital humanism.' And this is why *uBuntu,* making humanity together, and together inhabiting the earth, requires also taking care of the earth. The earth is the remedy for the human. This is also the meaning of 'the human is the remedy of the human.' This is why humans have a duty to take care of it. This is what I wanted to say as a presentation of my text, which is slightly different from what I have sent to you, much shorter obviously, because I would rather listen to Drucilla than to keep going. Thank you.

Drucilla Cornell

It's a great honor for me to be exchanging ideas with Bachir who is, perhaps, the foremost leading comparative African philosopher in the world. I'm always amazed by your knowledge and your humanity yourself, Bachir. What a pleasure it is to be here. I want to begin by making a couple of observations because *Nite* is a way of achieving our humanity together. It's never been more important for us to include African philosophy, not just for South Africa, not just for Senegal. It's a way of looking and understanding what it means to be a human being completely differently. I do want to say two things about the uBuntu Project. First it was a project. I didn't know anything about *uBuntu* and I ended up moving to South Africa and dedicating my life to understanding it. I think this is very important for those of us who are academics. Sometimes, you just have to really push yourself to realize that there's a whole different perspective that you didn't grow up in, didn't understand, but that you must understand in order to move forward if we are to really have a meaningful chance of developing of what Senghor calls 'a civilization of universals.'

The *uBuntu* Project began as an on-the-ground project in the townships, with a sewing collective and a vegetable-growing collective, to begin developing cooperatives that were organized completely differently than capitalist forms of organization. The *uBuntu* Project also advocated and fought very hard for the creation of an *uBuntu* jurisprudence. This goes to your point, Bachir – the idea that *uBuntu*, or *Nite*, is against people's rights is completely misconceived. At the time the *uBuntu* Project began, the Constitution of South Africa had removed the epilogue that explicitly referred to *uBuntu*. Even so, we fought to develop an *uBuntu* jurisprudence. Emeritus Justice of the South African Constitutional Court Albie Sachs at first argued that dignity could be a justiciable principle, but not *uBuntu*. I said he was wrong about that, and he came to agree with me. Then, with Justice Yvonne Mokgoro began the development of what is now a very rich *uBuntu* jurisprudence. So, the idea that there's something about *uBuntu* or *Nite* that is anti-rights, anti-constitutionalism, is completely misguided because, as Bachir tells us, both *uBuntu* and *Nite* are always constructed and therefore, their meaning is always in the future.

I want to speak to three burning issues of our time. The first is that in the United States, we have an anti-vaxxer movement. Now this movement is not only very much against public health, but it's against being human. The anti-vaxxers are operating on instinct. They're not operating on humanity; they're operating on fear. They're operating on 'maybe the antibodies cause the government to be able to spy on you, so we don't need any vaccines.' But what really is motivating that? I want to suggest that it's precisely instinct: it's terror, it's fear, and it's rage. And those three aspects together are absolutely dangerous in the United States right now, seriously dangerous. It's not really about this vaccine.

Here I want to bring in my other comrade, Amartya Sen, a big supporter of the uBuntu Project. What we have lost in the United States is capability freedom: exercise your own creativity, your own space, which always comes collectively. Capability freedom is an idea of justice that rests on how much people can actually exercise their options in life so as to flourish as human beings. When you don't have freedom to have a good job, when you don't have freedom to have health insurance, then you don't have freedom. I'm very proud to say that there are now 51 strikes going on in the United States. My daughter is a union organizer, so she's part of this movement to say, 'We must have decent jobs with decent benefits. We have the right to have a good job. We have the right to have health insurance. We have the right, if my wife or my mother or my sister gets sick, to make sure she gets the best care.' When you don't have capability freedom, what does freedom become? You no longer can be a person who can meaningfully

The other big issue of our time right now is the right to abortion. In South Africa, for example, the right to abortion has never been contested. Am I pro-abortion? The answer is that to be simply pro or against abortion does not consider the bigger issue at stake. What is it that feminists in the United States are for? We're for reproductive freedom. I personally entered this debate through the ideal of what I called the 'imaginary domain.' We, as women, need to have an ability to see who and what we are in terms of our power – what is a very scary power to many people – mainly men – that we can produce life. Therefore, we should have all the support and all the sustenance, and of course men, too, because they're there in the parenting process.

We shouldn't say abortion is about choice. If you are pregnant and you didn't want to have a baby, you didn't choose. The liberal language isn't adequate. But it also shows us our vulnerability, our need for sustenance, our need for maternity leave, our need for free childcare, our need for all the things that make it possible to be a human being who is kind not only to those who are currently living, but to the next generation as well.

There's a very threatening and scary movement right now in the United States called 'the Black Flag movement.' The black flag was from the early days of the confederacy in the civil war in the United States, and it led to two very brutal massacres. The flags were a sign that there would be no Union soldier left standing after these massacres. Now we have people putting up black flags. Last night, five young African Americans; October 14, 2021, Black men, doing nothing except walking down the street, were shot and murdered. And their murderers put black flags on their bodies. What does this tell us? What kind of fear or despair has turned into murderous rage? This takes me back to something Bachir emphasizes: *uBuntu* and *Nite* are philosophies of life. The Black Flag is a racist symbol of murder. It was then at the beginning of the civil war, and it is now. We must really take seriously that African philosophy allows us to think completely differently about our co-dependence and think against, if you forgive my word, the impotence of an individualism that gets pitted against tribalism. The individualism that you cannot get a vaccine, that you cannot walk down the street safely, but you can buy a gun anywhere. But what you cannot do is have a meaningful life because capability freedom only comes when we act together to create an entirely different world system other than racialized capitalism. Thanks.

Bassey Antia

Thanks a lot, Drucilla and Souleymane. Sinfree will now pose a couple of questions to you.

Sinfree Makoni

Thank you very much, colleagues. These were fascinating presentations and I also enjoyed reading the papers that you sent. Let me try to apply my mind to some of the things that you are saying to see whether I understood the core of the argument. Souleymane was saying, for example, that *uBuntu* is unfinishable – it is an unfinishable project. Is it that *uBuntu* is an unfinishable project or is it that *uBuntu* is an incompletable project? Is it that unfinishable or it is completely incompletable?

Souleymane Bachir Diagne

Thank you. Thank you very much for that question. I would say that it is an open-ended movement. That would be the best way to characterize it. I was here paraphrasing, as I said, the famous title by Jürgen Habermas, *Modernity: An Unfinished Project* (1997). That definition of modernity as an unfinished project is an ethos, so to say, a kind of disposition vis-à-vis what is to come. The idea that our humanity is always to be achieved as an open-ended process is what I meant. So, if I say 'unfinishable,' the reason why I would prefer 'unfinishable' here to 'unachievable,' is that the word has a nuance of failure. If you cannot achieve something, if something cannot be achieved, it means you will always fail to achieve it, while unfinishable is open-ended. That is what I was trying to say.

Sinfree Makoni

So to some extent, you will never get to a steady state of *uBuntu*? You are always moving towards *uBuntu*?

Souleymane Bachir Diagne

Right. You are always pushing its frontier and bringing it to new fields. Let me give the example of Drucilla's paper. I did not think of *uBuntu* as a way of dealing with feminism. It was not in the first writings of Desmond Tutu, or Nelson Mandela, and so on and so forth. But the project itself has the potential of going in that direction. So, it is not just that that finish line keeps moving in front of you, it is that while you are going, while you are thinking within that project, new possibilities continuously open in front of you.

Sinfree Makoni

Okay, so within this cosmology, let's say, of *uBuntu*, where does death fit in? How can we frame death through the analytical apparatus of *uBuntu*? What does death become through the lenses of *uBuntu*?

Souleymane Bachir Diagne

Well, if I think the cosmology of 'ntu,' and I'm doing this by comparison. Again that is the work I do. I do comparative African philosophies. I'm not saying that all

African cosmologies are identical, but they are comparable, and I'm looking at comparison here. We deal with emerging cosmology. These are not closed cosmologies, but emerging cosmologies. When they are cosmologies of vital principle – if you consider that all existing beings are forces, to 'be' is to 'be a force.' You are not in the logic of attribution. You are not saying that the being has force or that force can be attributed to the being. You are saying that 'being' and 'force' are one and the same thing. So you may ask yourself, what is a force for? What is the goal of a force? The goal of a force is to become more force.

We could compare this with Spinoza's philosophy of *conatus*. To be is to be always intention. And this is why this is not the closed cosmology; instead, we are talking about an open-ended cosmology and always emerging cosmology where in particular, the goal of the human force is to be more force. And what does that mean when it comes to death? It means that the goal is to become an even higher force as an ancestor. In many African traditional cosmologies, the goal of a person is to become an ancestor. This means that paradoxically, as you grow older, provided that you have learned to become a person within your own community, you are supporting your community and, in return, your community is supporting you in becoming a person. Becoming fully a person is actually being a force out of reach of death. You are, in that sense, immortal. Your death will only mean a passage toward the state of being the force of an ancestor.

If we look carefully at many cosmologies, both in West African cosmology that I am more familiar with, but I believe in the cosmology of 'ntu' as well, this is the idea of achieving your humanity to the point where it is out of reach of death. And by the way, let me just add that this is not particularly specific to African cosmologies. In a way, you can read even the Bible along those lines. When it is, say in the Bible, 'let the dead bury the dead,' you are saying that when death comes, it only takes what is dead. Fully achieved life is out of its reach. So this is how I would answer your wonderful question. Thank you for it.

Sinfree Makoni

Since you are interested in comparative philosophy, how does *Nite* or *uBuntu* play itself out when we are talking about Africans in the diaspora, whether they are in the US or in South America, et cetera? Are there parallels between the morphological characteristics and the philosophical characteristics of *uBuntu* in West Africa and *uBuntu* among those Africans who were, let's say, taken forcibly from Africa into South America or into North America? What are the parallels there? What happens to *uBuntu* in this case?

Souleymane Bachir Diagne

Well, let me give a very factual answer to that. I would not have been able to respond to that question before, but a couple of years ago, I travelled to Brazil. I was invited for the first time to Brazil, and I stayed awhile in Salvador da Bahia in particular, where I was invited to present my work. Even more recently I did a webinar with the friends I made there because they were interested in what I had to say about N*ite* and *uBuntu*. The reason why they were interested is that they were doing the same comparative work I was doing. The force of life, that is expressed both in *uBuntu* and *Nite,* is something that remains through the transformation and changes that the diasporization of Africa has created.

And I would even add that we talk very much about restitution of African art these days, so France has been returning artifacts. These art objects, which are, in a way, a visualization – the visual language of this cosmology of life – when they were taken from the continent, often through violence, and kept in these ethnographical museums in places such as Europe, their force was still manifested there. And this is how they had a transformative role and function in modernism and modern art. What these objects have produced in the history of art, and human art in general, can be seen as a translation of the *uBuntu* or the *Nite* force that they've carried with them. So, I believe that, yes, in a way there has been an 'uBuntuization' of modernity in art that is the manifestation of the capacity of this force to continue to be alive, even in exile or when they became diasporic objects.

Sinfree Makoni

Okay, thank you very much. Let me ask a couple of questions to Drucilla and then we can move on. Drucilla, you have been in constant exchange with Souleymane. My question is this: For over a long period of time, what has been the impact of Souleymane's ideas on how you have conceptualized issues about feminism?

Drucilla Cornell

Thank you. That's a great question. For me, when I first spoke of ethical feminism, it expanded the idea that feminism was not simply about the battle for women or transgender or gays and lesbians. Of course, it's about all those things, but more importantly it was about fighting against anyone being thrown under the bar of humanity. And I initially called that ethical feminism. But now, I would call it *uBuntu* feminism. And this gets to what Bachir just said. If you think *uBuntu* conceptualizes humanity as in an affective field, it is what Bachir was referring to as a force of life.

This is why we need to rethink the battle of abortion. It's not only about the right to abortion. It's about us supporting one another. The other side of being an ancestor is that there are human beings that are not yet born. Now if we really cared about human beings that are not yet born, then we would make sure that the horrific inequality in the United States did not exist. So that if you understand that we are together in this, then women's reproductive freedom is freedom for all of us. In this way, we can understand why Bachir keeps using the term life force, and I think he's right to do so. Because if everything we do has moral and ethical force, then feminism must be part of understanding that vulnerability.

Sinfree Makoni

How do you reconcile your notion in your article of conceptions of transindividuality with the argument that Bachir was making that one realizes or brings their humanity to fruition through the group? The group helps you to bring your humanity to fruition. In your paper you are talking about trans-individuality, so how are these ideas compatible or are they a slightly different emphasis?

Drucilla Cornell

In the text that Bachir sent us, he reinforced the point that tribalism is rooted in instinct. The notion that you are in this group, and not in this other group, is a form of what Bachir rightly calls, 'tribalism based in instinct.' When we start to see that we are human together and this is a struggle, then it's important to see there is force in our efforts to be human together. But does that mean that what it means to be a human being will always be an ethical task? The answer is yes.

Sinfree Makoni

Let make the last comment and then I'll give it over to my friend Bassey. This conversation is very exciting, but there's a tension between the arguments, Drucilla, which you are putting across, and what Bachir is arguing, I think. Bachir is talking about humanity generally and how we become human through other people. You touch on this, but once you introduce the notion side of ethical feminism or *uBuntu* feminism, aren't you breaking down that notion of humanity into certain divisions? Isn't it the case here that Bachir is trying to come up with a sort of non-global notion of humanity, but your instincts on feminism are drawing you into drawing distinctions within that humanity when you talk about ethical feminism or *uBuntu* feminism? So whereas Bachir sees unity, you see difference?

Drucilla Cornell

The way I understand your question is how did we grapple with the reality of difference?

Sinfree Makoni

Yes.

Drucilla Cornell

The way that I did that theoretically is distinguished between identity, identification and position. I'm an unrepentant Marxist socialist. In my position, I am a white woman and that means something. I can't just jump out of being a white woman.

When I walk down the street I don't feel particularly threatened by the police, a little bit particularly when I'm demonstrating. And in my earlier days I was constantly on strike and the police were against picket lines. But then what is an identity? I was raised as a woman. Now what did it mean to be a woman? Oh, it meant something. It meant: you can't do. You can't be a firefighter, you can't be a cop, you can't be a lawyer, you can't be a doctor. Ruth Bader Ginsburg was told when she graduated from law school that she could work as a secretary. Ultimately, she became a member of the Supreme Court as we know.

The importance of identity is that we are finite beings. This gets back to what Bachir said about the force of life. We are vulnerable. We grow up in a language. We grow up in a position. We grow up understanding and coming to terms with that. Our identifications are more fluid, but we have identities and, at the same time, have positions. Out of that – this is the point – they don't completely determine us; out of that we struggle to be human together. But if you can think you can just step out of being white, if you think you do not have to be an active anti-racist, you're missing my point, because this is what Bachir keeps emphasizing. It's the future and the future is in the struggle to become something other than the way we're positioned, the identities we grew up in, and the identifications we have.

Sinfree Makoni

Okay. Thank you very much. Now the future belongs to my colleague Bassey Antia to invite the global audience to interact with you.

Bassey Antia

Thank you very much, Sinfree. And thanks again to Drucilla and Souleymane. We have a couple of questions in the (Zoom) chat. The first one is addressed to Souleymane. The question is, 'How would you compare your open-ended notion of the human and humanity with that of Sylvia Wynter's conceptualization of the human (McKittrick, 2015)?'

Souleymane Bachir Diagne

By first confessing my ignorance because I'm not familiar with that conceptualization unfortunately. Can I have a sense of what it is?

Bassey Antia

Yeah, Linden, would you like to jump in here to elaborate somewhat?

Linden Lewis

It was not my intent to say anything. But I'm talking about her attempt to render the human from the notion of a European conceptualization of humanity. That has been the way in which she has talked about it in terms of a delinking of that colonial concept and inspiring in people a different notion of humanity that is not caught up in an entirely European context.

Souleymane Bachir Diagne

Yeah, thank you for clarifying this. I believe that we agree here. If I try to look at the modern European concept of humanity, we should not be also simplifying. There is not such a thing as a European essentialist vision of what a human is. We can say that there is a modern concept and identify it, for example, with a philosopher such as Descartes. Descartes believing that the human being is to be constituted in his – and I'm using *his* because that is the gendered notion he had in mind, his view was excluding women – that the human being is constituted by first isolating himself from others and defining himself in total isolation. Whereas to come back to the exchange between Sinfree and Drucilla earlier when Drucilla says transindividuality, it means that you do not reach the point where the individual defines himself first as an individual and then tries to look at connection with others. He is right from the beginning defined in this transindividuality into subjectivity, if you wish, into humanity in the first place.

But Descartes's notion of the individual – self-defining individual – and then that individual defined as master and possessor of nature, this is something you find also in Descartes. This refers to how the individual not only separates himself from other individuals, but also separates himself from nature, and turns nature into natural resources. That would be a definition of the modern individual of triumphant capitalism that we are suffering from. That capitalism of greed of the powerful individual is also what is destroying our planet. I would oppose that to what I was saying about this emergent cosmology where the human being considers herself in the chain of being – in this continuous chain of being from the pebble to the force of forces. So, defining yourself in separation vis-à-vis other human beings and defining yourself in separation with other living beings would not make sense in a cosmology such as that one.

And what we say, Drucilla and me, is that we need to capture the meaning of that philosophy for our times and put these concepts to work. When we need that definition of the human to fight inequalities. For example, take vaccinations. Two percent of Africa is vaccinated while anti-vaxxers here are frowning upon what is given to them to protect everybody else. These are the kinds of inequalities we are trying to fight in the name of the definition of the human being that is radically different from this modern European conception of the human as separated from other humans. A being so fiercely individualistic and separated from nature, that he allows himself to turn into natural resources. Our planet is dying from that, from having been turned into natural resources. So thank you very much for that question and the precision you made.

Bassey Antia

Okay, thank you very much. Drucilla, did you want to jump in?

Drucilla Cornell

I just wanted to say, Sylvia Wynter makes it very clear. There's Man1 and Man2. Man1 is the notion that some of us are to be saved, to put it very simply, in the notion of the Christian Man. And then the long debates over whether Africans or South Americans have souls are what she calls Man1. It's a simple summation. Man2 is the Biological Man in meritocracy – we have seen this again and again and again – the notion that some human beings are just born superior and that other human beings are born inferior. That for her was Man2. So what do you have in Wynter? There isn't any human yet. Now what I think – and I hope, Sylvia, you're listening somewhere – is that what *uBuntu* and *Nite* give us is an understanding of the dynamism of our engagement in bringing new ways of being human into our social reality. She tells us that the human has not even begun yet, but *uBuntu* and *Nite* tell us that it always has already begun.

As soon as you're born into this force field, this affective field with other human beings, at least in South Africa in other African countries, happens through ritual. The cutting of the umbilical cord is when you enter the symbolic community, and that's a ritual. That ritual gives you your symbolic name. Now you are part of a community. That future is yours to build. The only problem I see in Sylvia Wynter's wonderful work is that Man1 and Man2 seem to dominate so as to obscure human possibilities in *uBuntu* and *Nite*. And what she has trouble coming to terms with is how we struggle to realize the human. We're saying that human is already here. But when we construct what it means to be a human being, when we fight for humanity, when we struggle to be a human being, there's always more to be done.

Bassey Antia

Thank you. There is a question from Hilary to you both. Hilary would like to know how you would explain *uBuntu* as going beyond humanism and responsibility for one another. The backdrop to this question is your reference to human entanglements, ethical responsibility to both human and other, or more than human entities from the tree to the pebble to the earth. How do you see *uBuntu* going beyond humanism and responsibility for one another?

Souleymane Bachir Diagne

Okay, let me just say that I agree that, in a way, the backdrop to the question bears the response to that. This is why I spoke probably very quickly when I indicated toward the end of my short presentation that in the humanism of *uBuntu*, the term *humanism* should not blind us to the fact that when you get down to the cosmology of 'ntu' from which the word *uBuntu* is formed, 'ntu,' the vital principle, goes beyond the human being. In other words, if there is any centrality of human life, it is the centrality of responsibility. Not a centrality as kind of ontological priority, however, as the only priority would come from the particular responsibility of the living human being to maintain the chain of forces from the force of forces to the pebble. If you go back to the vital principle, that is what makes it naturally beyond simple entanglement of humans. Drucilla, you want to clarify that further?

Drucilla Cornell

I think that is an extremely important point, Bachir, because what we're talking about is that humans are immersed in an ecological world in which we're just one part. It'd be very helpful if we stop being such a destructive part of it because we can't escape it. It's not like we can walk away from the violence that human beings have done to the world around us. This is where you're right about a certain brand of European philosophy. I mean, Kant thought it was okay to torture cats. Why? The answer is because there's something unique about being human. But what we're saying in a certain way is that what is unique about being human is that it gives us responsibility. Have you ever met an elephant that made an atomic bomb? But that means not only that we are part of it, but we're more responsible for it. We are the ones right now that can guarantee that the wonderful beings we share this planet with can flourish. That is part of what it means to be uniquely human.

Bassey Antia

Thank you. We have a question here from Adrien for Souleymane. Adrien first pays tribute to Souleymane for having situated *uBuntu* in the global discussion the same way Senghor did with universal civilization, and also notes that he has worked on *uBuntu* in the context of Mbiti's work. His question for Souleymane is: 'What relationship would you establish between the consciousness of 'sociologists of risk' such as Anthony Giddens, Beck, Jürgen Habermas and theologians such as ML King, to the concept of social destinies being related to *uBuntu*?'

Souleymane Bachir Diagne

Thank you very much, Adrien, for that question. It is important, I believe, that your question brings us squarely within the field of social political power of *uBuntu* – in particular when it comes to social issues that you raise and socialism as well. Drucilla mentioned socialism and Marxism and I do believe that *uBuntu* can be identified with socialism. Let me give you an example which takes us out of Africa, because we should not think that these concepts are unique in a specific way to Africa. When the French Communist Party was created in the beginning of the 20th century, the first leader of the French Communist Party was Philosopher Jean Jaurès who created the French newspaper *L'Humanité* (Humanity), which still exists. It is still the daily newspaper of the French Communist Party, or what is left of it today.

Why did he call it l'Humanité? This idea that giving yourself a notion of a humanity to be built, to be achieved against the fragmentation introduced by capitalism, the simple word, *humanity* in that sense, became a 'machine de guerre' against capitalism. What he writes in the first issue is that claiming humanity as something that needs to be achieved is a way of opposing the dissolving forces of capitalism.

Capitalism fragments humanity, while socialism – he had even a kind of cosmological sense of what socialism means in terms of achieving humanity.

Achieving humanity is not just singing some kind of 'kumbaya' where we would say 'we are identical, we are all brothers and sisters, let's sing together,' et cetera. It is to say, 'achieving it (humanity) is going against the forces of fragmentation and division represented by capitalism.' So this is a struggle, we are not talking about some kind of peaceful romanticized lyrical illusion, we are talking about the principles upon which the struggle is going to be constructed. When you claim your humanity, when you claim *uBuntu*, you are claiming socialism as well. That is what something I take from this. Let me just add that I'm glad you brought in John Mbiti who left us not so long ago also.

Usually his definition of *uBuntu*, 'You are, therefore I am,' is misunderstood as saying, 'well, the collective needs to be in order for the individual to be, and the individual is nothing, the collective is everything. And the individual draws her being from the being of the collective.' It is reciprocity precisely, this individuation with the support of the community that Drucilla made precise in her definition of the philosophy of *uBuntu*.

Bassey Antia

Thank you very much. (In the chat) Hilary is grateful for your answer on the issue of entanglements and is quite intrigued by the cosmology referred to in the 'ntu' of *uBuntu*. So just a comment. I wonder if anyone would like to jump in with a comment or a question?

Sinfree Makoni

Let me ask Drucilla a question. When you look now at your intellectual trajectory from the time that some extant notions of *uBuntu* intervene in your intellectual work, what has been the impact of *uBuntu* on your own intellectual trajectory? How different would you have been as an intellectual if you didn't know about *uBuntu*? What did *uBuntu* do to you or what forces of thinking did *uBuntu* unleash in you and how has that affected the type of scholarship that you do?

Drucilla Cornell

uBuntu gave me an entirely different way to think about individuality and what it means to be human through its notion of our ontological interconnectedness.

Bassey Antia

Thank you. There's a question from Cristine who would like Drucilla to comment on the differences or similarities she sees between the ethics of care and *uBuntu* feminism. I'd like to add on to this by also asking what your view is on the different flavors or geographical specifications and qualifications of feminism. So, is there an

African feminism? Is there an American feminism? I think, Amina Mama is in the audience and may wish to comment on this as well. Drucilla, you go first.

Drucilla Cornell

Sure. Thank you for that question. You see, this is one of the ways that African philosophy has changed my feminist politics. Again, we're so lucky to have Bachir because of his work in comparative African philosophy, not just South African *uBuntu*. *uBuntu* feminism can make us think differently about the important debate in the United States between justice and care. The ethics of care surrounds the meaning that there's something about the way we are together, and we need to care for one another, and that supposedly goes against the notion of the autonomous person of justice. In *uBuntu* there's no conflict between justice and care. Firstly, we're not autonomous people, that's a fantasy. Secondly, justice is the best way we care for each other. When we organize together and fight for a better world that is not for capitalism but instead, for socialism, we're caring for each other.

Bassey Antia

And perhaps the bit in respect of different flavors of feminism? The other question surrounding African feminism, European feminism, North American feminism – what's your take on such distinctions?

Drucilla Cornell

Well, I should be perfectly honest. If you think of feminism through *uBuntu* or what I earlier called ethical feminism, then all those feminisms have one project which is to absolutely refuse anyone being thrown below the bar of humanity. There's going to be different struggles obviously. Struggles tend to be somewhat local. But I'm with Bachir – what we really need now is the effort to create a common global good. We can unite around all these various different struggles. Now, does feminism have to be anti-racist? You bet.

Bassey Antia

Thank you. There's another question from Adrien: 'Mbiti's conceptualization of the African world view, as well as Senghor's theory of *Negritude*, place emphasis on how we relate to visible and invisible beings. Is this concept operative or operational in African political discourse or practice today?'

Souleymane Bachir Diagne

Thank you, Adrien, for this question. I would say that yes, but when I say yes, what I'm looking at is not the ontological side of the philosophy of *Negritude*, but connected to that ontological side, the political side, which has been articulated as African socialism. This is very important to look at. Now that we are in a phase – to quote from the title of Axel Honneth (*The Idea of Socialism: Towards a Renewal*, 2016), we are in a phase of the reconstruction of socialism. This is a time when socialism is rethinking itself and reconstructing itself. I belong to a generation of people who were very skeptical to say the least about Negritude in African socialism. We were saying that there is only one socialism which is the scientific socialism as articulated, for example, by my former mentor Althusser.

In this time of reconstruction of socialism, I believe that socialism must revisit all the different forms that were, at one point, dismissed as utopian, et cetera. It must retrieve its own force, the driving force of the dream of utopia and spirituality. The spiritual force of socialism, as expressed in African socialism by the likes of Senghor and Nyerere, must be part of the reconstruction of socialism in this global rethinking of socialism. This is why I think that yes, indeed, it is or should be operational and operative in current political practices and discourses today.

Sinfree Makoni

I think this has been a fascinating conversation. We need powerful argument for the relevance of African cosmologies; it is a way of explaining some of the contemporary challenges that we are faced with. What I found quite interesting in the conversation is the commitment to a future in which African ideas and African cosmologies play a key part. So for example, Bachir's insistence of the future and the role of *uBuntu* or *Nite* in shaping that future are quite encouraging. What it does is it destabilizes the view of *uBuntu* as a philosophy of yesterday. If I take anything from what Bachir is saying and, in some sense, what Drucilla is saying, is that *uBuntu* and *Nite* are philosophies of the tomorrow that is yet to come. To some extent, it gives us confidence and makes us feel much more optimistic about our capability of controlling the ideas which will shape our tomorrow.

The other thing that I thought was quite interesting was – which Bachir also talked about in his paper – the role of *uBuntu* in influencing and in shaping how we respond to this pandemic, with issues about vaccinations, et cetera. I think this is an encouraging way of understanding that intellectually, there are certain ideas that can enable us – if we see ourselves as interconnected – to make sense of the current circumstances that we find ourselves in.

Bassey Antia

Thank you, Drucilla and Souleymane, for sharing your expertise with us. We are really very grateful. And we'll be going back home much richer than we were a little over an hour ago. We are really very grateful for the inspiring conversation you both have had.

References

Diagne, S. (2021) UBuntu and Nite pioneers of Africana philosophy. Unpublished manuscript for the African Studies Program's Global Virtual Forum.

Habermas, J. (1997) Modernity: An unfinished project. In E.M. Passerin and S. Benhabib (eds) *Habermas and the Unfinished Project of Modernity: Critical Essays on the Philosophical Discourse of Modernity* (pp. 38–55). Boston: MIT Press.

Honneth, A. (2016) *The Idea of Socialism: Towards A Renewal*. Chichester: John Wiley & Sons.

McKittrick, K. (ed.) (2015) *Sylvia Wynter: On Being Human as Praxis*. Durham, NC: Duke University Press.

7 Foundational Concepts and Struggles for Dignity and Life

Catherine Walsh and Walter Mignolo

Catherine Walsh

I would like to begin by thanking Sinfree, Bassey and also Magdalena, my former student and longtime friend.

I believe that for both Walter and I, this book *On Decoloniality* has a lot to do with our different lived histories and, relatedly, our different ways of thinking and practicing the interdependence and continuous flow of theory-and-as praxis and praxis-and-as-theory. It is this difference and the making of it present that makes the book especially unique.

In the short time I have here, I want to share three points of reflection that help reveal the relation between my history – or, better said, 'herstory' – and what I understand and assume as decolonial praxis, including in these times of pandemics (in the plural) and COVID.

My first point has to do with my relationship to decoloniality, a relationship grounded in a long history/herstory of activism and social struggle, particularly related to the structural oppressions of race/racism, language, knowledge and patriarchy/gender. It is from praxis that my processes of theorization come, processes most often tied to collective analysis and thought.

I first came to think about the colonial and decolonial with Boricua or Puerto Rican communities in the US; they taught me about the lived reality of colonialism and the necessary struggles *against* the colonial tare and *for* something else. For 16 years, these communities were a central part of the contexts of my everyday life, education-based work and shared battles against the still-present colonial system or matrix of power.

I still recall the phone call I received in 1980 from a lawyer who worked with the Puerto Rican Legal Defense and Education Fund-PRLDEF. He asked if I would be willing to work with him, PRLDEF, and a Puerto Rican community-based organization in developing a lawsuit against the Bridgeport, Connecticut schools. His argument was that the colonial nature of both language use and the educational curriculum was the reason for failure among Puerto Rican students. He asked me if I could work with them in building the case against educational and linguistic colonialism and for decolonizing language and educational practice. Of course, I said yes. This case, and many others that followed with PRLDEF, the Lawyers' Committee for Civil Rights, META-Multicultural Training and (Legal) Advocacy Project, and the NAACP Education and Legal Defense Fund, along with work with Puerto Rican, Dominican, Haitian and other communities and students of color, helped me see how systemic racism works in both the US legal system and US schools. It also made me think about how race, along with gender, language, knowledge and existence-based ways of being in the world are constitutive parts of what we refer to in this book as the colonial matrix of power. Up until I migrated south in the mid-1990s, confronting the operation of this matrix was part and parcel of my praxis with communities and in the institutions we call schools.

While it was only later that I began to use the terms 'coloniality' and 'decoloniality,' the concrete experience for me of working *against* systemic oppressions, *with* communities of color and *for* a radically distinct educational practice for almost two decades in the US is a foundational part of my herstory, of my beginning to learn to unlearn in order to relearn and of what I understand and describe in the book as decolonial praxis. The years spent working collaboratively with Paulo Freire and within the network of critical pedagogy in the US were also crucial in giving me ways to understand the political significance of pedagogy – pedagogy not only in the context of schools, but also, and even more crucially, in the context of social struggle. As Paulo argued, pedagogy and praxis are deeply related.

This takes me to my second point. In 1995, I immigrated from the north to the south, from the US to Ecuador. Although my relationship with Ecuador began in the late 1970s, for more than the past 25 years Ecuador has been my home, my place of existence, thought, work and praxis-based struggle. Here, my herstory has taken somewhat different but related paths. While there are certainly parallels with the ongoing struggles in the US and in other places in the world against systemic racism and settler colonialism (and the obvious relationship between the two), the differences of territory and collective memory are also great. Over 500 years after the colonial matrix of power took form here (in Latin America, or what some of us prefer to call Abya Yala) and then began its global travel, coloniality, with its ongoing mutations and reconfigurations, continues to mark most aspects of existence. Here, in Ecuador, I have learned that decolonial struggles are struggles of and for existence and life.

While Aníbal Quijano (1992) gave me the words and structural arguments to understand and name this reality, social movements have taught me about the living nature of their significance, including and most especially the meaning of the decoloniality *for*, and about the necessary insurgencies of decolonial prospect, praxis and project. Even before I made my permanent move, Ecuador's Indigenous movement (recognized in the 1990s as a strongest in the Americas and possibly the world), approached me, giving me 'tasks' or charges or responsibilities to assume, one of which was to help think in an Indigenous university. Another from the mid-90s on was to think with the movements' concepts and principles of plurinationality and interculturality, including with respect to knowledge, and the rethinking of state, concepts and principles that came not from academia but from social movement thought-practice. Putting the Indigenous movements' decolonial, political-epistemic project in practice, including in my university work, was part of my charge, part of the tasks that they gave me. In 1999, the country's black movement insisted that they, too, had charges or tasks for me to take on. So began a very different process of shared work, including the formation of what Bassey Antia mentioned of the Afro-Andean documentary and oral history project, the largest living archive of black collective memory in Latin America.

With both movements and their community base, I was pushed to unlearn and relearn, to confront what I thought I knew, and to deeply question the supposedly universal nature of Western being and thought. Decoloniality came to me, for me, the praxistic and never-ending work of my own decolonization, as well as the ongoing political, epistemic and existence-based pedagogies and methodologies of movements, collectives and communities to not just resist, but more crucially to re-exist. Decoloniality's significance and sense, again for me, became intricately tied up with the question of the how or hows; that is with the action, the labor, the struggle-based work, the pedagogies-as-methodologies and methodologies-as-pedagogies of decolonizing. It came to signify and mark a politics of responsibility and ethics – a thinking *from and with*, rather than studying *about* – and a praxis, including most especially in the university, that works to fissure or crack the white, Eurocentric, westernized and disciplined frames of knowledge and higher education. The doctoral program that I began more than 20 years ago, and in which Walter Mignolo has been a crucial part, is one example of this cracking – it's a crack within the university.

It is this politics and praxis that drive my thinking, my doing and my writing, including in this book; a politics-of-as-praxis that, and again for me, is aimed at the crack-making, and in shifting the gaze away from coloniality's totality and toward its fissures or cracks, those increasingly present in Latin America or Abya Yala but also throughout the world, including in the United States. What does and what could it mean, I ask, to think from and with the cracks? To urge and enable a kind of crack thinking?

This takes me to my third and last point, which has to do with these present times of virus pandemics – in plural – but also with the cracks. I share many of the suspicions about the orchestration of a well-planned global project (I prefer the word 'project' rather than conspiracy), in which COVID is both strategy and instrument in the new configurations and mutations of capital, and the colonial matrix of power. Capitalism and coloniality are not affected by the virus, but feed off it.

In the case of Latin America, but certainly not just here, what is at work is what I understand (in part through ongoing conversations with numerous collectives and communities) as a project/plan of 'targeted de-existence.' Targeted understood as racialized, gendered, heteronormative, territorialized and generational, and part of the strategies of extermination, access and social control (in reality of existence itself), that intend to eliminate all those who hinder, disturb or are simply not useful to the reconfiguring system of power. Here, COVID is a tenacious, effective and useful tool.

The Amazon is a particularly clear case in point. Since COVID began, the destruction of the Amazon Forest has increased by more than 60%. While set fires, massive deforestation and the uncontrolled advance of state-sanctioned extractive industries of mining, oil and agro-industry, among others, are eliminating the flora and fauna and the lungs of global life, state-sanctioned military protect the rights and access of companies and workers to enter Amazonian Indigenous communities, including those in voluntary isolation, thus, propagating the virus in horrendous proportions, killing off the elders as guardians of ancestral knowledge, practically wiping out many of the smaller tribal groups, and eliminating large numbers of the general population.

Moreover, in both Indigenous and Afro-descendant territories and communities throughout Latin America, the new strategy is the targeted elimination of children and youth – to kill off the children and youth that are the future generation. In Brazil, the targeted assassination of black youth by police has reached pandemic proportions since COVID began, as have feminicides, transcides and racialized genocides throughout the region. In Colombia, one Indigenous or black leader a day has been killed since COVID began in March 2020, and more than 70 massacres occurred in 2020 in Indigenous and black territories – territories rich in natural resources. All this is further exacerbated by the limited access and often outright denial of healthcare as COVID continues to spread. I think of the parallels with African-American and Native American communities in the US, but also the parallels in African nations and many other places in the world. Is there any doubt, I ask, about the targeted de-existence in process?

For many, including myself, the critical question today is how to sow life in these times of death, how to plant re-existence in these times of de-existence? Such questions – without a doubt decolonial in substance, project and motivation – are what are pushing the creation and making of small fissures or cracks in both rural and urban spaces today, enabling some hope and cultivating local spaces and forms of re-existence – no matter how small – against the real threats of de-existence. I wonder how such cultivation might also be taking place elsewhere in the world. Is this not what decoloniality, at least in part, is all about? That is, about struggles of and for life against, despite, without, and in the borders, cracks and fissures of the racist, heteropatriarchal, capitalist and modern colonial system, and its mutations and new configurations in the era of COVID?

These are the central questions and concerns that are crucial for me and, in many ways, of our book.

Bassey Antia

Okay, well. Thank you very much, Catherine. Walter, the floor is yours.

Walter Mignolo

Alright, thank you very much Bassey for the introduction, and Magda and Sinfree for organizing this. There is a lot to talk about and a lot to do. I will talk for about 15 minutes, too, and I have three points. Also, I don't know if I will manage to talk about the three points, but I'll stop after 15 minutes. How do we get to 'coloniality?' My story, I came without knowing it – the experience, the discomfort. It started as a son of Italian immigrants in Argentina. Feeling on the one hand that I didn't belong to the country. The country belonged to the people who possessed the land since the 19th century, the kind of families that came from the 18th century. I didn't know that, but I feel that kind of discomfort in a small town of Italian immigrant in the whole area, in the west of Buenos Aires. I went to the university, and I don't know why but I remember that they start reading Gramsci (1971), because they were studying philosophy. I started reading Gramsci and joined a group discussing Marx (1973) and Marxism and that was in the 60s, with professors but also with the majority of students.

One day, I discovered the second discomfort. I realized that my friends, my wonderful, wonderful friends and their wonderful minds were Marxist, but at the same time, they came from middle-class families. They were sons of dentists, of lawyers, of doctors, etc. My father was a 'jornalero.' I mean, he worked in the countryside employed by the people who owned the land. When I was 7 years old my parents moved to a small town so I could go to school. So my father became a proletarian working on a small factory making plows. That was a second of discomfort, how could I relate to my friends from middle-class families concerned with enthusiastically endorsing Marxism and the proletarian revolution while my father was a proletarian and did not know about Marx and Marxism? Those are the experiences that you carry with you and you don't know what to do with them. After finishing high school, I moved from the small town to the city of Cordoba to attend the university and connected with faculty that were traveling back and forth from France, mainly Paris. I ended up becoming interested in semiotics. I went to do the PhD (Doctorat de Trosieme Cycle) in France, and then the discomfort increased because once more I felt out of place. At first I thought it was a personal problem, but with time I began to understand that was systemic and Anibal Quijano found a word for it, 'coloniality.' At the time, Latin Americans migrating to Europe (and I was one of them, so second experience and migrant), Spain mainly but also France, Germany, England, Sweden, were identified as 'sudacas,' people from the South (Sud). 'La palabra **sudaca** es, según la definición del *Diccionario de la lengua española* de la Real Academia Española, una expresión despectiva utilizada para referirse a los naturales de Sudamérica.'[1] En Francia, la novela del boom hacia furor y en ese sentido las y los sudamericanos y sudamericanas eramos 'le denier gadget d' outremer.' (We became famous in France due to the popularity of the Latin American novels, we were the 'le denier gadget d' outremer'.) From all directions, coloniality was coming and felt. But at the time only 'modernity' was on the table and the talk of the town. Coloniality was non-existent because the general idea is that, in South America, 'colonization' ended in the 19th century. Quijano taught us that yes, colonialization ended in the 19th century but coloniality is well and alive.

I then came to United States, and again, the discomfort continued. I was again a migrant. Soon after arriving at Indiana University my colleagues and students were talking about 'Chicanos.' It was 1973. 'What are the Chicanos?' I asked. I have no idea. And then, I learned who the Chicanos and Chicanas were, little by little. I became more informed, and in '87, I read Anzaldúa (1987), *Borderlands/La Frontera, The New Mestiza*. It was a shock. Remember, Quijano (1992) introduced coloniality in 1992, and I encountered the world around 1994. At the time I read Anzaldúa I was already doing research, teaching and writing on the colonialization of the Americas. Reading Anzaldúa was a triple shock.

The Darker Side of the Renaissance (Mignolo, 1992) is an autobiographical narrative in disguise. I do not tell my personal story. It's a scholarly book, certainly, but I wrote it not because of disciplinary concerns to explain to myself and for all those in similar life experience. What I mean is what Frantz Fanon (1968) said: the colonizer is not satisfied with controlling material resources but with a perverted logic that enters the memory of the colonized and distorts it. He was talking about the experience of settler colonialism in Algeria. The situation in Argentina, where I was born, was not the same. Colonialism ended 150 years before I was born, but coloniality persisted and is still with us. The *Darker Side of the Renaissance* attempted to underscore the colonization of languages, of memories and of space based on my own lived experience rather than on disciplinary demands.

In 1993–94, I encountered Quijano's coloniality. The manuscript of *The Darker Side* was already finished. Coloniality was an epiphany. I understood that the book was digging into the very foundation of coloniality. Coloniality put everything together. I began to understand that what happened to me happened to a lot of people. Coloniality is a short hand for coloniality of power and *patron colonial de poder* that was translated as *colonial matrix of power* into English, 'patrón.' They brought their colonial matrix of power is a logic that is underlying all the kinds of Western colonialism since the 16th century, and I began to understand (and Cathy said something in that line in the beginning), that the colonial matrix of power is the underlying structure of Western civilization. Western civilization is the youngest of all world civilization after since the Axial Age (900–300 BC). There is no Western civilization before the Renaissance (1350–1650 AC). Greece and Rome are Western in retrospect after the Renaissance. Greece was connected to the South, Egypt, and East, Persia; and Rome connected to Istanbul (during Constantine times, Constantinopla) and to Moscow (the third Rome). What was Western about that? Coloniality opened up the can of worms, that was the epiphany that reoriented my life and reoriented my research and my research became related to my life and vice versa.

I am making this connection because understanding coloniality is not a question of definition – *what is* coloniality? Rather it is a question of life, *where I sense coloniality, where is coloniality affecting me. And where do I see coloniality around me, in everyday life, in the news, in what people say, at the university, etc.* Then comes the conceptual work, understanding conceptually and at that moment decoloniality emerges because coloniality is always already a decolonial concept. The entry point is your own sensorium Where do you feel it? And if you do not feel it and realize that other people do, you have to ask yourself why you do not sense and see coloniality, only sense and see modernity. Coloniality, as a student of mine said it brilliantly – 'Coloniality is not over. It's all over'; and that's that. We are all in the coloniality matrix of power, not outside of it. Therefore, it cannot be 'studied' by any of the existing disciplines because the disciplines are tools of the colonial matrix of power to control and manage knowledges, subjectivities and intersubjective relations.

And this brings us to the current widespread talks on decolonizing the university, the curriculum, the museum, knowledge, or what have you. All those conversations presuppose that coloniality is all over those instances, but there is not much analysis of coloniality. It is presupposed, I suspect, that something like 'coloniality' needs to be decolonized. However, and in my view, to aim at decolonization without knowing and understanding the mechanisms of modernity/coloniality, the structure and mutations of the coloniality matrix of power, is a shot in the dark. It would be similar to claiming a psychoanalytic cure without understanding how the unconscious works, or claiming to democratize society without understanding when the concept of society was created to regulate social relations and by whom and why.

Now the conversations on decolonizing the curriculum, the university, the museum, etc. imply knowing what regulates and controls knowledge and the subjective and intersubjective relations that manage knowing and knowledge. We are talking then of the larger domain of the public sphere, let's say the intellectual sphere is large, not just the academic. Academy is one small place of that sphere. It touches journalism, television, social media. It touches all of us who are involved in the intellectual domain of the public sphere, as well as those who are not and do not care about us and our work because they have other preoccupations but they have televisions and iPods are bombarded by slogans, images, sounds, hideous advertising portraying a happy and smiling human being before the news of the last bombs that destroy such and such a city or the massive number of refugees that are fleeing the country. When you start thinking about all of this (and this is the tip of the iceberg), you begin to realize that there is something absurd and perverse in what we take for granted: announcing the latest toothpaste before showing the images of destroyed cities and massive migrations of refugees. For all of us who are in this intellectual sphere, one of the main concerns is to be constantly vigilant and aware that we are controlled by Western vocabulary, imagery, formulaic expressions, disciplinary formations, esthetic sensibility, artistic taste (and culinary taste as well) so that we cannot think without going through Western vocabulary, art history, natural and social sciences, the humanities in a word, the disciplinary formations that discipline schooling from kindergarten to the university and the museum. We may like democracy or be critical about the uses of democracy, but for many people it is almost impossible to imagine political or horizons beyond democracy. Democracy is a trap. What is crucial is to live in harmony and conviviality. Democracy may be a road to that, but not the only one. But the problem is that the goal of democracy is confused with the mean of democracy: one citizen one vote – not a citizen, then no vote. Well, that is a small example of the rhetoric of modernity hiding the logic of coloniality.

Let's now touch on the COVID nightmare. One of the main tasks after the COVID pandemic – if there is an after-COVID – is to be aware of our limitations, without losing track of our possibilities. Authoritarian states come in many cloths and with many masks. We, the people, protest, critique and complain. We, the nationals, are admitted in the public spheres but repressed if we go too far. The non-national (refugees, non-national migrants, called illegals), have more limitations. In China, the US, France or Iran, the population is controlled and managed in different ways. There may be more room for maneuvering according to the locations in which people have been placed in terms of gender and sexuality, ethnicity, religion, etc. More room for protest, criticism of the State, the banks, the corporations, doesn't mean that those of us who have those privileges will have a significant impact on the State institutions, the official mass media, the corporations or the police of the military structure. What is left to us, the us I was referring to above, is to delink from what the rhetoric of modernity (the state, the market, the advertising, the media, the university, the museum, etc.), wants us to do and to re-link what 'we' (and this we refers to all of us who will follow this or similar paths) would like and want to do and what we (always this restricted we), would like, want and can do, is to rebuilt trust, respect, love and the beauty and pleasure of thinking today shuttered by digital entertainment. The analytic of coloniality is a necessary decolonial task to know what are our possibilities of recovering our joy without losing our indignation, to recall the telling dictum by Lorena Cabnal (2019), Maya-Xinca communitarian feminist. These are questions of decolonial praxis, and Catherine explained that very well in her previous intervention. Decolonial praxis does not mean just going into the street: to do so it is not necessary to embody the decolonial, to do so it is necessary not to lose indignation. The massive protests in Chile a few weeks ago (Walter refers to the protests in October 2020, https://www.bbc.com/mundo/noticias-america-latina-54594783) (at the time this conversation was taking place), in Bolivia, the Gilets Jaunes in France, in the US after the killing of George Floyd – to do that, you don't need decoloniality, you need common sense confronting the brutality of the authoritarian states of any states (be those with more than one party called democratic or one party state called authoritarian by speakers of democratic authoritarianism). The question is this: what does decoloniality offer to those who seriously want to engage with it, in body and soul, so to speak? I have no doubt that the decolonial option is one option, among the existing ones (religious, ideological, disciplinary), that have much to offer, although is not sufficient to invoke its names in vain.

To be more specific: race and racism permeate the life of the people all over the world today in the public domestic sphere, in the relations between the State and the nation and it permeates the international relations, as we are witnessing in October 2022, in the conflict between US and Russia as a result of the conflict in Ukraine. But also with China, Iran and all the former Third World. We all know what racism means in the public and domestic spheres. But it is coming to the open in international relations. The recent dictum by Joseph Borrell, Foreign Policy Chief, speaking at the inauguration of the European Diplomacy Academy: Borrell called Europe 'a garden' and most of the world a 'jungle' that 'could invade the garden.'[2]

Racism is not a question of skin color, pure white being visually the absence of color; it is not a question of blood as it was for the Spanish Inquisition wanting to preserve the purity of Christian blood, nor yet of the purity of the absence of skin color. Racism is epistemological (in the specific sense that is theological and secular scientific knowledge that warrantied the truth of the existence of races) and of the sensorium: knowledge making people believe that what authoritarian discourses said there is, it is what there is. The decolonial task here, yes, it would be to protest, but mainly to build discourse, images, teaching, workshop showing the false premises in which racism have been built, *the assumptions that what authorities said it is, it is, and not just what someone (actors and institutions) said it is.* By changing the assumptions, we change the terms of the conversations. By protesting we attack the content, but not the terms. From here we can delink from the assumptions of modernity and relink with decolonial assumptions that there are just 'persons' and that racial classification and ranking (as well as sexual, and national, and gardens and jungles) are all illusions and mirages of actors mounted on institutions built in the process of building the colonial matrix of power.

Decoloniality teaches us learning to unlearn in order to relearn (a motto from the Pluriversity Amautay Wasi in Ecuador). That may be probably of the decolonial task following the re-orientation that Anibal Quijano offered to us in 1992: decoloniality/ decolonization as epistemological reconstitutions. I'll stop there.

Magdalena Madany-Saa

Thank you so much, Catherine and Walter. Usually we start with a question from Dr Makoni. We will follow this tradition. Dr Makoni, over to you.

Sinfree Makoni

Thank you very much to Catherine and Walter. I've got two questions for Catherine and two questions for Walter. As I was preparing for this talk, I went and reread the book edited by Reiter (2018) called, 'Constructing the Pluriverse,' in which, you both have chapters. My questions to Catherine would, to some extent, be partially based on my reading of that book and my listening to your talk. In this particular book, concerning the 'pluriverse,' Reiter for example, in the introduction, makes the following suggestion and makes the following claim: 'Western approaches to European science do not contain the tools to ask different questions and find new and different answers.' Let's assume that he is right. If he is right, the question then I'm posting to Catherine is as follows: How then do you turn non-Western ontologies and epistemologies into research programs and research designs in a university? You are assuming that Western science cannot enable you to ask these other new questions, so you're then left with one of the alternatives is that you didn't have to turn to non-Western ontologies. The question then becomes: How do you design research programs and projects based on these non-Western ontologies?

Catherine Walsh

Thank you, Sinfree. Let me put it a little bit in the concrete context of the doctoral program that I mentioned that Walter has also participated in over the last 20 years that we have here. When we began this doctoral program (and maybe some of Magda's experiences at UASB in the masters were similar). The issue was first how to think from here, that is how to think from Latin America, but also how to think from the Souths of the world first. That's not the rest of the so-called Western world exists, but it's to reverse what usually happens in universities. In other words, first, usually, it's the study of so-called universal knowledge, the canon, right? And then, later, when we get to the local context, in terms of sort of case studies, right? Here, the process has been to turn that upside down. What does it mean to think from here and particularly from the world senses, the world knowledges, the worldviews constructed in this territory? The challenge – the still-white control that's present within Latin America. In other words, one can talk about South geographically, but oftentimes, the Westernization of Latin American universities takes a parallel to the North, right? Sort of what today is called the Global University. Parallels that I know also exist in South Africa. One could begin to think about, as we did here, what does it mean to ask the question, who do we want to think with? Why, and with what project? That sort of paralleled the issue of who the students are.

In the process of acceptance of students into the program, one of the key criteria is those students that come from all of Latin America and, occasionally, from other places in the world. They have a strong base: the processes of social struggle in their own countries. Some are social movement leaders, others work in schools or academic spaces, but we had a large percentage, a large number of Indigenous, of black students, growing numbers of women, including women of color. It's sort of how to change that base and how to think from and with the knowledge that is produced in this part of the world, and not to study about something that I mentioned before. In that sense, as Sinfree mentioned or asked in the question, non-Western ontology, epistemologies, cosmologies are the base of our thinking. In other words, it's how to build a thinking from a different logic. That's not to assume that all students that enter the program, or that all faculty that work in the program, necessarily understand or think from those logics, but it's how to create a sort of different space where we challenge Westernized logics and ways of thinking. Not to eliminate, but to challenge them as the only possibility and to construct what we might call, and as the book Sinfree mentioned, has in its title 'the pluriversal,' in other words, other ways of thinking that oftentimes the universal tends to shroud or race-eliminate.

Those processes have been particularly key. Twenty years of experience with many, many graduates from all over who take the seeds of that program back to their own spaces, to their own territories, to their own countries and to universities and other countries have enabled this to grow. One could say this is a kind of way of building a decolonizing project in praxis where ontologies, epistemologies and existence-based ways of thinking and being are central to the kinds of questions that we ask. I could say much more, Sinfree, but I think for reasons of time, I should probably stop there.

Sinfree Makoni

Yes, then that leads me to my second and last question to you. I can understand the logic of trying to mobilize Indigenous ontologies and epistemologies and using that as the basis, but as I reflected on your work, I read the couple of articles in which you were talking about 'Buen Vivir.' This is in a 2010 article that you wrote called Development as Buen Vivir: Institutional arrangements and (de)colonial entanglements. As I came to the end of the article, I wasn't very sure what was the nature of the argument you were making. Because you begin by saying this concept of Buen Vivir is at the core of the Ecuadorian constitution, but toward the end, you seem to have been suggesting that there is some incompatibility between that concept of Buen Vivir and the Ecuadorian constitution. The question then became to me: Is it that these Indigenous ontological concepts are incompatible with notions of constitutional arrangement, or is it that the notion of Buen Vivir is multilayered, fluid and it cannot be easily used in a constitutional arrangement? Those are the questions to me, but I wasn't sure what exactly the core of the argument was you were making.

Catherine Walsh

If one understands, I guess, a translation of Buen Vivir into English, it would be life in plentitude, and what Walter mentioned Sumak Kawsay is a way in Quechua, one of the principal Indigenous languages to talk about that. The way that a philosophical or existence-based notion of being in life is constructed. One could say in Indigenous communities, but also in a similar sense but different, and black communities where the notion of collective wellbeing is very much parallel, one could say to *Ubuntu* is also very key. What happens when those notions are put into a constitution? One could say 'instrumentalized,' right? Many that are listening may not know that in Ecuador, as Bolivia went through in 2007 to 2008, a rethinking of the Constitution in radically different terms. Some say that Ecuador's Constitution is the most radical in the world. Not only does it name the status 'plurinational' and 'intercultural,' but also uses the notion of this living in plentitude, which is not capitalist living, which is not a neoliberalized notion of living, but living as part of nature with nature, and a different philosophy of life gives the face to the entire Constitution.

I had the privilege to be an advisor to the Constitution and participate in that process. I had the privilege to be an advisor to the Constitution. I participated in a lot of debates which were not with political parties, but rather with representatives from different social sectors of the country. In those processes, the hope was that with a different philosophical base that was very different from the typical neoliberal, capitalist-based logic that organizes constitutions could serve as a base to sort of refund society. That hope was basically wiped out or denied in the processes of state and government. Basically, what we learned in this process is that when a philosophy, a way of being that's lived is put into a constitution, and then given in the hands of state, and the state constructed as a way to rethink development, but basically, to use many of the same tools of westernized notions of development, of Eurocentered development, of what is sometimes called in European nations, 'Integral Development,' it lost its hold. Basically, the problem that I outlined in that article that Sinfree mentioned that I wrote many years ago, was how the hope was constructed and that took base in this philosophical notion of changing the way that we live, to live in harmony, one could say, with others and with other beings that aren't necessarily human beings, including with ancestors.

When that was put into state, it became instrumentalized. It became functional to the state project. Basically, the learning here is the danger of what happens when state co-ops, uses concepts that have a different or radically distinct base of existence and tries to use them as a new way to control and instrumentalize the population. The learnings were great. The learnings, I think, in a simple sense, taught us not to put our hope in state itself. That change happens from the bottom up, it doesn't happen from top down. And when state takes control of concepts that are constructed from the bottom, from the basis – from community basis, and instrumentalizes or functionalizes them and then uses them against the very populations that constructed them, there is the problem. So Buen Vivir became sort of the slogan – a slogan that we could say has parallels today with the use of the word 'decolonial,' when it's manipulated, when could it mean anything? It could mean good food to eat, to be able to eat in a good restaurant, it could mean to have access to open tourism that takes over communities, it could mean extractivism – it began to become manipulated in a different way. In summary, Sinfree, my argument would be, that the problem is that when something that's constructed from the bottom up that's producing a different way of thinking is taken on by state and controlled by state, it not only loses its significance, but it becomes a dangerous tool where development, in the worst sense of the word, takes over people's life.

Sinfree Makoni

Thank you very much. I think this gives us an opportunity. This gives me an opportunity to shift to asking Walter just two questions, as well, then we'll open up the floor. Walter, in the papers that you sent me recently, your 2020 responses to discussions about decoloniality, let me read you back one passage that stood out to me. You said that 'there is no object of study that decoloniality can exhaust objects or events will always exceed decoloniality. There is no single method that will exhaust the objects or events, decoloniality is an option among others.' Now, my question is this, if there are no objects that can be exhausted through decoloniality, it implies that in any analysis, you would require to mobilize decoloniality and other analytical operators. My question is, from your experiences, what are the other frameworks that you tend to use to complement your decolonial analysis of events or text?

Walter Mignolo

I don't remember the text I sent you that you refer to but I will address the question. I think that the question is very important because it touches a nodal point of the politics of decolonial investigation. Decolonial investigations could be academic, but the need of investigations exceeds the academy. As Argentine philosopher of German descent, Rodolfo Kusch (2020), brilliantly stated: 'se conoce para vivir, no por el simple hecho de conocer.' (It is known to live, not for the simple fact of knowing.' Notice that the impersonal 'se' is very common in Argentina, even in philosophical discourses.) The Zapatistas have shown through the years the outcome of their investigations, they argue with foundations. Sherlock Holmes was a tremendous investigator, but he was not working at the university. He was not an academic. The first point to be addressed in your question is the mirage that knowledge is the relation between a knowing subject and a known object, and the object *must* be known!! Well, the object is an invention of the subject, there is no object outside the knowing subjects, the disciplines or the beliefs that invent 'objects.' The second point, why shall we accept and believe that what must be known are 'objects' and not 'relations?'

The second point is more strictly relevant to you question. The only 'object' of decolonial investigations after Quijano is the colonial of power and the colonial matrix of power. The only object of investigation for psychoanalysis is the unconscious. Neither of them, coloniality of power and the colonial matrix of power nor the unconscious could be analyzed beyond decoloniality and psychoanalysis. We can add 'society' as the object of sociology. *The point is that there are no other frameworks than decoloniality, psychoanalysis or sociology that can analyze coloniality/ colonial matrix of power, the unconscious and society.* To believe that knowledge means to known 'an object' from a different perspective is one of the most damaging beliefs that is modernly instilled in all of on the binary assumptions that there is a distinction and separation between the knowing subject and the known object.

Now what is then the point of decolonial investigations? The decolonial investigations are geared to understanding work of the colonial matrix of power works. Why would we want to do that? Not because we want to find the truth, to improve a discipline or to introduce a new one (decolonial studies, disoriented people say), but because without knowing and understanding that our subjectivities and intersubjective relations management are managed by the colonial matrix of power it would not be possible to delink from regimented ways of living to re-existing, as Catherine said. There could not be decolonial tasks without understanding coloniality; there cannot be decolonial healing without understanding colonial wounds. There cannot be psychoanalytic cure without understanding the work of the unconscious. Today, I will say that this is the field of the colonial matrix of power. That is the first point.

Let me expand the analogy with psychoanalysis to convey the idea of decolonial work and address your question about analyzing a text, an object, an event, a situation. It would be useful to remember your question, so I reproduce it here:

> My question is this, if there are no objects that can be exhausted through decoloniality, it implies that in any analysis, you would require to mobilize decoloniality and other analytical operators. My question is, from your experiences, what are the other frameworks that you tend to use to complement your decolonial analysis of events or text?

These are not goals of decolonial analysis or the analytics of decoloniality as Cathy and I argue in the book, *On Decoloniality*. What you ask Sinfree presupposes that the analytic goals are to exhaust something, an object, an event, a situation, a text and for that one disciplinary or interpretive option is not enough. That is done, and that is fine. It is call interdisciplinarity. That is not our goal, in my decolonial understanding. But neither is the psychoanalysis, to analyze the unconscious from a different framework. It doesn't make sense because the unconscious is not an object beyond psychoanalysis that invented it. Similarly, coloniality of power and the decolonial matrix of power cannot be analyzed from other frameworks because neither of them is an entity beyond the decolonial options introduce by Quijano (similarly to Freud introducing the Unconscious or Marx the Capital). With the caveat that coloniality and the colonial matrix of power are concepts created in the Third World, so to speak, not in the First.

So, I do not tend to use, and I do not use any other framework because for us (or at least for me) inter-disciplinarity is caught in modern epistemology: to have inter-disciplinarity means to keep the disciplines. And decoloniality is an un-disciplinary praxis of living, thinking, doing. This is what changing the terms of the conversation means. In that sense, decoloniality is what we (those following Quijano) embodied and enacted to introduce a turnaround in the water of modern epistemology. Decoloniality cannot be assimilated to epistemic break (Foucault, 1972) nor paradigmatic change (Kuhn, 1962), both wonderful Eurocentric critics of philosophical and scientific eurocentrism. But our decolonial critique of Eurocentrism is not there from the right, the center and the left. Sure, we could side with Foucault and Kuhn but our concerns are not theirs because of the legacies of coloniality that we inhabit and inhabit us. 'They' inhabit the legacies of modernity not the legacies of modernity/coloniality.

The bottom line is that decoloniality is not one more 'method' to analyze 'objects.' It is an option that enterd the field of all the options we are living in and by: religions, ideologies, disciplines, all the options that modernity created to manage and control knowledge. It created also the binary belief on known object and knowing subject. This belief was questioned by theoretical physics in the 20th century and by the early Frankfurt school (Horkheimer), but within Western cosmology. The decolonial option steps out from that illusion, from the Western regulations of what knowledge should be and how could be obtained. For that reason, I wrote *The Politics of Decolonial Investigations* (2021). But there are other important arguments in this direction; for instance, Linda Tuhiwai Smith, *Decolonizing Methodologies* (1999) and Leanne Betasamosake Simpson, *Dancing on Our Turtle's Back* (2011).

Sinfree Makoni

Okay. Let me ask the last short question, then I can open up the discussion. In one of your many publications, I think this one you wrote it with, I think he's a Russian scholar called – I can't pronounce it properly, but you refer to India and China as 'second-class empires.' The question that I'm asking is, how is coloniality carried out by these 'second-class empires' manifesting itself globally? In other words, is the colonial matrix of power manifested by the 'second-class empires' substantially different from the experiences that we have here, so far, with other empires?

Walter Mignolo

Thanks for this question that was relevant at the time of this conversation and is more relevant today, October 2022 when I am editing the conversation, we all in the planet have been experiencing the Ukrainian question for 10 months

The metaphor of the 'second-class empire' penned by Madina Tlostanova, a Cherkess/Circassian ethnicity, scholar, Russian citizen, visualizes one of the consequences of the imperial difference. Russia was never experienced settler colonialism, like India for example. But it did not escape coloniality, that is, the interference of coloniality. The first sign of the second-class empire was Peter the Great, founding Saint Petersburg, a window to Europe and changing the name of his role from Czar to Emperor. See, the King of France or England were not eager to call them Czar and to create a city that will be a window to Russia. That is an indication of what: of the entanglement of the colonial difference. While Ivan the Terrible was Czar, there was no entanglement: he was doing his business while at the same time Charles I of Spain was doing his. They were two powerful politico-economic and religious organizations. Charles was an Emperor and Ivan was a Czar, and that was that. By the time of Peter the Great, the West was already establishing itself as a civilizational model. Japan was not interfered as was China, in the middle of the 19th century, by the British specifically by means of the Opium War (Hong Kong is a derivation of that). Japan apparently was not eager to suffer the same destiny and moved to the Meiji Restauration, which entangled Japan with the Western model and the illusion of modernity. There is a long history here that made Japan into a second-class imperial force that expanded in East and South Asia until the WWII. Since then, Japan has become a nation-state which preserves domestically its own culture. However, in the international relations it became submissive to the US.

There is more, but that gives you an idea of why the imperial difference is important (which of course, implies racism in international relations), and why metaphorically Tlostanova referred to them as second-class empire: they follow the Western model while in the Western eyes Russia and Japan are second-class organization and people. This is still the case today.

Now, what does all of this tell us about the colonial matrix of power, which is the main thrust of your question. On the surface, it could be said that Russia and Japan, at certain points, were caught in the mirage of Western modernity. Trying to be the same, they admitted that they want to follow a model that was not emanating from their own history, but it was a mirage outside their own history. It means that the rhetoric of Western modernity attracts people, while the people attracted are racially classified and ranked. The initial moment of the imperial difference was the Ottoman Sultanate. But the Ottoman did not fall into the trap, and because of that, it was dismantled, and the Republic of Turkey (that is, the nation-state model) was implemented by Ataturk following the collapse of the Sultanate after WWI. Russia attempted to undo the imperial difference with the foundation of the Soviet Union. But alas in the process it continued to be trapped in one of the two models of Western modernity: Marxism/communism. The collapse of the Soviet Union was expected to open the gates for Western neoliberalism to bring Russia under its wing installing proxy-government. After a decade of turbulence, Vladimir Putin rebuilt the Russian Federation. Like China, it appropriated capitalism but rejected neoliberalism and started a process that continues delinking from Western dominance. *The colonial matrix of power entangles both projects. The Russian project of de-Westernization (e.g. liberating from the imperial difference) and the UN (NATO, EU0, efforts to maintain the unipolar control and management of the colonial matrix of power.* But this entangles not only the State's international relations, but also the people's subjective and intersubjective relations. And of course, the structure of knowledge that circulates through State and private colleges and universities, etc.

Today conflict between the West (US, NATO, EU) with Russia, China and Iran (with India and Turkey in the middle) is a dispute for the control and management of the colonial matrix of power. That is the decolonial interpretation of the conflicts of the world order today being played in the sphere of the imperial difference and the consolidation of second-class empire that reject Western interference. What is going to happen I do not know, but at this moment we are experiencing the efforts of re-westernization to maintain unipolarity and the efforts of de-westernization to march towards a multipolar world order. And this game is an inter-State game. Decoloniality doesn't have much say in the conflict, other that understanding what is going on to orient our doing, in the spheres in which we, the people in the public sphere, can do something.

As the students of mine said: coloniality is not over, it is all over. And the instrument of colonial power is the colonial matrix of power.

Sinfree Makoni

Okay. Magda, I hand over to you and I delink from the conversation.

Walter Mignolo

It's healthy to delink.

Magdalena Madany-Saa

You're doing the wrap-up, so you cannot delink. I would like to briefly come back to the concept that you both mentioned, and you both wrote extensively about Sumak Kawsay, and connected with the field of education, and particularly, language in education. In many Latin American countries, and Ecuador is a good example of it, we have English language policies that ask students, especially university students, to achieve a high proficiency in English in order to graduate from an Ecuadorian university. English became a mandatory subject from the second grade in Ecuador, so everybody is learning English. English is this language that will open the door to the world. Then, we have Sumak Kawsay, which is this ontological concept. I'm not talking about Buen Vivir, I'm talking about Sumak Kawsay as conceived by the Indigenous epistemic community of a plentiful life and taking care of the wellbeing within the community, so finding the endogenous solutions for the wellbeing. My question is, what can we educators, and also what can policymakers unlearn and relearn from Sumak Kawsay?

Catherine Walsh

Is there an order here, Magda, or do you want me to go ahead and then Walter or…?

Magdalena Madany-Saá

As you wish to answer it.

Walter Mignolo

Go ahead, Cathy, since I already talked too much.

Catherine Walsh

There's a debate today, Magda. If because of the association of Buen Vivir for its functionalization or instrumentalization in the Constitution, and Sumak Kawsay being considered by the state as the same, why is it important that communities themselves rethink what this concept really means? Some communities say that before it was recognized in the Constitution, it existed, but people didn't necessarily name it. It's part of everyday life that's been constructed generation after generation, and passed down by the elders to the newer – to future generations. What does this all mean, like you ask, in education? I think at one sense, as you clearly stated at the beginning, there's a contradiction between an educational process that continues and increasingly looks to the North as the basis of universal knowledge, and universal language use, English being, as you mentioned, sort of the way into the future, the way into modernity, the way into Western civilization, leaving native civilizations behind. Worse yet, if we think about how educational structures mandated by the Ministry of Education require the same kind of evaluations and global instruments that exist now throughout the world. In the short time that I spent in South Africa and from conversations that I had with people, it became clear that the same instruments were being used in many Latin American countries, as well as in the US, etc., to evaluate faculty, to evaluate students. And what are the sort of global competencies that students should achieve and their language essentials?

If Sumak Kawsay is a concept, a way of being built on territory and built through native language – the logic of a native language, what happens when that gets translated into Spanish as the dominant language of society and, worse yet, into English? The contradiction here is very clear. Interestingly, what's happened in these times of COVID, where roughly 60–70% of students from primary school on do not have access to internet and cannot do virtual education, which is schools are still not open here. What happens is, that in many communities and in many urban neighborhoods, people are going back to creating their own educational process – an educational process that's connected to life, that's connected to existence and not connected to the global competencies that the Ministry of Education, UNESCO, etc., try to spread throughout the world. I would say we're at interesting moments. If one looks at the positive side of these times that we're living in, in the construction of new forms, of occupational practice, of rethinking education, as directly connected to the necessities of life and collective living in times where the collective is each time more fragmented, and individualism takes place. The fact that we can't touch one another, see one another physically, but have to look at one another on camera is part of this.

But, it's worse yet – what happens in how these times break the collective force of communities, and make one think about oneself and one's immediate family, and not the broader collective.

The processes taking place, I would say, are reconstructing Sumak Kawsay. Not necessarily saying that they're doing it, but are constructing and practice it in small spaces, in an urban neighborhood, in a rural community context, because of the necessity of thinking about what life means in these times when life is put up against the de-existence that I mentioned that's happening. I think times are interesting, because they make one wonder, and as Walter said, if there's a post-COVID, which we don't know if there is or not, whether in fact, this marks a new route for education to take. Education that's based on the needs and issues and desires and knowledge that exist in that space, rather than global competencies or global demands that have taken form. And if in fact, those who will stay in the so-called formal or official education system will increasingly become those students who are white or white in up-higher class – privileged, because they have the apparatus, the computers, the technology to connect through the internet, etc. What we're seeing is a reformulating of what education means – education in the official sense, and education in a community collective sense, and I think that brings into reflection today possibilities of building a notion of Sumak Kawsay, not just in Indigenous communities, but one could say, as a social project. It's taking place without necessarily naming it.

Magdalena Madany-Saá

Thank you so much, Catherine.

Bassey Antia

Okay. Well, thanks a lot, Catherine. We do have a number of questions. If there are any outstanding questions, they can be taken up in the cost of the after-party session. So, Teboho, you have a question?

Teboho Motaboli

Good morning, and I thank everybody who's attended. My question is, for both of our speakers or presenters: the dominant opinion-makers in the west, you could take the example of global ranking of universities, you could take Ivy League schools in America, are bound by their own pursuit of what they consider to be 'excellence,' and they probably have no regard to decoloniality, etc. They don't think it is relevant. We can look at the example of, at the moment, the vaccine for COVID-19. For them, it's the competition to see that they show excellence by finding the cure for COVID. Forget about others, like the Russians claim that they have a vaccine, the Chinese, but I think it just passed over our head. We don't even know that they did anything at all. What I'm emphasizing is the dominant opinion-makers of the west are concerned with what they consider to be 'excellence' and domination just follows, and decoloniality is, in my view, a response that is probably struggling to make itself recognized. Maybe, ideally, in the future, decoloniality hopes for a universality that is represented by a convergence of scholarship, philosophies, etc., where we think all of us belong and is important. Is there ideally any chance in the future that there will be any universality other than the universality of competition, domination, and action and response – the dominant North as acting in dominance and decolonial South acting in competition to see if they catch up or they become as important as well? Is there any point in the future where there could be a convergence of the two?

Walter Mignolo

What are the two? Decolonial –

Teboho Motaboli

I'm saying dominant North blazes its own path. Our decolonial response is that we would like to be part of the creation of knowledge in the world.

Bassey Antia

Let's see. Catherine or Walter, you would like to fill in the question?

Walter Mignolo

I would like briefly to connect and respond to both Magda and Teboho's questions. Let me answer Magda's question first: *My question is, what can we educators, and also what can policymakers unlearn and relearn from Sumak Kawsay?*

Walter Mignolo

Cathy, who is more into these issues than I am, already provided reach comments and insights. So, I go directly to the point. What I have learned, as educator, is *learning to unlearn in order to relearn*. For perhaps 15 years I taught an undergraduate seminar under department request. The title was provided by the DUS: 'Maya, Aztecs and Incas: The World According to the People of Latin America.' I did not question the title. Before that I asked: why do you think undergraduate students would be interested in this topic, specially at Duke, where there is an emphasis on the present and the future rather than the past? 'Let's try once,' the DUS, responded, and then we decide. It was a seminar, so 18 max. Four hours after registration opened, it was full and 20 or so students on the waiting list. It ended up being a course with two TAs. I did it twice, but it did not work.

It was difficult to engage in sustained conversations since the course became one lecture. After two years the course returned to its original format, a seminar format. From then to 2022, the seminar is always full. The first day of class, after welcoming them, my first three sentences: This seminar is about education, not about schooling. Schooling is not education; you are schooled not educated. Education happens in conversation. And in this seminar, we will converse on learning to unlearn in order to relearn. My third sentences are: in this seminar we use a minimum of non-Indigenous material (written text, oral exposition or interview, videos and YouTube). Around the seven week we get to Amawtat Wasi and the curricular structure. The goal of the Amawtay Wasi curriculum is *Kawsay*, which means, both life and knowledge. For the simple reason that living is knowing and knowing is living. As we also know *Sumak* is a superlative. Hence *Sumar Kaways could be interpreted as living and knowing in plenitude*. Through the semester students go to a volta-face because they began to realize that they are trapped in Western cosmology (controlled by Christian theology and secular science and philosophy, politics and economy), and that there are other cosmologies that they learn from the very Indigenous thinkers, intellectuals, artist, activist that are re-building and re-emerging in the reconstitution of their destituted memories. Students began to realize their ignorance, which is a very healthy outcome of all education.

So, what is the point I am making for educators and policymakers? To become like the students, and if students had that experience, it is because I am one of them, learning from the cosmology/philosophy of First Nations, and sidelining Western cosmology/philosophy that we cannot ignore, it is in all of us, including Indigenous thinkers and scholars and activists, but we do not have any obligation to obey. Hence, delinking is the move. We, educators, can work on that, in and outside the university. Policymakers have a more difficult task since public policy is enclosed in the web of modernity, ignoring coloniality. When policymakers can bring coloniality to the fore, then policymaking will make a decolonial contribution to which Indigenous thinking, living and doing have much to offer. Sumak Kawsay is just the tip of the iceberg,

Now to Teboho Motaboli's question

What I'm emphasizing is the dominant opinion-makers of the west are concerned with what they consider to be 'excellence' and domination just follows, and decoloniality is, in my view, a response that is probably struggling to make itself recognized. Maybe, ideally, in the future, decoloniality hopes for a universality that is represented by a convergence of scholarship, philosophies, etc., where we think all of us belong and is important. Is there ideally any chance in the future that it will be any universality other than the universality of competition, domination, and action and response – the dominant North as acting in dominance and decolonial South acting in competition to see if they catch up or become as important as well? Is there any point in the future where there could be a convergence of the two? [...] I'm saying dominant north blazes its own path, and the decolonial response is we would like to be part of the creation of knowledge in the world.'

Walter Mignolo

Your comments and questions, Teboho, opened a can of worms both in the assumptions of your comments and the expectations of your questions. I try to simplify a set of very complex issues.

Let me first agree with your comments on universities. Yes, like the nation-state and museums, universities, institutions that were exported-imported since the 16th century, the university of Mexico, San Marcos in Lima was founded in mid-16th century and Harvard towards 1635. Now there are Western model universities all over. And museums. And nation-states. If that happened, depending on the place and the time, it is because in many (not all) occasions the locals were eager to import institutions and knowledge from the West. But overall, the coloniality of knowledge has been centrifugal on three interrelated spheres: actors, institutions and languages. Knowledges in other languages that were not the Western modern vernacular grounded in Greek and Latin were destitute from the house of 'sustainable' and 'relevant' knowledge. Mandarin has five times more speakers than English, but English controls and manage knowledge industry, both in the content and in the regulation of the ways of 'serious' knowing. Confucius is not Aristotle, in this view. Why not? Or the Aristotle of the great Muslim thinkers (Al-Ghazali. Ibn Shina or Ibn Rush, Ibn Khaldum) are out of what 'has to be known.' This is the first point.

The second point. Today there are *three not two* trajectories: the west is in the process of re-westernization of the 'Great Reset' in the political, economic and technological arena (Davos) and 'reset Modernity' (Latour & Leclercq, 2016) in the arena of culture, for a better term. And re-westernization is confronting two raising trajectories to be contained to maintain the privileges of Westernization of the world (1500–2000), that re-westernization is attempting to 'reset.' The scenario is no longer that of the Cold War, when there were two possibilities in the same cosmology: liberal capitalism or state communism and decolonization, which was fundamental to a project to form nation-states on the ruins of former colonies, as it happened in the Americas in the 19th century (except the US did it in 1776). Sure, capitalism is global, but it is no longer managed by Wester liberalism and neoliberalism. The monster scaped Frankenstein's lab. And the third trajectory is decoloniality at large. What I mean by decoloniality at large is the emergence of the global political society, the people taking their/our destiny in our own hands. Decoloniality at large is not a move by a universal ideology (like Christianity, liberalism or Marxism) but by the Constitution of destitute values, memories, all that Fanon expressed saying that coloniality (he used colonialism at the time) distorts and destroys the memories and self-esteem of the colonized, making them believe that they are lesser and deficient. Within the sphere of decoloniality at large there are specific ways of carrying on and embodying decoloniality. What we, Quijano followers do, is one particular decolonial way of living, thinking, doing.

A caveat though before answering the last part of your question, Teboho. Today, October 2022, a debate arose in the file of the various feminisms. As we know, feminism is not one – nobody has the golden key to universal feminism. Feminism, like decoloniality, is a connector of people that struggle to get out of the gender binary trap that Western civilization, starting with the Bible, installed in the mind of many people. Liberalism only secularized binary oppositions. Briefly, De Giorgi *et al*. (2023) Meloni in Italy removed the debate of women liberation and the right to occupy high-profile positions that only men in the past had the privilege to occupy. In the past Condoleezza Rice provoked similar concerns, although in her case, the question of gender and race were at stake. Meloni is white and Catholic. Narendra Modi, in India, is promoting the reconstitution of Indian past to nourish national fundamentalism. In China the consolidation of 'socialism with Chinese characteristics' supported by capitalist economy and the reconstitution and valorization of China long history (as the West does with Greece and Rome), are politics to delink and confront Western neoliberal global designs to homogenize the planet under Western tutelage.

So that the reconstitution of the destituted is not a privilege of decolonization (see for example the exemplar works of Linda T. Smith and Leanne Betasamosake Simpson in this respect). What is common to de-westernization and decoloniality are the needs to step out of the regulations and traps of Western modernity in all areas of experience. My answer to your last question Toboho, is no, there is no chance for the moment or the near future for convergence. The utopistic (what our work should contribute to) horizon would be not convergence but respectful co-existence. That is what the word *pluriversality* means: the explosion of Western *universality into pluriversality as a universal project*.

Bassey Antia

Thank you very much, Walter. I'll just read out some two, quick questions all addressed to Catherine, and then we will move to the after-party session. The first one is from Valleta. She wants to know how Catherine relates her own concept of de-existence to Mbembe's (2008) necropolitics. Are there any divergences between Catherine's concept of de-existence and Mbembe's notion of necropolitics? And then the second question for Catherine comes from Tembe. Tembe asks, 'In thinking with and by centering traditional epistemologies, how do we avoid the danger of anthropologizing?'

Catherine Walsh

Thank you, Bassey. And thanks for the questions. Let's think a little bit about the relation and the distinction between de-existence, as I was explaining it, and Mbembe's necropolitics. In a basic sense, I understand necropolitics as related to the use of social power to dictate how some must live and how others must die; that is, about the creation of death worlds in which certain populations are subjected to conditions of life that, in essence, are a form of living death. As Mbembe makes clear, necropolitics and necropower are tied in many ways to Foucault's notion of bio-power. In the present-day pandemic of COVID in Latin America but also elsewhere in the world, necropolitics and de-existence seem somewhat related: what is at play is the elimination of certain sectors of the population, most particularly – in the case of Latin America – Indigenous and African-descended peoples and those living on lands rich in natural resources. However, I also see a clear distinction. First, I am thinking with and from the ways that people who live with the constant threat of violence-dispossession-war-death name and describe it, as well as how they not only resist but more significantly struggle to re-exist despite of it. Second, my thinking and analysis are not grounded in Foucault but in coloniality's long-lived horizon – the colonial matrix of power that Walter and I describe in the book – in which the ideas of race and gender, but also heteronormativity, became key components of the so-called Conquest, 500 plus years past; ways to mark from then on – first in Abya Yala/Latin America and then throughout the world – of who's more human and who's less human, who's dispensable, and who's an obstacle to the advance of capital, civilization, development and progress. I am thinking with Fanon's description of the zone of non-being. Is this not what is occurring today in many territories of the world, including, as Walter said, in countries of the East but also in African nations, where certain sectors of the population that are no longer seen as useful are being eliminated.

De-existence is not just about death. It refers as well to the practices of violence, de-possession, war and death that begin to interweave. Obviously this existed before COVID, but with COVID the strategies of de-existence are further enabled, eliminating lives, knowledges, ways of being in the world, and territories as the place of and for life. While I can see parallels between the notion of de-existence that I am describing here and Mbembe's necropolitics, I believe that our thinking comes from a different perspective, analysis and place. We might agree that yes, there's a so-called social power that's working to enable some to live and others to be eliminated. But what's happening in the ways that that elimination takes place? And where it takes place is crucial to think about today. How, as I said, the elimination of knowledges, of ways of being in the world, are tied to extractivism and the take-over of territories, of extractive industries aligned with state but also aligned increasingly with narcotrafficking – all this is part of the de-existence taking place in Abya Yala/Latin America as well as elsewhere in the world.

For me, de-existence is not a concept, like necropolitics is, that we can apply, but it's rather something that's being constructed in daily struggle, in different places of the world. What happens when we connect those struggles? What happens when we begin to analyze and theorize collectively from below, not from the application of academic concepts but from and with the relation and connection of the struggles for existence in life in different regions of the world today under a new, what we might call 'global regime of control,' where, as Walter said, imperial colonial differences are key, but also where the colonial matrix of power is continually mutating and reconfiguring. I could go on, but in terms of time, I'll stop there with the Mbembe connection or non-connection.

In thinking with Tembe's question about how traditional epistemologies could be anthropologized, I agree there is a danger. If we think about the structure of universities, but also the structure of education, of schooling itself, the danger is clear; the tendency is to *study about*. All too often, the introduction or inclusion in educational curricula of Indigenous, African, or black-diasporic epistemologies has been through a perspective of cultural relativism anthropological observation.

How do we observe and study these other epistemologies or traditional epistemologies, as Tembe said? For me, and from a decolonial perspective, practice and pedagogy, the distinction is between *studying about* and *thinking with*. To think *with*, I need to challenge my own thinking. I need to consider the ways that I've been socialized, to critically recognize the epistemologies or structures, the logics, philosophies, etc. that have been part of my own formation or deformation, and to open toward other logics that both make tense and expand my own. What does this mean in praxis? In my context of teaching in Ecuador and Abya Yala, this means reorganizing what and how we read, and who we choose to think and dialogue with. It means creating space within the classroom among the racially and ethnically diverse participants – including of students and faculty for whom traditional cosmologies and epistemologies are a way of life and social movement leaders who move within and out of the university on a daily basis – to construct together forms of interrogation that fissure or crack the supposed universality of academic knowledge. The issue is not let's learn about this other way of thinking, but rather how this other of thinking – thus connecting directly to what Walter was describing before – challenges my own way of thinking and thought.

As Walter Mignolo mentioned, many white or 'whitened' students get angry or enter in crisis. Now, how do I think about myself, they ask? How do I continue my own thinking and being in this situation where I know now that what I've been taught is not the only way of being and thinking? How do I challenge myself? How do I see the ways that privilege continues to create itself? That, I think, is the difference. It certainly ties to a pedagogical praxis. I noticed in the chat that someone else asked about pedagogy and about what this means in teaching. Such questions are central. What Walter and I are talking about is not an abstract conceptual theory that has no base of practice. The issue is not to make decoloniality a new universal, but rather a praxical/analytical way of questioning how we are in the world. Who do we relate to? How do we define not only our identities, per se, but our sense of being? And how in these times particularly, the stark individualism that capitalism has made the normality enters into crisis? How do being and thinking with others create a new sense, or a necessary sense or an urgency that many of us feel and becomes increasingly frustrating when, in these times of COVID, we can't leave the house!

In my own case, the years that I worked with Paulo Freire and was involved with critical pedagogy, gave me a base to think about not just how to teach in a school or a classroom, but how actually teaching is part of life, part of our own learning and unlearning and relearning. Today, my understanding, perspectives and praxis, and my learning to unlearn and relearn, are much deeper, constitutive, in essence, of decolonial work. This includes, but of course is not limited to, the classroom. How we ask the questions, how we construct the questions and how we begin to look not just for a simple answer, but how we understand that the questions lead to other questions, where the base is really about existence in life itself, particularly in these times. In that sense, I think, the notion of the *with* and *from – thinking with and thinking from –* is very important in challenging anthropological modes and building forms of decolonial praxis.

Decoloniality is not about Indigenous peoples; some say it's a new anthropology where the Indigenous has the center. This is not true. Decoloniality is about all of us. It brings to the fore the necessity of pluriversality, not universality; of ways of rethinking and otherwise thinking, of other ways of knowing, and other ways of being that have existed for centuries not just in Latin America, but in other places of the world. Decoloniality challenges the notion of a singular logic and rationality. It challenges, opens up and fissures the universal logic that so many assume as natural. I think that's what decolonial work is about. It's about questioning ourselves, rethinking ourselves, but always in conjunction *with*. It's not an individual project, it's necessarily a collective project. In that sense, it's something that we all need to consider, assume and address.

Walter Mignolo

Let me make a quick observation, there is a myth, an illusion, false belief or just unfamiliarity with what decolonization and decoloniality means, not in abstract, but in the history of the word and the events to which it is attached. One of those false beliefs is that decoloniality has to do ONLY with what the Indigenous people have to do. Of course, it has, but Indigenous people have been taking their destiny in their own hands and claiming decoloniality based on their own history, memories and experiences. Non-Indigenous, we have our own memories, experiences and histories of coloniality *and have much to learn from them not to talk about them*. I refer to this issue above, referring to Amawtay Wasi. On the other hand, decoloniality is not about middle-class intellectuals justifying our guilts, but we have work to do where we are, in this case, at the university, in the public sphere. It is there that we can contribute to twist the idea, images and prejudice that the middle-class in South and North America have about 'Indians' and 'Blacks' and 'Gays' and 'Lesbians' all those targets that the alt-right in Argentina, the US, Canada, Italy, France, Germany, UK, Holland, etc. are targeting as threatening the 'common sense' of family, heterosexuality, whiteness and Christian religions. It is ridiculous to think or expect that a non-Indigenous could teach Indigenous people that they have been colonized!!! And it is disingenuous to *talk about* Indigenous people to a middle-class audience to show that we are progressive or revolutionary decolonials!!

Magdalena Madany-Saá

Thank you so much. We still have questions. Some of the questions Catherine already answered by expanding on education, because many of them were related to education, but there's some more questions.

Bassey Antia

I would like to ask Desmond and Ted, perhaps to post their questions at this point in time. Kindly keep the questions brief, so that we can take a few more. Desmond?

Desmond Odugu

Thank you so much, Catherine and Walter, for this wonderful opportunity. It's wonderful to meet everyone here. Some of you who were with us last week might remember me asking the question about the nation state and I'm leaning on that question to ask this, because it seems like this idea keeps coming back to our conversation. There are a few ideas that Dr Mignolo and Dr Walsh talked about here, that I think are relevant to the question I'm asking. Some of this also is grayed out of my current work that conceptualizes coloniality, not just as systemic but also structural. I see the nation state at the heart of that matrix that is the power and ability of the nation state to use violence. When I think of what Dr Mignolo said regarding decoloniality as an 'option,' I wonder if what part of the exercise of that option is to just maintain the current matrix of power. For some people, not for everybody, but for some people. To get back then to the question about border crossing, the idea of moving from the north to the Global South, which I consider as such a powerful enactment of that idea. Is it really possible for us to ultimately get to that point where the order of existence in the world is no longer directly controlled under the superintendency of nation state? I will also say, by extension, academic institutions or intellectual institutions, the way that you are conceptualizing this, Dr Mignolo, not just universities, but the media and so forth, which I think have very clear, aggressive hold on people's lives, and in many ways, in destructive ends.

There are many instances in which the work of decoloniality in the world, it's been done even before the academia to conduct project, have been confronted with state violence or corporate violence. My sense is that the structural element of coloniality does not accept these options. That is the option for people to be different. Whenever the exercise of those options come in contact or context with the nation state or with corporate politics and so forth, there is violence. And I wonder if there is any possibility for coexistence between the structures of nation state, global corporate capitalism, institutionalized structures of knowledge production in universities and elsewhere, and also this project of decoloniality? Or do we really have to look forward to a completely new era, a post-state, post-capitalist, post-university in a world where people can begin to enact these existences? I can comment on this further if it is helpful, but I'm just wondering how much decoloniality is possible as a lived experience given the structures of power we have in place today.

Bassey Antia

Who would you like to respond? Either speaker?

Desmond Odugu

This question is to both of you. Sorry for not clarifying that.

Walter Mignolo

I can go. You want to take another question?

Bassey Antia

Okay. Alright. There is a question from Ted, who regrettably is in a library and can't ask the question himself. It's all about education. He's inviting a comment, and

I think this may also be addressed to Catherine. He says, 'In Bolivia, with the Reform Education Act requiring, for instance, that all Bolivians were supposed to learn both Spanish and Aymara, but in practice, this only applied to Indigenous peoples and not the majority population, because they would go to the private American schools.' Some contradiction there, which Ted would like to comment on. He says, 'Various groups who have fundamental and radically different ways of living always risked being co-opted or exterminated by the states. How might a coalitional, anti-capitalist, and decolonial politics be formulated at a global level across and between these groups against nation states, constitutions and the hegemony of, say for instance, the EU, the UN and the IMF?' Now, this is a powerful one. 'Is it possible to formulate a politics of refusal against citizenship in the traditional sense, and a glocal redistribution of goods and care outside of the monetary developmentalists mode in loose networks of care? Or are we so entrenched globally in the system of political institutions of the state and the market that we cannot overcome it?' Perhaps, we could take these two for now. The previous one and this one from Ted.

Walter Mignolo

Let me just make some general points about the Global South, the nation-state, the media, the university and the co-existence, which I already addressed in the previous comments. And the decolonial option. I try to be brief.

The Global South doesn't stand. It presupposed the Global North, and the Global East and the Global West. Furthermore, is the South of Europe equivalent to the North of Africa? Is Portugal in the South of Europe equivalent to Mozambique, Angola and Brazil? Is the South of the US not Global South? Third, First Nations in Canada have been as active, eloquent and efficacious in the Global North as Pueblos Originations in the Global South. Under Mao Zedong China was Third World, and therefore Global South after the collapse of the Three World division. Now is in the Global East, or East Asia. Fourth, the Global South in in the Global North (migrations) as much as the Global North is in the Global South (debt, extractivism, military bases) with the acquiescence of people and institution from the Global South.

Second the nation-state. The nation-state was created in the late 18th and 19th centuries in Europe. It was on the one hand, an outcome of the Treaty of Westphalia (1648) and on the other hand of the advent of an emerging ethno-class, the European bourgeoisie. It became THE instrument for the control and management of authority in the colonial matrix of power. The mistake of decolonization during the Cold War was to believe that decolonization could be achieved by founding nation-states in the former colony's rules by the native. In Latin America we knew that it happens in the 19th century. 'Internal colonialism' was the felicitous expression to describe the situation: coloniality managed by native elites following the manual of the former colonizers. Now, the state has become an instrument to the corporations or, if the state confronts the corporations, the officers of the state will soon be removed by judicial forces or by elections, where many people will vote against their own interests (as it was the case of Macri in Argentina and Bolsonaro in Brazil). So, yes, decoloniality cannot be a state-led project. Decoloniality is the connector of many projects of the political society in the public sphere, despite the state. However, the struggle for decolonization in Asia and Africa has left a wealth of thoughts and ideas that has become the foundation of decolonial thoughts – Gandhi, Cesaire, Cabral, Lumumba, Biko, in the same way that Machiavelli, Hobbes, Locke, are at the foundation of Western political thinking.

Co-existence I already addressed. I would add that today de-westernization, decoloniality and re-westernization co-exist in conflict. And will continue to co-exist with constant mutations for a foreseeable future. So, co-existence doesn't mean only pacific co-existence. If one day it happens that the co-existence is pacific, it will not be because of a grand-master plan of one ideology but because people will realize that to live in harmony in plenitude is preferable to live in conflict and war because we hate X and we want to destroy it and want to dominate Y.

The media, meaning here I guess, main-stream media, of course are at the service of the state and the corporations. There are certainly 'dissident' media that are there precisely to offer to the population narratives that the main-stream media do not, cannot and do not want to offer. So, there is a 'war of images and narratives' to which decoloniality could, should and it is contributing since our (decolonial) task runs parallel to many independent media that are not and do not have to claim decoloniality, but whose task is akin to ours.

The university is like the state, an instrument of the colonial matrix of power. There is a history of Western university, and University is a Western institution. It doesn't mean that all other civilization does not have crucial institution for higher education. Of course, they did, but the Western colonial expansion carry with it the university. Then the university as the state, and the museums, are institutions engrained in the colonial matrix of power: the state to control authority, the university and the museum to control knowledge, memories and the sensorium. Most of us here are at the university. Well, we have decolonial work to do within the university (but not only at the university), but the university cannot be decolonized. To decolonize the university means that you want to have the cake and eat it. Knowledge and knowing is not a property of the university, although it manages to make us believe that that is the case.

The decolonial option. Decoloniality and decolonization were not born at the university and are not contained in and by it. Be aware of the important but at the ame time limited function of decoloniality at the university. As for whether the decolonial option could be at the service of the colonial matrix of power, I leave it to you to decide. And whether the decolonial option is possible in the current scenario dominated by re-westernization and de-westernization is possible, I leave it to you too. There are many people that find in the decolonial option a way out of the mess and the way into rebuilding the communal. Is up to you to decide what to do.

Bassey Antia

Okay, thank you.

Catherine Walsh

Bassey, can I follow up on that as well?

Bassey Antia

Yes, please.

Catherine Walsh

Okay. Sort of tying into what Walter said, I think Desmond's and Ted's very clear questions and comments lead us toward important issues that may not have been part of our initial reflections. I think it's important, Desmond, to think about the myth of nation-state; if it ever existed, today we can say that nation-state no longer exists anywhere in the world. The denationalization and the transnationalization of state are part of the current moment. We're still led to believe that the nation-state is there. The notion of left and right party politics is part of that, right? Of whom to elect as the president of the nation, as if that person has a sort of individual power that's not transnationalized. Elections anywhere in the world today are really transnational elections. What's at stake, who's involved, who's behind the candidate, not just in terms of funding, are concerns very clear in the US with the Trump campaign, but present as well most anywhere in the world. I think it's important, as Desmond suggests, to dismantle or undo this myth of nation-state, particularly in these current times, and to think about the ways that the nation-state *is* being dismantled. This takes us beyond the old binary of left versus right. This is something that we've learned in recent years in Latin America from so-called progressive governments and presidents who, despite a left discourse or avowed leftist perspective, continue the projects of capitalism and coloniality.

Wide-scale extractivism, particularly in ancestral black and Indigenous territories, continues regardless of the left or right designation as does de-existence. I think that's one point important to think about, but it's also to think about the prospects of and for change. What are the actions of the dismantling that are taking place, that have taken place and are being retaken up in these current times? Certainly, in both Bolivia and Ecuador, the notion of the plurinational is key, a plurination that does not necessarily mean the insertion in or the taking over state. Here there is an important tension at play within Indigenous movements. In both Ecuador and Bolivia, many of the contemporary debates have been with reference to the idea, significance and project of the plurinational state. Experience in both countries shows the difficulties and problematics when the plurinational becomes an add-on within the same state structure and top-down system of power; rather than dismantling the state, state structure and power are maintained and strengthened. Yet state per se was not always or necessarily the center of discussion. This was true in the idea and prospect that began in the 1920s in Bolivia, and in the 1970s in Ecuador; in both instances, it was the plurality of nation and the plurinational that were of interest, possibility and concern. Such concerns, of course, have also existed in other places of the world, certainly in different nations in Africa, and most particularly South Africa. The plurination is part of the debate, right? Part of a long history of debates about the problem of the South African state, during apartheid and now post-apartheid. How to think about reality today, including when those in the townships and those in power may look the same physically, but obviously have very different notions of how the society should be constructed. That sort of ties to Ted's long question.

For me it is helpful to begin to connect the ways that nation-state and its myth and practice are being dismantled in different places of the world today. Making these connections can enable us to think, I would say, not globally, because the notion of the global has also been co-opted and used in the wrong ways, but instead to think about connecting fissures or cracks. One of these connections, particularly key and that Ted alluded to in his question, is with relation to Kurdistan, a territory that crosses a number of different so-called nation-states – Turkey, Syria, Iran, Iraq – but also includes Kurds in many other places of the world. For many involved in the Kurdish struggle and movement today, the project is not for a new state, but instead, and following the proposals of the imprisoned leader Abdullah Öcalan, it is for a confederalism that crosses territories and nation-state borders. Geographic unification is not necessarily the project here, nor is it nationalization in the western sense. Here it is revealing to consider the connections between the Kurdish movement and social movement and community-based processes in Latin America. Kurdish movement representatives frequently move in and out of various Latin American countries, building ongoing relations and conversations not with government or state, but with communities involved in imagining, thinking and making radically distinct forms of society, without the myth of nation-state that's been maintained for so many years. Made evident is a connecting of the system's cracks.

While one could say that the context of Kurdish people is radically distinct from the context of many Indigenous and black communities and collectives in Latin America, the dialogic exchange has been rich. The notion of the plurinational and the notion of confederalism, both have this aim of rethinking the very notion of democracy, this a western concept that's been universalized and applied throughout the world. This rethinking in, with and through different words, terms, languages, practices and contexts, *is* taking place. These kinds of connections enable what Ted referred to in his question as a kind of politics of refusal. They also evidence the building of what the decolonial feminist María Lugones (2003) referred to as a coalition politics. At work here is relation across differences, across geographic location and in a shared project of sorts that doesn't collapse into one, but recognizes difference. I think that's particularly key today, not to solidify or continue to fight for the nation-state and its myth, but to recognize its transnationalization, to recognize the limitation of electoral politics and to begin to think of other forms of social governance that enable other forms of relation and decision-making, including participatory assembly-based forms of decision-making and governance. This isn't to say that electoral politics don't matter or that, in the US context, Trump and Biden are the same. What I am saying is that their projects, while discursively distinct, continue to maintain the interests and structure of capitalism and coloniality.

I am not suggesting a simple movement from coloniality to decoloniality. But I am arguing that the decolonial cracks are all over. The decolonial happens and it is made. However, it doesn't always have to be named. It's not a new paradigm, theory or route, nor is it an adjective that can be lightly applied to most anything (including decolonial tourism and decolonial foods!). It's also not a competition in which some are more decolonial than others, about who can raise higher the decolonial flag. I return to decoloniality's praxistic call, to the urgency, particularly in these present times, of thinking, doing and struggling together, of connecting the fissures and the threads from different places in the world, taking into account what needs to be done and what is being done, and of beginning to weave new possibilities.

Bassey Antia

Thank you very much, Catherine. I would crave indulgence to just take two very short questions from Brett and Sheneez, and thereafter, request Sinfree to summarize the evening or the morning for us. So, Brett?

Brett Diaz

My question was prompted by what Walter was talking about, but of course, Catherine, you're also welcome to chime in if you want to. First, I want to say, thanks for mentioning Gloria Anzaldúa's work. I also had a sort of similar experience to you, because my last name is Diaz. I come from California and my family, both of my grandparents, generation families, come from immigrants – one from Cuba, Spain, from France and Quebec. I also learned a lot about myself reading Anzaldúa in a place where understandings about language and linguistic identity inform how you are taught to be a Chicano or how you were taught to be a Latino or whatever. I very much appreciate that reference. What I wanted to ask you about, Walter, is drawing more on your semiotics background and where it intersects with Marxism and class understanding, it's how to use the historical material in our culture, in our places, to break apart from the sort of second-order issues such as color, for example. I'd like to see the issue of class and commodification, objectification and exploitation so that we can find those, as you said, borders and counting the fissures or cracks, to show how people are together and to be less drawn to these physical manifestations, if you will, of class that actually make it more difficult to renew and to show together the causes that we have. It would be really interesting to see how your thoughts on semiotics and historical materialism kind of come together to accomplish that.

Bassey Antia

Walter Mignolo, you have the floor.

Walter Mignolo

Thanks Brett Anthony for picking up on Anzaldua and inviting me to think on how semiotic and historical materialism come together. I am not sure what you mean by historical materialism. Historical materialism in the Marxist sense of the expression I have nothing to do with it. I share Quijano's several observations distinguishing coloniality of power from historical materialism. The evolutionary and unidirectional perspective of historical materialism and its limitations of social class and class societies has many complications, Quijano insisted. His own alert that race and racism were foundational classificatory technology to justify slavery and the exploitation of labor, his own concept of structural-historical heterogeneity to explain the foundation of capitalism in the 16th century (before the Industrial Revolution) that Marx observed in the 19th century, are alien to decoloniality in the sense that we inherited from Quijano.

Racism is already an early strategy to transform human beings into commodities: African slaves were a commodity in two senses: they were bought and sold and, as all commodities, once it is used and it is no longer necessary it becomes disposable. So, there you have objectivation of human life and then of 'nature,' in the economic structure objects could become commodities. Objects that become commodities are related to exploitation of labor, and racism justified exploitation of labor before chattel slavery ended because it was too expensive, waged labor replaced it and the industrial revolution profited from waged labor.

How did I get to this through semiotics? Because I learned from semiotics to read sign and signs are all over, everywhere. A cloudy dark sky is a sign that it will rain, and the leaves coming back on the trees are sign that the Spring is here. Signs on the road tell me what the maximum speed is and 6/34 tells me that I was assigned room 34 on the sixth floor of the hotel where I am staying, or that such number and such street is my house address. But then when I encountered colonialism and coloniality, I began to read historically the signs. I investigated the role of Latin alphabetic writing in advancing colonization. Arabic and Russia have alphabetic writing, but that was inferior to the Latin and the vernacular languages. Anzaldua was doing something similar I learned from her in 'How to tame a wild tongue.' Anzaldua taught me that borders separate and unite two sides entangled on power differential. That power differential is coloniality. Then I read the signs of historiographical discourses and of cartography, the Western signs of controlling and managing memory and space.

Bassey Antia

Thank you very much. Sheneez Amara, next.

Sheneez Amara

Hello, thank you very much for your talks. I've really enjoyed this. I just wanted to ask about education and the practice of education, in light of everything that you both are saying, because I think what interests me is that I feel like in theoretical discussions or the intellectual kind of debates, we say many different words, but we often mean the same things. Oftentimes, I think we're very – not universally, but oftentimes we similarly want to be anti-racist. We want to conduct research in this way. I'm very interested in how we teach this. How do we bring that into the classroom and spread the message? I'm a PhD student, I haven't actually taught yet, but I remember something you said, Professor Mignolo, in a talk you did earlier on. I think it was a couple of weeks ago, you said, 'We cannot decolonize the university, but we can do decolonial work in the university,' and you said about a key part of that is the hundreds of students who pass through. It would be interesting, I think, to think about what can we do and to kind of create a conversation about how we act within the university, which we know this is colonial institution. In order to encourage students to think in some of the ways that everybody has been thinking and speaking today. It's very inspirational. How can we spread the messages?

Walter Mignolo

Since Cathy has much more experience in pedagogical question, I go first and leave Cathy to have the last word.

A quick example of my own practice and theory of education related to coloniality/decoloniality for undergraduate. The seminar is on the cosmologies of First Nations. I teach the basic concept of Maya, Aztecs and Inca cosmologies, but I start with First Nations in Canada and close making connections with Native Americans and Macoris in New Zealand. The material (texts, documentary, videos interviews and written interviews) is 95% by Indigenous thinkers, activists, artists, intellectuals, and 5% by non-Indigenous. The goals are for them to have direct contact with Indigenous cosmologies told by themselves and the political relevance of the cosmologies for Indigenous praxis of living and thinking. That invites them to reflect about themselves, about the cosmology of Western civilization, disguised by theology, science and philosophy. At the end students learn much about themselves as they learn about Indigenous thoughts, praxis of living and thinking. Learning about themselves (the students) in the mirror of what has been either hidden or distorted by their previous education.

Catherine Walsh

To sort of weave with Walter, let's start with Rojava, with what's going on in terms of education, in a project that's women-led. That, I think, is the key element today in terms of rethinking and the redoing that we're talking about here. Who's leading, how are they leading and with whom? In Rojava, the Kurdish communities of women are leading the process and project in which education is thought of not as the institution of schooling but as a crucial component in the creation of communities of knowing, of thinking, of existing together, of care. How might we construct processes of education that are radically distinct, including but not only in places we call schools and universities? Rojava is one example that breaks the notion of institutionalized education, the education that takes place in Zapatista communities is another. But I want to insist here on the significance and force of women in the processes of social, educational, epistemic and existence-based change. Jineology, the science of women that the women of Rojava have introduced is another example Düzgün (2016). This is a science of life and existence that's being taught in schools and universities – the new universities taking form in Rojava, but also in spaces in Turkey, in Syria, in Iran, Iraq. It is the thinking of a new kind of social science conceived and taught from the perspective of women.

I recall bell hooks' (2014) arguments a number of years ago about how education and teaching must necessarily be postured and practiced as acts of caring and love. So seldom are care and love present in most classrooms. Worse yet, at the university level. What does it mean to create a context in the classroom of love and care, a space and place where students feel that they can talk honestly about their own feelings, bring up the tensions that may exist in the group or classroom, and actually begin to process and work through them? Yes, in conversation like Walter says. But I think that doesn't just happen in any classroom. One has to create, Sheneez, the environment, the sense that it's safe, that we're talking – that we're watching each other's back, and that we're taking care of one another. And that means, as teacher as well – I'm not just talking about students. It's also to sort of take a step down from that notion of 'the teacher' or 'professor.'

I always say I'm not an academic. Yes, I work in the university. I've worked in the university for 40 years, but I don't identify as an academic. Academia is not what defines me, and it's not what gives me the impetus of what I understand as pedagogical praxis, that which can take place in the classroom but elsewhere as well. As Walter well knows, this pedagogical practice of love and caring is a crucial part of the doctoral program that I coordinate in Ecuador, and in which Walter has, since its beginning, always been part. Considerations of collective sustenance and environment, including the sharing of food and beverage to give force to our body as we're conversing, reflecting and thinking, the noncompetitive sharing of knowledge and thought and the building of a kind of collective notion of caring about one another, are all part. That doesn't mean harmony, it doesn't mean we're all the same or that we necessarily all get along, but it means that we can put issues on the table and critically address them. I think, going back, certainly to the work of bell hooks, but also looking at other ways that issues of love and caring are part of a real teaching; teaching not as transmitting knowledge and information, but rather building together a space where we begin this kind of interchange of sharing, where thinking is built. Thinking as being/becoming, of supportive learning, unlearning and relearning in both an individual and community sense, of shared existence in a classroom space, but outside the classroom as well. Decolonial pedagogies, as I understand them, are not limited to a certain space. Moreover, they don't just happen. They are constructed with others, in shared processes of thinking and doing, and with the aim to begin to create other possibilities of thinking, of sensing, of feeling, of being/becoming, and of action – of actional thought and thoughtful action – that endeavor to undo, fissure and crack the dominant order, including the dominant order that universities continue to maintain.

That's my reflection on your question Sheneez. All this is very much in the doing, there's no manual to follow. Certainly, there are many examples; while they are not all led by women, I think women are leading today many of the most important processes of radical decolonizing change. But I'm not excluding Walter, because I know Walter's classrooms are spaces of caring and loving conversation as well. But how do we create this different way of thinking about what teaching is about? And teaching as thinking, as being/becoming, as co-existing but also as creating. That's my sense of the urgency of the work to be done. Sheneez, you may not be in the classroom yet, but think about the other spaces that you're in, spaces and places where those kinds of pedagogies occur, can be strengthened and learned from. To me, the notion of planting seeds is essential, that the idea is not to reform the minds of our students, or those that we may work with in collectives or social movements, but rather to think about the seeds. What are the seeds that we can plant? What are the seeds that have been handed down to us? What are the seeds that are out there that can be taken care of, that can maybe germinate and be cultivated? And how do we assure that they grow, not just in our classroom spaces, but in life in general? I think that's what we need today, to think about those seeds and to think about their cultivation.

Bassey Antia

What a wonderful place to be around at this point. So much has been planted by, well, seeds, over the past two and a half hours, and the tall order is Sinfree's now to summarize the seeds that have been planted and send us to our respected homes.

Sinfree Makoni

Yes. Thank you very much, Catherine and Walter, and thank you to everybody for participating. I only have two things to say, which I think, are related to this discussion. What I learned from this conversation was that everybody, in respect to race, class or ethnicity, is affected in one way or the other by issues of coloniality. If that proposition is a valid one, then issues about decoloniality should be of interest to most people, whereas decoloniality that provides you with a way of thinking about how coloniality has an impact on you. Now, if I didn't shift and started thinking, as an applied linguist, what is the relevance of this? What are the questions that I ask? The question that I then don't want to ask are questions like, 'What is decoloniality?' et cetera, et cetera. That is not the question that I would like to ask. The question I'd like then to ask is, what is the impact of coloniality or decoloniality on the nature and type of Applied Linguistics that I do? I shift from being preoccupied with providing definitions of decoloniality, to being more interested in thinking about the impact decoloniality or coloniality has on the nature and type of discipline that I'm engaged with. That, I think, is my summary discussion. Although, I would like to hear what Ofelia García thinks. You've been very quiet.

Ofelia García

Sinfree. Thank you, of course, Walter and Catherine. It's wonderful to see you after these many years in a different place. I think that this is all related to language, of course. Because coloniality has gone through language and the way we think about language and teaching languages is certainly impregnated by coloniality.

Sinfree Makoni

Yes, that's right. In a way, you see, since the way we think about coloniality is influenced by language, then decolonizing language and linguistics as the discipline, one of the disciplines that deals with language becomes an important and urgent issue. And from my perspective, some of the theoretical models in linguistics are Applied Linguistics – which are grounded, no longer called a universal speaking subject – don't capture the experiences that I think are relevant, and which should be centralized in how we should be thinking about language, with how you think about languages and impact on how we are going to be handling issues about the nation state, issues about literature, issues about semiotics, etc.

Walter Mignolo

Do we need linguistics to talk about language?

Sinfree Makoni

Yes, we don't need linguistics. You could say, in a sort of effect, linguistics provides one way of talking about language but that is not necessarily perhaps the most fruitful or productive way of thinking and talking about language. That you would argue seriously that linguistics is taking us into a blind alley in terms of thinking about language.

Walter Mignolo

One of the first books that we published as a collective modernity/coloniality and Cathy was one of the co-editors was titled *Indisciplinar las ciencias sociales*. Decoloniality is an undisciplinary way of thinking. Why? Because the disciplines do what they promise: they discipline the future experts in the disciplines. That is coloniality of knowing and knowledge.

Sinfree Makoni

Yes. The point I'm trying to make, if I try to articulate it in a more robust way, is to say that linguistics constitutes one way of thinking about language. But whether, for example, that is the most productive or most useful way of thinking about language for one's purpose is an open question. The second issue is that I believe that there are many more, maybe infinite ways of thinking and talking about language, for example, which have not yet been brought to the fore, which cannot be incorporated in contemporary linguistic thinking. What I'm interested in, for example, personally, the other alternative ways of thinking about language, et cetera, which may draw their expression whether from land, from water, or from skyscrapers, et cetera. Because of what I think are the inherent limitations in the objectives of linguistics.

Walter Mignolo

Yap, that is a big, big issue. But I think we cannot frame the problems that are involved in that. And the disciplines prevent us to ask questions on issues that are related but that the disciplinary frame dismiss and disregard.

Sinfree Makoni

Yes. Thank you very much to everybody. Thank you very much. This has been fascinating stuff. Thanks.

Desmond Odugu

Thank you so much, everyone. It's been fantastic.

Shaila Sultana

Thank you. Thank you.

Notes

(1) The word sudaca is, according to the definition of the Dictionary of the Spanish language of the Royal Spanish Academy, a derogatory expression used to refer to the natives of South America.
(2) https://edition.cnn.com/2022/10/18/world/uae-eu-borrell-racist-comments-intl/index.html

References

Anzaldúa, G. (1987) *Borderlands/la frontera*. San Francisco: Aunt Lute Books.
Cabnal, L. (2019) El relato de las violencias desde mi territorio cuerpo-tierra. *En tiempos de muerte: cuerpos, rebeldías, resistencias* 4.
De Giorgi, E., Cavalieri, A. and Feo, F. (2023) From opposition leader to Prime Minister: Giorgia Meloni and women's issues in the Italian radical right. *Politics and Governance* 11 (1).
Düzgün, M. (2016) Jineology: The Kurdish women's movement. *Journal of Middle East Women's Studies* 12 (2), 284–287.
Fanon, F. (1968) *The Wretched of the Earth*. New York: Grove Press.
Foucault, M. (1972) *The Archaeology of Knowledge* (trans. A.M. Sheridan Smith). New York: Pantheon.
Gramsci, A. (1971) Hegemony. In *Selections from the Prison Notebooks of Antonio Gramsci* (pp. 95–123). New York: International Publishers.
Harding, S. and Mendoza, B. (2020) Latin American decolonial feminist philosophy of knowledge production. In S. Crasnow and K. Intemann (eds) *The Routledge Handbook of Feminist Philosophy of Science* (pp. 104–116). New York: Routledge.
Hooks, b. (2014) *Teaching to Transgress*. New York: Routledge.
Kuhn, T.S. (1962) Historical structure of scientific discovery: To the historian discovery is seldom a unit event attributable to some particular man, time, and place. *Science* 136 (3518), 760–764.
Kusch, R. (2020) *América profunda*. Buenos Aires: Editorial biblos.
Latour, B. and Leclercq, C. (eds) (2016) *Reset Modernity!* Cambridge, MA: MIT Press.
Lugones, M. (2003) *Pilgrimages/Peregrinajes: Theorizing Coalition Against Multiple Oppressions*. Lanham, MD: Rowman & Littlefield Publishers.
Marx, K. (1973) *Karl Marx on Society and Social Change: With Selections by Friedrich Engels*. Chicago: University of Chicago Press.
Mbembe, A. (2008) *Necropolitics* (pp. 152–182). Basingstoke: Palgrave Macmillan UK.
Mignolo, W.D. (1992) The darker side of the Renaissance: Colonization and the discontinuity of the classical tradition. *Renaissance Quarterly* 45 (4), 808–828.
Mignolo, W. and Walsh, C. (2002) Las geopolíticas de conocimiento y colonialidad del poder. *Interdisciplinar las ciencias sociales: Geopolíticas del conocimiento y colonialidad del poder. Perspectivas desde lo andino*, 17–42.

Mignolo, W.D. and Tlostanova, M.V. (2006) Theorizing from the borders: Shifting to geo-and body-politics of knowledge. *European Journal of Social Theory* 9 (2), 205–221.

Mignolo, W.D. (2021) *The Politics of Decolonial Investigations*. Durham, NC: Duke University Press.

Mignolo, W.D. (2020) On decoloniality: Second thoughts. *Postcolonial Studies* 23 (4), 612–618.

Reiter, B. (ed.) (2018) *Constructing the Pluriverse: The Geopolitics of Knowledge*. Durham, NC: Duke University Press.

Rodriguez Castro, L. (2021) 'We are not poor things': territorio cuerpo-tierra and Colombian women's organised struggles. *Feminist Theory* 22 (3), 339–359.

Quijano, A. (1992) Colonialidad y modernidad/racionalidad. *Perú indígena* 13 (29), 11–20.

Simpson, L.B. (2011) *Dancing on Our Turtle's Back: Stories of Nishnaabeg Re-creation, Resurgence and A New Emergence*. Winnipeg: Arbeiter Ring Pub.

Smith, L.T. (1999) *Decolonizing Methodologies: Indigenous Peoples and Research*. London: Zed Books.

Walsh, C. and Castro-Gómez, S. (2002) *Indisciplinar las ciencias sociales: Geopolíticas del conocimiento y colonialidad del poder. Perspectivas desde lo andino*. Quito: Editorial Abya Yala.

Walsh, C. (2010) Development as Buen Vivir: Institutional arrangements and (de) colonial entanglements. *Development* 53 (1), 15–21.

Walsh, C. and Mignolo, W. (2018) *On Decoloniality: Concepts, Analysis, Praxis*. Durham, NC: Duke University Press.

8 Decolonizing Methodologies: Research and Indigenous Peoples

Linda Tuhiwai Smith

Linda Tuhiwai Smith

First of all, let me respond[1]. I want to greet you wherever you are and hope that you are well and that your families are well. If you are grieving for someone who is lost, my sympathies to you. Grieve as long as you wish to grieve and rejoin life when you are ready. My heart goes out to you all. I speak to you here from New Zealand, from a small town called Whakatane. It is the weekend, it is Sunday, and I am visiting my father who is 94, and who is also a very distinguished Māori studies scholar. I am sitting in my home territory of Ngāti Awa at the moment. I cannot see all of you and all your faces, but I want to say, *Tena koutou Tena koutou katoa*, greetings to you all.

I'll talk a bit about the *Decolonizing Methodologies* (1999) and where we are at now. Firstly, the third edition of *Decolonizing Methodologies* (2021) was published by Zed Books, who have now been bought out by Bloomsbury Books.

I want to talk to some of the changes in the book – as a way of explaining where I think we come to in decolonizing methodologies. My first point would be the following: We still need to decolonize methodologies, decolonize theory, decolonize institutions, decolonize society because, if anything, the pandemic has shown us the deep inequities, the deep racism that exists, particularly in what are called settler colonial societies. But even those societies that have been colonized by other, non-Western countries experience the same institutional inequities that we have. As I speak, there are groups, Indigenous communities, minority communities all around the world who are excluded, who are suffering and who take the brunt of a dominant population's hatred and anger, and resentment and jealousy.

Building on this, I think the work of decolonizing methodologies is important. I know some of you will come from communities like the ones I come from, where they say things like, 'We're the most researched population in the world.' I've been all over the world, and I've heard that expression, 'We're the most researched people in the world.' To me, the issue is not whether that is empirically true or not. The issue is: What compels people to say that? What is it that has made them feel like they are the most researched? I think it is this overwhelming sense that researchers have just come, and taken and left. There are a lot of terms for that now, like helicopter research – fly in, interview, fly out. As a master's student, I was intrigued by methodologies because [. . .] that is really where I started to confront what it meant to do research. But that was many, many, many years ago. Having experienced beyond just doing a single piece of research, my concern now is the whole institution of research, the institutions of knowledge that prop up colonizing and racist research.

During the pandemic, you would all have heard the responses to science. I think one of the interesting debates in Indigenous methodologies is whether Indigenous knowledge is a science or not. I do not think any Indigenous knowledge should be made to fit into a box determined by the West of what is science or what is not science. But I know our scholars like Gregory Cajete would argue that there are many aspects of Indigenous knowledge that are absolutely based on empirical knowledge and deep observations of the environment. And that there are also many aspects of Indigenous knowledge which are based on our worldviews, our relationships with the Earth and the environment, our ability, and belief, and dreaming, and spiritual awakening, and spiritual wellbeing – that those things are also part of our knowledge system and are often stripped away, if not ridiculed, by Western science. What the pandemic has shown, especially now in the delivery of vaccines, is that the biomedical research scientists have no clue whatsoever about *how* to deliver a vaccine to our communities. You need different kinds of scientists to do that. They might be people in the logistics area, truck drivers, community activists, people who know our communities, elders – those are our scientists that we need right now. I think the pandemic, in a way, illustrates the importance of building our capacity as Indigenous and people of color who do research, meaning people who have this dual responsibility to be critiquing and contesting Western sort of ideologies but also having the credibility to work with other knowledges, to work with peoples who have been excluded from research. It is a big burden if you are doing that research. I acknowledge the kind of dual, if not, multiple burdens that you carry. But, in a way, you have no choice. I think if you are Indigenous or a researcher of color, there is no choice, in a sense, about the work that we do. And rather than bemoan the fact and try [to] be like a White researcher, I think we [should] embrace our difference, and we make out of that difference a life and a career worth living and worth doing.

In the new edition, I have added a new chapter with some new projects. What I have done over the last two years at conferences is to ask younger scholars, emerging researchers, postgraduate students, whether that chapter, the 25 projects, was still relevant to them. One of the challenges of doing a new edition of a book is whether there is a point to it. There are questions like, 'Why can't they just reprint it?' 'What else can I say, or is it even still relevant?' Because there are so many new, fabulous books by our scholars that maybe the message of decolonizing methodologies is now being diffused and dispersed, and it is no longer required. But the young scholars assured me that the original 25 projects are still relevant and still important to them. But, in the workshops that I used to do, we have identified 20 more projects. I use the word 'project' in a really down-to-earth way. I am not good at inventing flashy new terms. To me, a lot of what we are doing is work. I remember an Indigenous elder asking me, 'What does an academic person do? What do *you* do?' Most of our people do not know what we do – they think we drink coffee all the time. I tried to explain to him, and he said, 'darling, you work, you do work, and that's what's important.'

So, that is my approach to everything: We do work, and our work is in the theory, research space and teaching space. There is nothing fancy about that in terms of a hierarchy of work, in my view. The kind of work we do is with our minds, our intellectual training, but we think we are really clever. But many academics that I know are emotionally undereducated and underdeveloped. We are not the greatest of human beings in terms of how we have been schooled and educated, and we need to be humble about what we know and understand, that we have been trained to do certain kinds of work that contributes to the wellbeing of our peoples. I think it is as simple as that – that is our role as teachers, scholars and researchers.

In the third edition of *Decolonizing Methodologies* (2021), I have added 20 new projects, and I have enhanced some of the original 25 projects because some of those original ideas have been advanced, if you like, and broken out into a number of other categories, which shows the growth of work. The way I have identified the projects is not just by looking at the literature. In fact, when I started writing *Decolonizing Methodologies* (1999), there was really no literature. So, because I was already traveling around different parts of the world, I paid attention to where people put their energy. When I went to Indigenous gatherings, I looked at what our peoples were doing, where they were putting their hearts and minds and their work. It is really out of that sort of approach that I came up with the original 25 projects, and I have used the same approach with the next 20. All I can say is that our peoples are doing more work, they are not subtracting any work, but there is more capacity to do some work than there is to do other work. To me, that is a reflection, in a way, of education, of development, of where certain communities are at, at present.

This morning I looked at the news on Brazil, and they are on the cusp of the collapse of their health system. So, when some of my colleagues look at Brazil, they look at the country, Brazil. I do not look at the country, Brazil. I look at the Indigenous context of Brazil, the Indigenous peoples in Brazil who, right from the start of this pandemic, have taken massive hits. I think it is almost like a genocide, the failure of governments to look after them. I know from what we have experienced, I know, in my heart, that, for many Indigenous communities in Amazon, there is no way that they will be getting the help they need, and the compassion they deserve. There are other places around the world where Indigenous communities are still fighting for their physical survival. They rarely have a choice about whether they are trying to protect their Indigenous knowledges or their lives. I think the scale of the Indigenous struggle is still from the sheer physical survival as a people to try to be self-determining, arguing in the United Nations for our rights as Indigenous peoples. The scale and the scope between those two struggles are really what we are about and what we always have to remember.

For me, working from the context of Aotearoa, New Zealand, which is a well-off country [. . .] that means our context here for Māori people is very different [from] the context of others. Those nuances in the Indigenous peoples' struggle are important, not just in the political sphere but also in our work. These factors influence the way we have to nuance our work and cultivate an understanding that, when we use the term 'Indigenous' or 'methodology' or 'theory' or 'decolonizing,' it does not represent a narrow idea about one possibility or one pathway for one type of configuration of being 'Indigenous' or being 'colonized.' I believe we have to keep terms and ideas open. Don't close the door. In our world, the Indigenous world, it is really important that you don't close the door because, in closing a door, you close the hope for a people who have not yet made it to the door. Leave an extra chair at the table because there are people that are making their way to sit at the table. If we think about that intellectually, it is the same idea.

There are some things we can be definitive about now because of the moment we are in. But it is also knowing that contexts change, and there are always other possibilities that we must bear in mind. It might not be comfortable for students who like things to be clear and definitive and certain. I am someone who is comfortable with uncertainty and comfortable with new possibilities that I have not kind yet imagined. That is the world that we are in, and the sooner you get used to it, the easier your life will be. But also, if you come out of our communities, you live with uncertainty. Intuitively, you know how to live with uncertainty. One of the problems of academia and scholarship is trying to define certainty: 'this is what it is, this is the theory of X, this is the theory of everything.' Intuitively, whenever that claim is made, I am thinking, 'No, no, that's not how it works.' We are still on this big journey, and it is important to keep these windows open, doors open, possibilities open for where we will be.

This new edition also has a new introduction. I invited some young scholars from different parts of the Indigenous world to help write the introduction. I asked them to introduce the book but also talk about its relevance to their careers. I did that deliberately because they are the next generation of teachers and researchers. I am retiring formally out of institutions. I will still be working, but my professional career inside the university is coming to a close, and I wanted younger scholars that are going to carry this work forward to introduce the book and the new chapter on the 20 projects.

To sum up: What does that mean? In the context of the #RhodesMustFall movement that came out of South Africa, the Black Lives Matter, the Idle No More, the Missing and Murdered Indigenous Aboriginal Women, there are struggles all around the world as we speak that, to me, speak to the ongoing significance of our struggles to decolonize academic knowledge, decolonize academic institutions because our universities, in particular, have been set up as arbiters of what counts as legitimate knowledge. These systems are global, and the ideas about race just circulate through academic institutions, and so our struggle to decolonize is also a global struggle. It's not just what some of us in South Africa or in Malaysia [are concerned with]. It is what all of us have to do because the system that we are trying to question and critique and transform is a global system that circulates ideas through a whole range of both obvious and then also mysterious academic processes. For example, publishing. We can decolonize methodologies all we want, but if a journal will not publish your work, then there is no progress. The whole publishing arena needs decolonizing. The fact that journals are often all-boys clubs, the editorial board is dominated by certain kinds of views, means that only particular ideas are circulated. In our context, we have had to start our own journals. We have had to seek publishers who will publish our work. So, the struggle is not just about doing a single research project, or your thesis, your PhD, or your first article or your first book; it is a struggle against a system, a very racist system. In that struggle, we are all together and we all have to be targeting different parts of that system. It is like Swiss cheese, in a sense. We are trying to make lots of little holes in a very sort of murky texture space, and it can be challenging to make a big enough hole to transform the object that we are trying to change.

Sinfree Makoni

Okay. Thank you very much for this informative introduction. I must apologize; I haven't read the third edition because I wasn't aware there's a third edition, but I can assure you, when it comes out, I will read it. So, the questions I'm going to pose come mainly from the second edition of your book. I want to concentrate on the issue of feminism and gender in decoloniality because throughout the book, throughout, [on] a number of occasions, you make reference to the fact that you are a mother, or when you went to do your postgraduate research, you had your kids, et cetera. And then let me read to you a quotation from page 190, where you are talking about issues relating to gender. You say this: 'so there is the possibility within Kaupapa Māori research to address the different constructions of Māori knowledge. A good example of this is the development of Māori women's theories about Māori society, which question the accounts of Māori society provided by men, including Māori men, but which still hold to a position that argues that the issues of gender for Māori do not make us the same as White women.'

So, are you saying that the Māori men's theories about Māori society may be different from those of Māori women, and then the theories of society by Māori women are different from the theories of society by White feminists? In other words, would you regard yourself as a Māori feminist decolonial scholar?

Linda Tuhiwai Smith

Well, there is a context, as always, to those kinds of ideas. Let me start with the latter part of your question, which is around White woman's feminism. For Black women, women of color, and for Indigenous women, in particular, the biggest flaw of feminism is that it didn't address race, racism or colonialism. And, so, there is a point at which the critique of White patriarchy – we can sit on the side as Indigenous women and say, 'Yeah, it's a patriarchal society,' but even when White women get into control, they're just as racist. It's a racist White society. So, there was a departure point, I think, in feminism – and I'm really going back into the sort of '80s and '90s versions of feminism and including Marxist feminism. There was a failure to address racism and colonialism in fundamental ways and an arrogance about speaking for Black women, and speaking for Indigenous women, universalizing the experiences of all women based on the experiences of white women.

Here in New Zealand, and I know elsewhere, Māori women, partly in reaction to feminism and particularly in reaction to White feminists' speaking on our behalf, developed our own kind of resistance and ideas about what it meant to be an

Indigenous woman. But we are also in a society in which the White colonizers were very good at recreating in their image [of] what our society should be like. For example, they never recognized that we had matrilineal power systems, that we – in fact, for Māori, it's bilinear. We descend equally and claim our tribal identities from the women and from men. Both those lines are equally important. The patrilineal kind of approach – I always call it the 'take me to your chief' mentality. When White people landed, it's like, 'take me to your chief,' because they thought there was a chief and that the chief was male. But when Captain Cook arrived, one of the early descriptions in Captain Cook's journals and journals of others on his ship was of a very powerful woman who is an ancestor of mine, an ancestress of mine. She was the most powerful woman in the territory. All they did was describe the fact that she was wearing a spectacular cloak in red. What they did not recognize is she was a chief above all chiefs. Colonization tried to recreate in Indigenous society the patriarchal structures of White society. In doing that, I think a lot of our men, because they were educated specifically to be the new generation of leaders, bought into a lot of that patriarchy and sexism. I think, as Māori women, our fundamental position is that it is up to us to sort out our own internal gender relationships, but our struggle is for our sovereignty, our *mana motuhake*. Once we get that, our relationships as men and women fall back into place.

Sinfree Makoni

Okay. Thank you very much. Let me then continue with another question. You spent some time talking about critical theories, and you suggest something on page 188 which reminds me of a statement I had read from Ellen Cushman who works among the Cherokee, and you write this: 'Bishop goes further to suggest that critical approaches to research have, in fact, "failed" to address the issues of communities such as Māori and the development of alternative approaches by the Māori people.' Now the question I have is: Are you saying that the critical research approaches failed to engage with the Māori as a society, or is this a reflection somehow of the limitations inherent in critical approaches when they deal with Indigenous communities? Because I read a similar argument made by Ellen Cushman when she's talking about the Cherokee that the critical approaches somehow fall flat when they are trying to engage with the Māori people. The question is *why*.

Linda Tuhiwai Smith

I think the big failure of critical theory as well as critical approaches is they are good at describing the problem but not good at seeing the possibilities of different kinds of solutions. What Indigenous communities and peoples have most to offer is that we still have these active paradigms of knowing, of being in the world. Some of it has to be reclaimed and restored, but we have, almost [at] our fingertips, ways of interacting with the world, being in the world, and being ourselves in the world that I think offer a different kind of hope and a different kind of future. I think the problem with a lot of critical approaches that I see is that people are good on critique, but they are not good on 'so, what do you do about it? What are the solutions? Where do you go?' Because you can critique, critique, critique; the urgency for us is that is not enough. In our communities, it is not enough just to critique. If you are critiquing a government or the crown, and you slay them in your critique with your fabulous logic, and you walk away and leave the people exactly where they were before, it is profoundly unethical. So, I think we are obligated to say, 'Here are some potential solutions; let's try those. Let's try these solutions. Let's think through into the future.' That is where I think we depart from critical theory and critical approaches.

Sinfree Makoni

Okay. Now, this is my last question before I give this over to Bassey. You say in this book, for example, that it is written for the researched when they become researchers. Can you help me think this through? If, for example, you were to write a book in which the researched, let's say the Māori, were now going to research the White New Zealanders, what type of book would that look like?

Linda Tuhiwai Smith

There are some really great critical researchers who have talked about the idea of 'researching up,' researching up the power. I think any good Indigenous researcher who is trained in the decolonizing methodologies should be able to research up to power and talk up to power, speak to power. Our skills have to help us do that. So, I do not think that that is the issue really. It is about the challenge of where we focus our efforts.

Sinfree Makoni

Okay.

Linda Tuhiwai Smith

Yeah. But the other part of that is – and I do hear that from some of my students – is whether the work they do as Indigenous researchers working with communities in itself will be transformative. Like, to what extent can you just do that and not address issues of power? I mean, when I think critical methodologies, I'm thinking fundamentally we're trained to think about the relations of power in any social setting that we might be working with. And I think if we lose sight of how power works, then we lose sight of the criticality of our research.

Sinfree Makoni

Thanks. I've got more questions, but I will stop here and give [this] over to Bassey for the time being. Yeah.

Bassey Antia

Thank you very much, Dr Linda (Tuhiwai) Smith and Sinfree. Esther has a question. Esther?

Esther Liu

Hi. Greetings from the University of Minnesota on Dakota land. My question is: To what extent are Indigenous research activities, let's say, and decolonizing methodologies mutual entailments? I know you write about this in your book, for example, when you raise the question of whether all research activities of a Māori researcher automatically constitute Kaupapa Māori methods or, kind of conversely, whether a non-Indigenous outsider could carry out Kaupapa research. But my question is more geared at how do we, [as] researchers, enter these tangles without then re-inscribing the researcher as the arbiter of what is authentically Māori and what is legitimately Kaupapa or another context, unsettling, or decolonizing. And even if one takes a more radical approach within some communities to say that you must be Māori in order to carry out Kaupapa research, then you're still making determinations of who is truly Māori and who isn't. So, I just don't see a way out of that.

Linda Tuhiwai Smith

What a good question and a question that often comes up about how essential it is for research with our communities, for example, to be done with Māori. I think I also say somewhere in the book, in the end, our communities choose who does research for them and sometimes we, or someone like me, will stand back and think, 'Oh, my God, look who they've chosen. Probably the worst person ever.' But that is not my right to choose. It is their right to choose. But it comes with consequences. And I would reinforce that, just because you are Māori and you do research, does not necessarily mean that you do a Kaupapa, or have what we call a Kaupapa Māori approach because many of our researchers are trained in particular disciplines, where they have inherited their discipline, and they have inherited the same arrogance of that discipline. So that, in itself, just being Māori, doesn't necessarily mean, in our view, that they are ethical, that they have a decolonizing approach, that they understand power, or that they understand that research can be exploitative. I would like to say that all Māori researchers would know that, but I have come across several who do not know that. I mean, they get – in the end, they learn it because they get told it later after their training. So, we cannot control how well our researchers are being trained. In Kaupapa Māori research, we are actually very clear that, to do that kind of research, you do have to be Māori. And if you are not Māori and you want to be in it, you cannot be the boss of it. You cannot be the principal investigator. You walk alongside us as a good ally. And, yes, that is political, but it is also an approach that works. We, in the end, bear the brunt of any accountability. And the problem with non-Māori or White researchers is they can always walk away. When it gets hot, they jump out of the fire. We cannot walk away, and that is the difference, I think. It is a difference for those of us who are having to bear the burden of a struggle and those who are our allies. Allies can walk away. Same in research.

Esther Liu

Thank you.

Bassey Antia

Okay. Thank you very much. There's a question from Cristine. She notes that your book is extensively discussed at the University of Santa Catarina in Brazil, so you're well known there. She notes that she's been working with postgraduate students in language policy on your book, and quite a number of the Indigenous students are really very engaged in the debate that you proposed. But she does have a question around building a global community cross-border approach to Indigenous studies. She asked if you see the possibilities of a cross-border approach to Indigenous studies – one that is able to cope with singularities of local experience that simultaneously builds on some global movements that may be able to support local initiatives.

Linda Tuhiwai Smith

Thank you. Great question. I think there is the beginning of quite a bit of collaborative research across different Indigenous contexts. Obviously, language differences mark these collaborations and how we go about doing them. And it's raised some interesting issues about whether we are, in fact, doing comparative studies. I think in the end, we have had to develop a whole ethic about what does it mean to work in collaboration – what are we trying to achieve when we work across borders? Of course, the borders themselves depend on what our concept of borders is because there are many Indigenous nations whose nation has been cut in two by colonial or imperial borders. So, for some, the border itself is unreal or real, but I think it is across, say, jurisdictions, if I use that term, political systems, whether we can work at that level. It depends on the topic. For example, in the area of water rights, there are a range of collaborative projects going on in Canada, New Zealand, Australia, where it is easier for scholars to kind of work together. I have been involved in this three-country collaboration around HIV, and that was really hard. It was really hard to work across different systems and different contexts and different capabilities. But I think we have to go there. So, your question is timely and hopefully that is what you are going to do because I think it is a new arena where we have to develop the right protocols because you do not want one Indigenous population building capability and then colonizing the next one. I think we always have to work in relationality. It is an important principle, and we have to work out how that operates. So, thank you.

Bassey Antia

Okay. Thank you very much. And Lynn Mario also has a question.

Lynn Mario de Souza

Thank you, Bassey. Dr Smith, my question is related to something which you [stated in response] to the previous question. I'm speaking also from Brazil like Cristine.

Linda Tuhiwai Smith

Wow.

Lynn Mario de Souza

But from São Paulo. And just let me say quickly, we met many years ago at Waikato. You may not remember but through – what's her name? Well, anyway, let's get on with the question. My question is related to relationality and onto epistemics in the decolonial production of knowledge. For Indigenous communities, relationality is extremely important. Now, working within Eurocentric universities, even though we're in Brazil, our universities are extremely Eurocentric, all our processes, all our methodologies and our journals, et cetera, are all Eurocentric, meaning that they value the individual as a source of knowledge and not relationality or collaboration or whatever, right, which you've just mentioned. And one of the principles of relationality is interconnectedness and collaboration. We have one of our Brazilian anthropologists who has studied a lot about our Indigenous philosophies, Eduardo Viveiros de Castro. I'm not sure if you're familiar with his work?

Linda Tuhiwai Smith

Yes.

Lynn Mario de Souza

Yeah. One of the things that he has functioned more with – he has brought Indigenous philosophies into our academies rather than claiming to represent them. And one of the things he has showed us is that relationality to a large degree involves collaborative translation. Because when you assume that knowledge is produced collaboratively, you're saying that knowledge is produced, using Cristine's term, as a cross-border phenomenon, right. It's coming from different places, and it suffers – it goes through a constant process of translation. It is constantly and collaboratively being transformed. So, coming back to your critique of critique when you say we don't just make critique, it's very easy to critique but perhaps more difficult to transform. When we look at relationality, and relationality as ongoing collaborative translation, and involving transformation collaboratively and collectively, we have a different kind of methodology of knowledge production, right? I'd like to know what you think about this.

Linda Tuhiwai Smith

Yeah. You are right. It is different. Working in a relational space and even translating it into the Western Euro context as well to even explain what it is that we do because, in a sense, it is a whole system in itself, working in relational ways. It is all-encompassing. It governs our behaviors, attitudes, interactions. And you are right, it's the translation – transformational elements are deeply embedded in the relational elements, whereas in the more linear models of research, 'You do this, then you do that,' and then it goes to translation, and then it goes to action, and then it goes to impact, and it can still end up being absolutely non-transformational. Whereas I think our idea about relationality is also linked to the idea of sort of collective wellbeing, that collectively we move together, collectively we engage with knowledge, and collectively we experience the transformational components. But when our relationality is broken, when we are out of balance, for example, when the human world has almost been destroyed, and many aspects of our environment are unwell, then the struggle of our relational approaches, I think, is, 'How do we restore that balance?'

It is the same with gender. How do we restore our balance? And that is actually a big challenge for us because right now the planet is not a healthy planet. Terrible things are happening as a result of climate change, which Indigenous communities have anticipated. For instance, I know that Alaskan elders had predicted the melting of the ice caps years back, and people laughed at them. But changes to our environment change us and relationships with animals and other entities that then disappear off the landscape [and] are a loss to who we are and our identity. So, we have a huge recovery task that is not being helped by the green movement, might I add. The conservation movement is not our ally in this space.

So, that is a challenging question, but I do think, generally speaking, that these deeper Indigenous philosophies that inform our methods and inform our approaches are really important. Having them available and thinking about them deeply, I think, is transformative in that it provides our students and colleagues with a completely different model that they can work in.

Bassey Antia

Okay. Thank you very much. Perhaps I could read through a couple of questions so that you take them together. Again, from Brazil, Atila would like to know how values such as harmony, respect, balance and so on play out in projects in the Māori community, based on your observation. And he would also like to know what the uptake of academic scholarship by government by local governments is like from your experience. And then Rebecca is interested in Indigenous methods and wonders what Indigenous methods, approaches you would propose for emerging researchers.

So, what Indigenous methods and approaches would you propose for emerging researchers?

Linda Tuhiwai Smith

Yeah. Okay. So, there's three different questions in there. What was the first question?

Bassey Antia

Yeah. In projects you have observed in the Māori community, how do values such as harmony, respect and balance play out?

Linda Tuhiwai Smith

Yeah. Okay. So, my current research has been in the area of trauma, particularly, a nationwide project on family violence and domestic violence. So, when we are thinking about balance, harmony, those values, they are completely out of whack when we look at what's happening in the trauma space and in the domestic family violence arena. But those ideas of balance and of harmony are the aspirations of our communities. And, in a way, it gives them a vision to strive for. For example, working with families who experience family violence, what is it – what kind of family do they want to be? Well, obviously they want to be a family based on love because they still love each other but a family that can live well together, can live in harmony. And part of our role is to stretch those ideas, to move them away from some sort of romantic fantasy of harmony to something that they can actually achieve, step by step, by reducing violence. For example, physical violence, verbal violence. By participating together in programs that support them, by reengaging with Indigenous value systems and concepts which give them different tools to understand how a marriage or partnership should work, how parenting should work, the relationship between siblings.

So, in a way, those Indigenous values help drive many of our social programs and actually help drive the practitioners in terms of the skills that they use to engage our people. It's different if you're working on the environment space where those relational values are also important because they're often still practiced by many of our people who, for example, fish. They are fishermen, they are hunters and gatherers. For them, those are driving principles of how they do their work, and they get really distraught when they see others take too [many] fish, exploit the environment, leave rubbish around. So, in an interesting way, we can see those values are not far away from us. They are not entirely romantic. We can see parts of our community live by those values, and then other parts of our community where those values have not been part of their lives. And I think the biggest struggle is how do we put it all together. It is very fragmented. So that is that question. And what was the other question, Bassey?

Bassey Antia

The other one was about the uptake of academic research by the local authorities.

Linda Tuhiwai Smith

Well, if you are meaning the local White dominant authorities, the uptake there is that they still go to White mainstream journals and researchers for authoritative views. But in the New Zealand context, that is getting more and more difficult because we have some top researchers now who are Māori. You cannot avoid their work because they publish in the biggest journals. Their work is very influential. They are very articulated, and our younger generation of scholars are much better than my generation in influencing policy and being able to translate research into policy engagements. Local government is still challenging for us. Local government, unlike central government, [which] we refer to as 'the Crown,' started as part of the colonial agenda, as places for White settlers. Over time, local governments feel entitled to make decisions about what happens in a township, for example, with water, with rates, which is deeply racist. Our government has just passed an act that all local governments have to have Māori representation on councils, on decision-making authorities, and that is because it has been extremely difficult to get our people to vote because they are so disengaged with local government but also to break through this barrier of racism.

So, the context here is changing, and I think in a decade, things will be really different. But the other aspect I want to talk about is just how our communities regard Māori researchers. I am happy to report that we as researchers are slowly rising in the estimation of how our communities think about us. It used to be that they thought a *pākehā* or White researcher would make what they wanted to achieve more legitimate. But now they are starting to see that Māori researchers understand them better, for a start, and they can still be influential in the work that they do. Some of our communities are producing beautiful research in collaboration with Māori researchers, so that is a positive step. More significantly our communities are building research entities around their own researchers and trusting them to support their community aspirations. In other words, they have begun to see the work that researchers do as useful.

Bassey Antia

Okay. And the third leg of that was your suggestions with respect to Indigenous research methods and approaches for young researchers, for emerging researchers.

Linda Tuhiwai Smith

Well, it depends really [on] what disciplines and fields the young researchers are coming from. I mean, I think a good piece of research is a piece of research that is well done and completed, like a good PhD thesis. And I think for emerging researchers that is being able to do a project that's within their skillset, that stretches them, that enables them to build those relationships at a basic level. I am quite careful with my students and postgraduates about what they step into when they go out into the world. I think it is important that they achieve success and therefore not take on projects that are going to overwhelm them because our communities think, 'Oh, she's graduating. Well, we'll ask her to do this humongous research which is going to completely overwhelm her.' My job as a mentor and a supervisor is to pull that young person back and go, 'No, no, you're not ready. You're not ready yet. You need to get some good track record. You need to build your skillset,' because a PhD takes you basically to the beginning of a journey, a new journey and to becoming a researcher.

All I would say now is that I am a way better researcher now than when I first wrote *Decolonizing Methodologies* (1999) because you're on a learning journey, and things are more nuanced. You learn your own weaknesses and you learn, 'well, that didn't work,' Thank God, the world wasn't watching me when I messed that thing up. So, we become better as we do it. It is like work. We get better during the work. And so, for emerging researchers, young scholars, we want them to be successful. It's starting that with the first step set or setting them in that direction.

Bassey Antia

Okay. Just before I call on Salikoko, Nicole has a question. Nicole says, 'Based on your earlier comments where you noted, where you talked about allies and the ability to walk away when the going gets hard, how have you handled White researchers who have attempted to position themselves as the experts within your community and use their research to catapult themselves as transformation scholars in the spaces?'

Linda Tuhiwai Smith

I don't work with them. True. I don't. I know who they are, and you know, I'm not a person who attacks them. I do not really want to waste my energy. My energies are invested in our community and our scholars and our young people. That is where I choose to put my energy. Every now and again, we have a couple of well-known scholars who are constantly used by the media to be the authoritative voice on Māori, and the younger ones attack them on Facebook and social media on their part. You know, to me, I struggle in the decolonizing space. It's a long-term struggle. You know that one White person, they are a problem, but they are just one. Where we are going is a long journey, and I think some of us have to keep our sights on that long journey and not get distracted. The biggest way, ultimately, to overcome that sort of single White authority person is to grow our own authorities but also to grow the number of people we have in the media and journalism across society in order that they will pick, they will determine who the genuine authorities are. Thankfully, the number of White experts about Māori [is] diminishing. They are choosing not to speak, or they know better not to speak. They would defer to someone else. It's interesting that there is gender dynamics in there too because it tends to be White men (and a couple of White women), but when I was an undergraduate student, all the authorities were White. That is not true anymore.

Bassey Antia

Okay, then maybe we'll take a question from Salikoko Mufwene.

Salikoko Mufwene

Thank you. Before I ask my question, in the spirit of decolonizing things, can somebody give me hints about how to change the color of the raised hand? Because mine doesn't reflect my color. Thank you very much, Linda, for this thoughtful [. . .] presentation on methodology. In my office, and you can find this also online, there's a poster of Bob Marley, the singer Bob Marley, saying 'Emancipate yourself from mental slavery.'

Linda Tuhiwai-Smith

Yes.

Salikoko Mufwene

It suggests that you don't have to be an outsider to carry on the bias that you are pointing out. And in a way, we can also say that we are all, we have all been colonized in one way or another because we believe that academic knowledge is objective. And there are consistent criteria and methodologies that everybody has to practice to apply, but what is missing in that is the element of power. And I think it's Boaventura de Sousa Santos that speaks of [a] cognitive empire which is that connotation of power. And I also heard you and a couple of other people speak of authorities on this particular subject matter or on that kind of knowledge and so forth. And I think that conceiving of academic knowledge as objective is a matter of convenience because, as individuals, we are all subjective. And the construction of knowledge doesn't start in academia, it starts with how we interpret the world in a vernacular way around us and adapt to it. Every one of us that survives has developed their own theory of their world and so forth.

Nonetheless, those theories are very similar and [with] that comes the dimension of culture that we are more or less are prepared by our respective cultures to look at the world in particular ways, which really gives a lot of power to your suggestion that the Māori women, for instance, should have the right to present their own perspective on not only Māori culture but [also] the world as they see it, especially if they have been brought up in a culture that assigns specific roles to women that are different from the roles of men and things like that. And so, I'll just give another example and then I'll let you comment on all this if you can.

In linguistics, we have been talking about saving languages and language endangerment, and I have heard from a senior White American scholar, who I respect, the following thing. The best thing to do in the case of, say African languages – his name is Paul Newman – is train African students to do very good descriptive linguistics, and they can go and describe their languages and so forth. But when you put things in perspective, that training is provided in the United States by White American experts and so forth, and if the African students are not critical, how can we put an end to that colonial structure? Because they are going to apply what their professors taught them to do. And in order to get a degree, you have to satisfy your professors.

So, I think what I want to say here is that we cannot keep talking about decolonizing knowledge just in terms of Europeans who have developed a particular research paradigm as opposed to non-Europeans, but also in terms of people trained by Europeans stepping back and asking, 'Have I been taught the right things to do? Are there alternative ways of explaining things?' Should we be approaching, for instance, methods that have to with society, culture, religion and so forth, [in] the same ways that we should be approaching physics and chemistry and the like? So, I think what I want to suggest here is the need for self-introspection to see whether the training that one has received is adequate for the kind of inquiry that one is engaged in.

Linda Tuhiwai Smith

Well, you have just identified the classic dilemma of education and development, if you like, where decades ago, the young, bright native school student was identified and sent away to a metropolitan country to be trained, and they did not come home. And when they came home, they were considered utterly useless to the communities that they came from in the first place. This whole idea, in the end, was used as a tool of assimilation. You are right in that we have had generational scholars trained in the US and in the UK, and here in New Zealand, who were seen as the generation that could begin to save us or begin to do the work that was needed in our community to revitalize our language, and to begin the work of our culture. That is my family, in a sense, because my father did his PhD in the US in art and then came home as a professor of Māori studies. But he said he worked really hard to reestablish his credibility once he came home, and he has had a lifetime of scholarship here in Aotearoa.

My generation is a little bit different because we were not sent abroad. We were educated here in New Zealand's university system and educated primarily by non-Māori, non-native teachers. But many of my teachers were from either the UK or the US. So, there is this Anglo-American hegemony that is still powerful in our academies here in New Zealand. But where I am right now, we have started our own tribal institutions of higher learning, and my father is the founder of one of these institutions. We teach PhD programs: a professional practice PhD, and a PhD in Indigenous studies, and another PhD in Māori studies, which are accredited in the New Zealand system, and we are starting to produce our own graduates.

One of the insights, I would say, is because we have our own institution, we have our own scholars who received PhDs from all around the world who are teachers, [but this] does not mean we do not need to do the decolonial work in our own people and in our own communities. As you know, the power of colonization and colonialism – what Ngũgĩ wa Thiong'o had said is – it's in our minds, in the paradigms of how we think, and so that epistemic violence of colonialism is in the way we even engage with knowledge and what counts as knowledge and what's true knowledge. We see it all the time in our language revitalization school systems where they are learning and immersed in our language, but we have these ridiculous debates about whether, if you speak your native language, it means you are not colonized. My opinion is that, just because you speak your native language, [it] does not mean to say you are not colonized. You can be an idiot in your native language, and you will still be an idiot in another language because you're an idiot. And that is how I break it down.

Unless you think differently, unless your language and your cognitive processes are aligned, and what we know from colonization is that all the work the brilliant scholars have been doing in the space of cognitive justice [shows] we live with cognitive dissonance all the time – the legacy of colonialism. The big challenge for us is to wrestle with that dissonance and try [to] create a good way to live.

Salikoko Mufwene

Thank you.

Bassey Antia

Thank you so much, Linda (Tuhiwai) Smith. We'll just take our final question from Visnja, who wishes to know what your suggestions would be regarding giving voice to Indigenous students and people of color in White dominant institutions such as Penn State's students, who see themselves as underrepresented in this institution and who are very often misunderstood by the professors? Any recipe for talking back, fighting back, wrestling?

Linda Tuhiwai Smith

Yeah, so I don't know the context of Penn State, but I think the dilemma for all our young people and these academic institutions is how do they make space for themselves to be themselves and to be able to voice the things they need to. And how can they do it without sacrificing their own studies. That is the dilemma of activism in the academy. In the end, we want our young people to finish the degree, but we also want them to do a degree that is going to be useful in our community, and we want them to practice their skills and to use their voices but not at the expense of their success. So, that is a hard one. I think my advice is students are better when they have community; when they have strong senior leaders, and they are not exposed to fighting these battles as individuals. I think what students don't realize is that the academy is a huge global machine. It can clobber them. So, student movements are very important and powerful. I was part of a student movement in the 1970s. You learn a hell of a lot of skills being a student activist and being part of a collective of activists. It comes with a price as well, and it is really important to get the balance between your visions and sense of justice and your practices of justice, in other words how you practice what you want the world to be like.

But for Penn State, I'm not sure what your context is. I basically think all universities struggle with student voice, anyway, let alone the voices of students from communities of color and communities of difference.

Bassey Antia

Okay, thank you so very much, Linda (Tuhiwai) Smith. We'd like to draw the curtain on this part of this very lively set of engagements we've had. And I'll now yield the digital flow back to Sinfree.

Sinfree Makoni

Okay. Thank you very much. We're now going to move on to the more informal section where, if people have any questions which they want to raise, they can raise them. They don't get to direct them to Linda Smith. But before we do that, there's one emerging scholar called Rebecca Bayek who wanted to talk briefly about her research project. I promised her that this would help her give that project much more in the notion of visibility. So, she'll talk for about three, four minutes about what she thinks she's trying to do. Rebecca.

Rebecca Bayeck

Thank you, Dr Makoni. Thank you, Dr Linda (Tuhiwai) Smith. That was really powerful and very insightful. I enjoyed the session. I'm working on what they call in the game literature 'Indigenous game,' but I don't like that name. And I would rather call these games by the names given by the communities who designed them; just like chess, if you go by their own standards, chess is an Indigenous game, but they don't use that name to call chess an Indigenous game. So, I'm working on African board games. One thing that I'm interested in is creating some kind of bibliography on these games. I was wondering and just kind of have an open call to ask anyone who is based on the continent of Africa, who maybe has some information about [a] dissertation or somebody who's working on any African board game to reach out to me with any kind of resources, information or connect me to any scholar. So that was kind of the point I wanted to make and just use this network, this platform to reach out to folks out there. So, if you have questions, more questions, just please ask me. Thank you, Dr Makoni, for giving me the opportunity to share this.

Sinfree Makoni

Thanks a lot. Now we're getting to the more informal section. I'm really curious to know, my sister Oyeronke, what's your take on this?

Oyeronke Oyewumi

My take on which aspect of the –?

Sinfree Makoni

No, your take on all these discussions about decoloniality, gender, femininity that we're discussing. What's your response?

Oyeronke Oyewumi

Well, I was elated to listen to Prof. Smith, especially on gender and women's epistemologies because I have written about epistemologies of motherhood, and I see parallels between what she was saying, in which I think about Africa. There are lots of parallels there.

Sinfree Makoni

Yeah, there are lots of parallels. What's interesting, Linda, is that if you are dealing with issues about women epistemology, you can do that without telling you to consult the work by Oyeronke. So, when I was citing the issue about Māori women and Māori women epistemology, I was connecting it back to Oyeronke's work, without officially saying so in public. That's why I turned the conversation over to you, that you are the source of the idea, so you can, as well, articulate it more effectively than I can.

Oyeronke Oyewumi

Yeah, and then of course for me – the way I have approached gender and the whole idea that gender categories are Westernized, are Western categories – part of what I see is that they only focus on this dimension. So, I was so happy, Prof. Smith, when you talked about other levels, other ways, other epistemologies, really. Because in my work on motherhood, I said that, to understand the questions and the interpretations of Yoruba society in Nigeria that I was putting forth, you have to understand, first and foremost, that motherhood is a spiritual category. And once you understand motherhood as a spiritual category, you would ask a different set of questions, rather than, when people are in the family situation, who does the dishes, who doesn't, because then you already assume a nuclear family in places where the family systems are different. So, I told you, it's really resonated with me, the idea that knowledge is not just academic knowledge or the way it has been codified in the west. In people's communities, there are ideas about knowledge at different levels and in different sectors, so I related to that very well.

But one of the issues on my mind, and I don't know, you've spent 90 minutes, you've been talking all the time. I don't want to make you talk again but, you know, I haven't read your book in a while, so I don't quite remember how you dealt with certain issues. But I have to say to you that as Africans and as an African scholar, one of the major problems, we live now, in and out of the continent, is the degree to which we are thoroughly colonized, and we are colonizing ourselves and our knowledges. And it seems to me that one of the major issues that we're facing is what somebody called 'colonial Christianity.' Many African scholars don't want to look at Indigenous knowledge. Some don't even want to bear their own names anymore because they said that 'Oh, it's pagan.' It's calling upon on forces that are pagan and all that. This is how many centuries later? I thought we left that behind, you know? So that's one of the major issues, and I just wondered that, in New Zealand, in Māori communities, how has Western religion, what role has it played, or how do you navigate it in the community?

Linda Tuhiwai Smith

It is one of those big, heavy questions because we have been thoroughly Christianized as well. But our main denominations, the Church of England, Roman Catholic Church, have very strong Māori arms to them, and in a way, they have successfully navigated and indigenized many aspects of the way the church functions because the missionaries were the ones who translated our language, translated the gospels into Māori language, and so Christianity is a big part of who we are. I think the Fundamentalist Christian movements are ones that are much more recent and more antagonistic to Māori customs and Māori value systems. We have Māori religions that came out of the Christian faith in a sense. So, in a way, they are Māori in the way they do things, but they rely on the Bible, and they are basically Christian in their belief system. So, that is really complicated, and I think many of the sort of non-Christian ceremonies would still be held more in secret and more in particular kinds of groupings.

But, in our belief, we do not see ourselves as having had a Māori religion, but we do see ourselves as spiritual people, and that spirituality is really important and fundamental to our culture. That spirituality is also different from religion and the way religion is organized and institutionalized. But it is an area we have to navigate carefully, and, you know, it is often the reason families are split and divided because they have different religions. One funny story of my husband's family: When the different churches came to town, the grandmother thought she will hedge all her bets, and so she sent one child to the Mormon Church, one child to the Anglican Church and one child to the Catholic Church, and then they used to come home and decide which one had the best morning tea, served the best food, and then the other members of the family would go to that one. Her take on religion was not really about the religion but about what else they could offer the people.

My own family are Anglicans. I have a cousin who is an Anglican minister. This is what I meant when I said that we live with cultural dissonance. It is part of what we have had to incorporate. But I think the one thing that would bind us together are our relationships, what we call our genealogies. That is certainly what ties us together and then all our obligations as a community because Christianity has not been able to break that down. In the end, we come from a place, we come from a mountain, we come from a river, we come from a tribe, we go back to the land when we die. That is something that religion has not broken in our fundamental belief system.

Sinfree Makoni

Let me try and see if I can ask Christine Higgins, What's your take on these discussions. I wonder whether you are there or – Christine?

Busi Makoni

Josephine has had her hand up for a while though.

Sinfree Makoni

Okay, Josephine, yes.

Christina Higgins

Yeah, please go ahead. I'm happy to listen.

Sinfree Makoni

Okay, Josephine. Then I have to move on to Christine. Yes, Josephine.

Josephine

Okay, thank you. Good evening from South Africa, Pretoria. I'm from the University of South Africa and Nigerian. And I just listened to my sister, Oyeronke, and I hear what she said in terms of some of us from Yorubaland changing our names from Okun to Jesuit and all of that. But I also have a counterexample from my hometown. My hometown is Kabba, and we are known as the Okun-Yoruba people, and we have, like, the Catholic Church is very, very strong in the town, but there's been a lot of very interesting things that have happened in terms of enculturation. So, for example, when I was younger, our parents would give English names, but that has changed. We've gone back to giving our Indigenous names, even for our baptism and confirmation. But the best thing that has happened in my town is how the cultural ways of dancing, of singing, the tune of our songs and everything, they have been incorporated into the liturgy of the Catholic Church, so much so that, if you are in the church, you could be dancing to the tune of *iworo*. *Iworo* is like a particular kind of musical dancing ceremony that we have. So, all of that has come into the church and you could be a Kabba person in the Catholic Church, with all the religions and everything. And I think, like, maybe that should also come into light as much as we talk about those who are also changing from *Ifa anugo* to just [. . .] and all of that. I just thought that I should mention that. Thank you.

Sinfree Makoni

Thank you very much. Thank you very much.

Oyeronke Oyewumi

May I say something?

Sinfree Makoni

Yes?

Oyeronke Oyewumi

Yes. I just want to respond to that.

Sinfree Makoni

Okay, do.

Oyeronke Oyewumi

When you look at the history of Christianity in Yorubaland, yes, they went through a phase during which – in fact by the turn into the 20th century, Yorubas were telling the missionaries that when they are baptized, they can take new names, and they want to take new names, whether the new names need not be English or biblical names. So, Yoruba society went through all that. The liturgy, all that you said, incorporated all that. But since the '80s, there has been another shift with the Pentecostalist. People denouncing their mothers in church, and their ancestral blood. They tell you their mothers are witches, mothers are witches, the ancestral blood. So, the trajectory, things, are changing, and changing in all sorts of funny directions. And as long as people hold Jesus as a White man, it fits into White supremacy, and there's no question that, no matter how many liturgies you introduce, right now, with the fundamentalism, churches like the old school Anglican or Catholic Church, they are actually on the retreat because of the Pentecostalist. And they find themselves trying to catch up with the Pentecostalist Fundamentalist. And so, beyond the facts that people introduce Jesu in their names, I actually see Yoruba people bearing English names, and that's unusual, given the history. But you have somebody sitting in Ibadan. They've never been out anywhere else. They say, 'My name is Susan.' And I'm scratching my head. Where does this come from?

And then two years ago, I had a mentee in Ibadan, and her name had Jesus in it. So, they put Jesus in their names. Fine. And then she actually was saying that people would ask her, that name is so difficult. Local, right? Yoruba-speaking people, why can't you be Mary? And it's these processes that I'm talking about, post all that historical that you just recounted, that things are changing, and we're entering a new phase of coloniality that is so disheartening. Thank you.

Sinfree Makoni

All right. Now let's see if we can get Christina. I wanted to get a sense from Christina Higgins. What's your take on all this?

Christina Higgins

Thank you for inviting me to speak. I just have been a grateful listener. I'm at the University of Hawaii, and I often have many opportunities to think about the language and cultural representation of this place and my role in that, and it's very complicated. Most of our – most of my students are not from this place, and so far, I've only had three Native Hawaiian graduate students come through our program. And so, I'm really trying to find ways for academia to do better, especially in our local context of supporting Hawaiian students, of inviting them into the worlds that we have but also trying to remake or refashion those worlds at the same time, and I think that that's crucial.

So, here at the university, we have Hawaiian studies and Hawaiian language programs, where the majority of students are Hawaiian. But I think the problem is they're not seeing themselves represented or invited or as necessarily belonging in some programs like the one that – like linguistics, right? And so, I try to figure out from a more administrative or professor role, like, how to go about changing that. That's something that I'm trying to contemplate and work with other faculty very, very slowly toward. It's not a value even that's shared among many of our faculty. They see it as the cream will rise to the top, and those are the ones who we accept and that's it. So, there's no intentional efforts to think about where we're located in the world and what that means to it. Everything that we do, there's a universalist notion of knowledge and intellectual endeavors, which I think is problematic.

(Conversation continues in the 'after-party.')

Note

(1) To all of you in this time of a pandemic.

References

Smith, L.T. (1999) *Decolonizing Methodologies: Research and Indigenous Peoples*. London: Zed Books.
Smith, L.T. (2021) *Decolonizing Methodologies: Research and Indigenous Peoples* (3rd edn). London: Zed Books.

Epilogue: The South Writing Back

Clarissa Menezes Jordão

This epilogue was commissioned as a free text – 'write an epilogue based on your own understanding of what an epilogue should be, make it as long as you like, but as conversational as you can so as to line up with the series dialogical format,' the editors explained. How could I not celebrate this opportunity? It is a rare pleasure to be able to write freely in the academia. Further, it is high time we challenge the rigid imaginary lines we ourselves have been reinforcing from within academic discourse. It is time to blur those whimsical borders that separate and hierarchize discourses as they separate and hierarchize languages, peoples, cultures as if they could be more or less pure, as if they were neatly bound, as if language practices were not human and being human was filled with ideology and affect. It is time to stop pretending our texts are objective, our reasonings linear, our emotions detached from academic texts. It is time to go back to Humberto Maturana, the Chilean biologist, and his understanding that reason is nothing but another emotion (2001); or to Ailton Krenak, a Brazilian Indigenous leader, philosopher, poet who has been reflecting about the COVID pandemic and insisting that we cannot 'go back to normal' when this is over (2020). These are times for change and change in academic discourse is one of the elements this book is practicing.

Change in contemporary times has been connected to our experience with the COVID-19 pandemic, which has forced us to reflect on our interdependence, our fragility and the survival of our planet. It has enhanced inequalities and made it impossible to close our eyes to the injustices of the world that have been sustained by the three tenets that Southern epistemologies fight against: capitalism, colonialism and patriarchalism (de Sousa Santos, 2018). This is not to say that the pandemics created inequality up; instead, what was already there, and had been there since the beginning of time, was exponentially thrown in our faces, in our eyes wide-open. But we resist. We insist. We fight back. We write long sentences in English, we use the first person in academic discourse, we open our hearts on paper and do get published in high-impact journal, sometimes, even when we openly write about our emotions as scholars who cannot think without engaging, who cannot and will not pretend to do away with who we are being when we write. I do mean 'are being.' It is not an error committed by a non-native speaker of English; it is a creative use of English, an intentional instance of translanguaging.

Brazilian writer and literary critic Márcio Seligmann-Silva (2020) refers to one dimension of the political struggle we need to undertake in contemporary times, especially in Brazil, against 'the empire of death' with its two horsemen, Bolsonaro and the Corona virus. Seligmann-Silva postulates that such empire 'shall not triumph so quickly or without resistance' (para. 21), and he points out art, creativity, imagination and multiplicity as ways to resist. He claims that:

> A luta política se dá como uma *batalha de imagens* e pensadores como Kopenawa e Krenak, assim como artistas, poetas, trabalhadores e intelectuais, produzem a cada dia novas imagens que se opõem à pretensa verdade monológica que os donos do poder procuram impor. Essas outras imagens mobilizam nossas paixões e sustentam novas e robustas subjetividades, formam outras coletividades e amparam a resistência. The political struggle happens as a battle of images and thinkers such as Kopenawa and Krenak, as well as artists, poets, workers and intellectuals produce, every new day, new images that oppose the purported monological truth that the owners of the power try to impose. These other images mobilize our passions and sustain new and robust subjectivities, form other collectives and support resistance.] – my translation. (Seligmann-Silva, 2020, para. 22)

Inspired by Krenak and his image of colorful parachutes (2020), I started reading this book, already thinking of the epilogue I was going to write for it. I envisaged each chapter as creating beautiful parachutes of different sizes and colors, parachutes that helped me admire the view while falling. Parachutes that allowed me, as in Krenak's image, to fly in a space that is not confined by logical reasoning, stability of meanings and homogeneity – a space where I see myself entangled in nature, of which I am part, and away from the separability between human and other forms of existence. A space between body and mind, North and South, and away from the dichotomies created by colonialism/modernity, which projected one onto-epistemology as the best and only to construct and maintain 'civilization.'

So, with Krenak's colorful parachutes as a first movement towards survival, we can move on to the second movement of resisting fascism in its different dimensions (academic, political, cultural… you name them). As we have read in Professor Thiong'o's talk that constitutes Chapter 4, in Swahili 'we talk of age as the right to tell stories.' This right reveals our second movement in this epilogue. Imbued with the right to storytelling, allow me, dear reader, to continue my skydiving into our narrative journey of resistance, stating my locus of enunciation and bringing my body into this academic text.

Let me start with bits of my life story, briefly, as it is not an extraordinary tale. I am 58 years old. I have been in a de facto relationship for 29 years already – yes, with the same person (I mean, not the same exactly, for we both have changed a lot together). We have had cats – one, ferocious who died at the age of 12. Seeing him die was one of the saddest moments in my life. Now we have twins, both cats, at the age of six. 'But this has nothing to do with this book, the avid reader might be thinking… Why is this South American old lady babbling about her life?' Latinos (it comes into question if Brazilians can be included under such category but, us being in LATIN America, perhaps it makes sense) are emotional beings and keep talking about their personal lives whenever they have a chance. Anyway.… I bet the avid reader is now wondering whether they should skip the next few paragraphs to look for the 'real text.' Dear reader, sorry to disappoint you – there is not such a thing in this epilogue.

Please, do not be so keen to embark on the same boat as this avid reader. Take heed as not to believe there is that kind of text here, not even elsewhere: a 'real,' 'scientific,' 'objective,' 'transparent,' 'accessible' text does not exist. Language, my dearest (non-avid) reader, is opaque and can only be materialized through interpretation, in a combination between individually and culturally built meaning-making procedures. This is to say that we have no guarantees as to our mutual understanding of these words; we need to negotiate, in dialogical agonistic relations, our meanings. And even so, there are no guarantees. Is that chaos? Yes; it is beautiful, challenging, learning-provoking instability. This is the realm of decoloniality, where we move away from the tenets of modernity/coloniality such as homogeneity, separability, stability, consensus, permanence and presence. It is where we move in the direction of everything opposed to and different from these concepts. It is where we can appreciate the open possibilities for meaning making, their anchoring on specific worldviews, the political/relational dimension of everything we do – especially education. It is where we promote multiversality (Maturana, 2001) and relationality as organizing principles of the world, where every form of existence (both human and non-human) counts.

Opening up to 'equivocal translations' (Viveiros de Castro, 2004) is a must when we wish to make and take the most of our experience, of our age, of our stories. *Equivocal,* in meaning-making processes, are always multiple, equi-vocal. *Equivocal* also suggests that meanings are prone to other readings, to different interpretations, to learning with the Other. *Equivocal,* as much as it is open to mistakes and misunderstandings, demands negotiation. It is always provisional, always contingent. So, you are free to translate my life-story equivocally. But your freedom is limited by the size of your cage, as Thomas Hardy (1902) once put it. We need to remember that our meanings are produced *in relationality,* depending on who(m), where, when, what, why and how we position ourselves and are positioned in life. It is always equivocally, and always from specific loci of enunciation. The importance of such loci is explicit in this book, especially with the presence of the short biographies of each author establishing, even if in general terms, where the authors are speaking from. I thought it would be important to tell you about my own loci as well.

Allow me to tell you a bit of the story of my life within the life-story of this book, in the hopes that this story may have its moral revealed to you (or at least I like to think about it having a lesson…or more than one…to teach). Looking at myself as a character created under the circumstances of the present narrative in time and space, I think of my academic journey so far as having taught me to make peace with multiplicity, contradiction and instability in my positions as a teacher of English in Brazil, a profession I have exercised since I was 18 years *young* (again, *young* here is not a non-native-speaker mistake…). Being positioned once as a private language institute teacher, I felt tied to the market and I convinced myself that I could literally sell English to my students. By teaching *English,* we all understood, back then, this included grammar rules and vocabulary lists I had to help my students understand and memorize, in order to reproduce and succeed in exchanges with US and/or British native speakers. Yes, these were the main targets of my job of selling a language whose reference points were two powerful countries, two countries where it was believed this language was born and therefore, where it thrived in its purest forms.

Then, I took my Master's on English and American literature that only included literature in Great Britain and the USA; all the other countries were not included. The idea of America was restricted to one country only, despite the whole of Latin AMERICA. Then, in 1991, I started teaching English at a public university in the south of Brazil. There I learned many lessons, one of them being that teaching is labor (see Connell's chapter in this volume) and, as such, it is a political endeavor, an ideological activity that involves *caring and sharing* (at the time I fell in love with Moskowitz's 1978 book).

Three years later I started my third and last job, this time at a Federal University still in the South. That's where I retired from, but am still acting as a post-graduate supervisor, teacher and researcher. My most exemplary lesson there certainly comes from the relationships I established that taught me I do not need to please everybody, I can survive, and even if I live around people that dislike me, such people have every right not to enjoy my company as I have not to enjoy theirs. But still, having them around teaches me valuable lessons, as long as I am open to learning. During this time, I received my PhD at the University of São Paulo. My lessons there? It's hard to select one, but as I am not afraid of challenges, I choose to share this one here: there are good people in academia – great professors and researchers with great hearts. Knowledge and wisdom can go hand-in-hand; intelligence and affect are inseparable and come with generosity and engagement in the same pack. I saw this happen in the chapters of this book as well.

In my academic journey, I have been in contact with critical theory (Frankfurt School), postmodernism (Lyotard, Usher & Edwards), post-structuralism (Derrida, Foucault), critical literacies (Freire, Street), multiliteracies (Knobel, Cope), languaging (Maturana, Varela), translanguaging (García, Li), decoloniality (Mignolo, Walsh, Grosfoguel) and English as a Lingua Franca (especially as it has been developing in

Brazil, in the works of Siqueira, Duboc, Gimenez and others). This is, in a nutshell, makes up the library where I read this book and where I write this epilogue.

Why is my library important? Mainly because it shows that my trajectory has not ignored Eurocentric epistemologies, but it has also involved knowledges produced in, by and for specific spaces in the Global South. This has allowed me to read the chapters in this book from a perspective concerned with and directly impacted by the issues brought up here. These are issues that affect my life and the lives of people I personally know. They are issues that demand from me an attitude of *corazonar* that, according to Arias (2020: 89 – original emphases, my translation), places us in a position in which,

> [*Corazonar*] there is no center, quite the opposite, what it aims at is to decenter, to dislocate, to fracture the hegemonic center of reason. What *corazonar* does is that it positions at the front and foremost something that power has always denied, the heart, and gives affect to reason. *Corazon*-ar, in a way that *corazon* [heart] does not exclude, does not invisibilize *reason*, quite the opposite, *Co-Razonar* nourishes it with affectivity, so as to decolonize the perverse, conquistador and colonial character it has historically had.

I have still not fully learned the lessons I was taught, but that is another story. In the present story I am telling readers who got to the end this book, there are valuable lessons to be learned from reading the chapters that are integrated into this volume. Which lessons each one will learn depends very much on each reader's locus of enunciation at the moment of reading. The joy of being able to interact lies, to me, in the possibility of not only constructing our lessons, but also on sharing them in order to understand them better, to ignore some, to reinforce others and to build new ones. These are stories all along and stories that make us tick.

Is this an epilogue to signal the end? Yes and no. Yes, it comes on the last pages of this book. No, because it simply indicates it's time to suspend Volume Three, to take another breath, and move on to Volume Four. Beware, for you will certainly continue to be surprised, challenged and shaken. Enjoy.

References

Arias, P.G. (2010) Corazonar el sentido de las epistemologías dominantes desde las sabidurías insurgentes, para construir sentidos otros de la existencia (primera parte). *Calle 14 revista de investigación en el campo del arte* 4 (5), 80–95.

de Sousa Santos, B. (2018) *The End of the Cognitive Empire: The Coming of Age of Epistemologies of the South.* Durham, NC: Duke University Press.

Hardy, T. (1902) *The Mayor of Casterbridge: The Life and Death of a Man of Character* (Vol. 3). London: Macmillan.

Krenak, A. (2020) *O amanhã não está à venda.* São Paulo: Companhia das Letras.

Maturana, H. (2001) *A ontologia da realidade.* Belo Horizonte: Editora da UFMG.

Moskowitz, G. (1978) *Caring and Sharing in the Foreign Language Class: A Sourcebook on Humanistic Techniques.* Boston: Heinle Publishers.

Seligmann-Silva, M. (2020) Construir paraquedas coloridos? Corona e os sonhos para além do apocalipse e da redenção. *Arte! Brasileiros, 1.* See https://artebrasileiros.com.br/opiniao/construir-paraquedas-coloridos-corona-e-os-sonhos-para-alem-do-apocalipse-e-da-redencao/

Viveiros de Castro, E. (2004) Perspectival anthropology and the method of controlled equivocation. *Tipiti: Journal of the Society for the Anthropology of lowland South America* 2 (1), 1.

Index

Abdelhay, Ashraf 62–63, 86
abortion 108, 111
Abya Yala *see* Latin America
abyssal ethics 56
Achebe, Chinua 58
   Things Fall Apart 89
aesthetics 56
Africa 19, 28, 82–83, 84
   Belt and Road infrastructural
      development 31
   and China 31–32, 37
   education 96, 97
   Indigenous languages 57–58
   languages 6–7, 9, 57–58, 60, 88–103
   literature teaching in 90–91
   restitution of African art 111
   socialism 119
   tribes 94
   'uBuntu and Nite Pioneers of African
      Philosophy' 104
African Studies 14, 29, 30–31
African Writers of English Expression 95
Afrocentricity 5–6, 9, 10, 67, 70, 71–72, 73–82,
      83, 86
AIDS 30
Algeria 126
alphabetic writing 152
Amara, Sheneez 152–153
Amawtat Wasi 140
Amazon 123–124
American Journal of Sociology 28
Ancic, Ivana 34
Andalusia 50
Angola 23, 50
anthropology 8, 14, 33
Antia, Bassey 1–11, 53, 61, 108, 113–119, 123,
      142, 145–147, 155, 166–173, 175–176
anti-apartheid movement 68
anti-capitalism 53
anti-colonialism 21, 53
anti-patriarchy 53

anti-vaxxer movement 107
Anyumba, Owuor 90
Anzaldúa, Gloria 151, 152
   Borderlands/La Frontera 100, 125
   The New Mestiza 125
apartheid 23, 50, 68, 106
Area Studies 30
Argentina 125, 126, 147
Arias, P.G. 186
Aristotle 141
Asante, Molefi Kete 4, 5, 6, 9, 10, 66–87
   An Afrocentric Pan Africanist Vision 86
   *Erasing Racism: The Survival of the
      American Nation* 80
   upending the inhuman: decoloniality,
      postmodernism and Afrocentricity
      66–87
Asia 19
Atatürk, Kemal 135
Australia 18, 19, 100
authoritarian rule 8

Bagga-Gupta, Sangeeta 33
Bandung Conference 21
Battle of the Alamo 81
Bayeck, Rebecca 176
Bhabha, Homi 16
Biko, Steve 64, 148
bio-power 142
Black Africa 84
Black Linguistics 76
Black Lives Matter 29, 53, 162
Blake, Jacob 73
Bolivia 62, 128, 147, 149
Bolsonaro, Jair 59, 147, 182–183
Borrell, Joseph 128
Bourdieu, P. 15, 33
Boym, S. 17
Brazil 49, 50, 64, 110–111, 147, 161, 167,
      182–183, 184–185
Brexit 8

Britain 49
Buen Vivir 130–131, 136–137

Cabnal, Lorena 128
Cabral, Amílcar 44, 68, 148
Cajete, Gregory 160
Cambridge Journal of Anthropology 13
capability freedom 107–108
capitalism 10, 14, 17, 19, 21, 43, 53, 57, 65, 114, 116–117, 123, 141, 182
care 30, 106, 108, 111, 117, 118, 154
Chakrabarty, D. 13, 56
Charles I of Spain 135
Chicanos 125
children 17, 96, 100, 124
Chile 128
China 19, 31, 147
    and Africa 31–32, 37
    Huawei 32
    imperial ambitions 32
    Opium War 135
    politics 142
Chinweizuu (Ibekwe) 66
Christianity 19, 178, 180
civil rights movement 68
class consciousness 42
'cognitive empire' 22
Cold War 30, 31, 141, 147
collaborative research 47
Colombia 124
colonialism 7–8, 13, 21, 22, 33, 43, 47, 50, 53, 57, 60, 63–65, 72–73, 90–91, 121, 147, 182
coloniality 10, 123–128, 133–136, 141, 142–143, 146, 152–153, 155–156
colonization 71, 125
Comaroff, Jean 5, 6, 8, 10, 12–38
    Ethnicity, Inc. 35
commensurability 54
Communism 28, 66, 116, 135, 141
Conelli, C. 13
confederalism 150
Confucius 141
Connell, Raewyn: *Southern Theory* 18
Conrad, Joseph 90
Cook, Captain 164
Cornell, Drucilla 9, 105, 107–109, 111–113, 115–116, 117–118
corozonar 186
cosmopolitanism 20, 21
cosmopologies 110
Coutinho Storto, André 55

COVID-19 pandemic 5, 10, 30, 44, 123–124, 127, 137, 138, 142, 143, 182, 183
creolization 20
critical pedagogy 122, 144
critical theory 14, 164–165, 185
culture 76
Cushman, Ellen 164

Dante 97
Darwin, Charles: *On the Origin of Species* 74
data digging 45
De Giorgi et al. 141
de Sousa Santos, Boaventura 3, 6, 7, 8, 14, 18, 19, 53–59, 60, 61–65
    Decolonising the University 52
    The End of the Cognitive Empire 9, 41, 51–52, 56
    Epistemologies of the South 9, 10, 20–21, 41–46, 52
    Epistemologies of the South and the Future 46–49
    If God Were a Human Rights Activist 57
    Knowledges Born in Struggle 42
    Nuestra America 14
    Portugal 49–50
    Toward a Multicultural Conception of Human Rights 57
death 109
Decolonial Linguistics 82
decolonial praxis 122, 128
decolonial scholarship 1, 42, 72
decolonial studies 43
decoloniality 4, 5–6, 10, 17, 37, 71, 87, 121–124, 128–129, 132–134, 136, 138–139, 140, 141, 144–146, 147–148, 150–151, 152–153, 155, 166, 184, 185
Decolonising the Mind 95
decolonization 7–8, 14–15, 20, 71, 102, 127, 141, 145, 147–148, 152–153
    see also Theory from the South
Decolonizing Methodologies: Research and Indigenous Peoples 10, 159–186
    Māori 161–162, 163
de-existence 142, 143
Deleuze, G. 93
democracy 127
denationalization 149
dependency theory 26
Descartes, René 114
Deumert, A. 3
development theory 29, 67

de-westernization 148
Diagne, Souleymane Bachir 9, 104–106, 107, 109–111, 113–114, 115–116
dialogue 62–63, 64
Diaz, Brett 151
dignity 107
Diop, Cheikh Anta 75, 82, 84, 85
dispossessiom 22
DNA 84
domination 10, 42, 43
Douglass, Kirstina M. 29
Dove, Dr. Nah 74, 76, 85
   Afrikan Mothers 70
   Maaticity 70, 71
DuVernay, Ava 81
Düzgün, M. 153

Ebola 30
Ecology of Knowledges 44, 45, 61
Ecuador 122, 143–144
   black movement 123
   'Buen Vivir' 130–131
   Constitution 131
   education 136, 143–144
   English language 136
   Indigenous movement 122–123, 149
   plurinationality 149
Eda, Marian 51
education 61, 137–138, 143–144, 152–155, 184
   Africa 96, 97
   coloniality/decoloniality 153
   Ecuador 136, 143–144
   India 91–92
   Kenya 91–92, 96
   love and caring 154–155
   political significance of 122
   Puerto Rica 121–122
   women 153–154
England 7, 13
English as a Lingua Franca 185–186
English language 89–92, 94–95, 96–98, 136, 184
English language teaching 184
entanglement 54
environment 84
epilogue 182
epistemicide 6, 9, 20
   justice against 41–65
Epistemologies of the South 5, 8, 10, 41–65
equality 71
equivocal translations 184
ethics 55–56

Ethiopia: wireless networks 32
ethnic groups and ethnicity 24, 35, 94
ethnographic sentimentalism 8, 14
Eurocentrism 83
Europe 7, 13, 50, 68
European Diplomacy Academy 128
Evans-Pritchard, E.E. 28
evolution 85, 86
ex-centricity 16
extractivist research 51–52

Fanon, Frantz 13, 21, 68, 126, 141, 143
feminisms 48, 53, 111–112, 117–118, 141, 163–164
Feurbach, Ludwig von 42
First Nations 153
Floyd, George 56, 128
Foucault, Michel 59, 69, 142
foundational concepts 121–122
France 5, 47, 49, 116, 128
Freire, Paulo 59, 121, 122, 144
From the European South: Journal of the Postcolonial Humanities 13

Gandhi, Mahatma 50, 148
García, Ofelia 61, 155
Gathara, Patrick 24
Geertz, Clifford 18
gender 74, 141–142, 163–164, 169
Germany 50
Ghana 73, 79
Giddens, Anthony 116
Gikuyu 7, 9, 88, 92, 97, 100–101
Gilley, Bruce 46–47
Ginsburg, Ruth Bader 113
global and philosophical movements 3–5
global culture 18
Global Health 30
global inequality 14
Global South 22, 147
Global Virtual Forum (GVF) 1
goals 110
gold 49
Gomes, Rafael Lomeu 25, 27, 29, 33, 34, 41, 45–46, 51, 53, 54, 57, 58, 59, 94, 95
Gramsci, A. 13, 125
'Grexit' 13
Grosfoguel, Ramón 72
Guattari, F. 93
Guerrero, Vicente 81
Guha, R. 27

Habermas, Jürgen 64, 109, 116
Hall, Stuart 20
Hardy, Thomas 184
Hart, Keith 36
Hawaii 181
health 30
heteronormativity 143
hierarchy 37, 61, 69, 75–76
Higgins, Christine 179, 181
Holland 50
holocaust 50
Homer 68
Homo sapiens 67, 70
Honneth, Axel 119
hooks, bell 154
Huawei 32
Huffington, Ariana 10 17
human beings: ranking of 74
human knowledge 67
human reality 68
human rights 104
humanism 8, 14, 104, 106, 115–116
humanity 62, 113–114, 116–117

Ibekwe, C. 4
identity 113
ideology 25, 28
Idle No More 162
Ife 6
Imhotep 68
imperialism 16–18, 91–92, 96
importance 53
inclusion 55
incommensurability 54
India 19, 91–92
Indian Ocean civilizations 91
indigeneity 22
Indigenous feminism 48
Indigenous knowledge 35
Indigenous languages 6, 57–58
Indigenous methodologies 160
Indigenous movements 122–123, 149
Indigenous research 166, 167
Indigenous systems of thought 34–36
individuals 114
industrial–academic complex 30
intellectuals 97
intercultural translation 20, 57, 58, 63, 64–65
interculturality 47
internal colonialism 147
International Congress of Jurists 104

international relations 128, 135
Inzalo Y'langa, 'Place of the Rising Sun' 68–69
Ireland: *internal* decolonization 13
Islam 30
Italy 141
Ivan the Terrible 135

Jackson, Andrew 80
James, CLR 18
Japan 19, 135
Jaurès, Jean 116
Jenkins, A. 17
jineology 153
Jobson, R. 8, 14
Jolly, Rosemary 98, 99
Jordão, Clarissa Menezes 182
Joseph, John 7, 100–101
Josephine 179
Joyce, James 89, 90
justice 41–65, 118

Kaepernick, Colin 81
Kaiper-Marquez, Anna 1–11
Kaupapa Māori 6, 166
Kawsay 140
Kenya 9, 23–25, 88, 91–92
    education 91–92, 96
    Indians in 91
    languages 96, 97, 98, 101
    legal systems 91
    oral literature 101–102
    wireless networks 32
Kenya Land and Freedom Army 96
King, Martin Luther 80, 116
Kiswahili 88, 97, 98
knowledge 8, 25–26, 35, 93, 141
Kopenawa 183
Krenak, Ailton 182, 183
Kuhn, T.S.: *Structure of Scientific Revolutions* 28
Kurdistan 150
Kusch, Rodolfo 132

language 7, 88–90, 92–93, 94–95, 184
    African languages 6–7, 9, 57–58, 60, 88–103
    English 89–92, 94–95, 96–98, 136, 184
    hierarchy 99
    language endangerment 174
    mother tongue 96, 100
    musicality of 89

Latin America (Abya Yala) 19, 28, 47, 50, 122, 123–124, 144, 147, 149
Latour, B. 18
Lawyers' Committee for Civil Rights 121–122
Lee, Jia Hui 15
Lenin, V. 13, 66
Lewis, Linden 113–114
L'Humanité 116
liberal humanism 8, 14
liberalism 8, 141
liberty 71
life force 111, 113
linguistic gentrification 6
linguistics 155–156
literacy 101
literature 90–91, 100
Liu, Esther 166–167
Liyong, Lo 90
Lück, Jacqueline 25
Lugones, María 150
Lumumba, Patrice 148
Lyotard, Jean-François 68, 69

Maaticity 70–71
Macaulay, Thomas Babington 91–92
McCarthy, Joe 28
McGirt, E. 17
McKittick 15? 113
MacShane, Denis 17
Madany-Saá, Magdalena 129, 136, 139, 145
Makoni, Busi 132, 179
Makoni, Sinfree ix–x, 1–11, 18, 22–23, 36, 46, 49, 59–61, 75–79, 82–83, 87, 88–93, 102–103, 109–113, 117, 119, 129, 131, 134, 155–156, 163–165, 176–177
  intellectual career 59–61
Malik, Hosea 100
Mama, Amina 118
Mamdani, Mahmood 23
Man is the remedy for man 104–105
Man1, Man2 115
Mandela, Nelson 105
Māori 161–162, 163, 166, 170, 171, 178
Mario de Souza, Lynn 54, 61, 87, 101, 168–169
Martin, Trayvon 73–74
Marx, Karl 13, 59, 125
  Theses an Feurbach 42
Marxism 19, 66, 135
matriarchy 75
Maturana, Humberta 182
Mbembe, A. 13, 142, 143

Mbiti, John 116, 117, 118
media 148
Meeuwis, M. 6
Meloni, Georgia 141, 142
memory 93–94
Meneses, M.P.: *Knowledges Born in Struggle* 42, 93
mestizaje 20
META (Multicultural Training and (Legal) Advocacy) Project 122
methodologies 45
Mexico: slavery 81
Michel, Samora 58
Mignolo, Walter 5, 6, 10, 72, 136, 139–142, 143, 144, 145, 146–148, 151–153, 156
  The Darker Side of the Renaissance 126
  On Decoloniality 121, 123, 124–129, 132–136
  The Politics of Decolonial Investigations 134
Mills, Charles 104
modernism 71
modernity 6, 19, 109, 125, 128
Modi, Narendra 54, 142
Mogstad, H. 13
Mokgoro, Justice Yvonne 107
Monteiro-Ferreira, Ana: *The Demise of the Inhuman* 68, 69, 75–76, 78
Moralies, Evo 62
Moskowitz, G. 185
Motaboli, Teboho 31, 79–80, 138–139, 140
mother tongue 96, 100
Mozambique 7, 47, 50, 58
Mpumalanga: Place of the Stones 68
Mudimbe, Valentin 45
Mufwene, Salikoko 82–83, 85, 86, 173–174
Multicultural Training and (Legal (META) Advocacy) Project 122

NAACP Education and Legal Defense Fund 122
Namibia 50
naming 94–95
national identity 94
national imaginaries 16
nation-states 135, 141, 145–146, 147, 149–150
Ndlangamandla, Cliff 57
Ndlovu-Gatsheni, Sabelo 72
necropolitics 142
Negritude 118–119
neocolonial capitalism 14
neo-liberalism 17, 62, 141

'New World (Information) Order' 70
New Zealand 159, 161–162
  academic research 171–175
  feminism 163–164
  Kaupapa Māori 6, 166
  language 174, 175
  local authorities 171
  Māori 161–162, 163, 166, 170, 171, 178
  religion 178–179
  values 170
Newman, Paul 174
Nigeria 73, 95
Nit nitay garabam 104–105
Nite 4, 9–10, 104, 105, 106, 107, 108, 110, 111, 115
Nkrumah, Kwame 50
Noah, Trevor 29
Northern Theory 18–19
nostalgia 17
'ntu' 110
Nyerere, Julius 57–58, 119

Obama, Barack 105
Odera Oruka, Henry 45, 54–55
Odugu, Desmond 27, 145–146, 149
Ogunnaike, Oludamini 6
oral literature 101–102
oral tradition 101
Ottoman Sultanate 135
Oyewumi, Oyeronke 177–178, 180–181

Padmore, George 86
palimpsests 54
Pan-Africanism 4, 86
pandemic climatic catastrophe 8, 44, 59, 160
Pan-European Academy 4, 67
patriarchalism 182
patriarchy 10, 43, 53, 57, 75
Peter the Great 135
plurinationality 149–150
pluriversality 37, 52, 129, 130, 142
Polanyi, Michael: *Tacit Knowledge* 28
politics of language, memory and knowledge 9, 88–103
Poor Theory 16
popular university of social movements 61–62
Portugal 19, 49–50
Portuguese 58
post-colonial studies 43
postcolonialism 10, 71, 72, 82
postmodernism 68–70, 71, 78, 185

power 19, 35–36, 50, 55, 64–65, 71–73, 80, 100
  colonial matrix of 122, 133, 135
Prinsloo, L. 32
psychoanalysis 133
Puerto Rican Legal Defense and Education Fund (PRLDEF) 121–122
Putin, Vladimir 135
Pyramids 68, 70

quarantines 4
Quecha 48, 131
Quijano, Anibal 122, 125–126, 129, 141, 151–152

race 56, 74, 128
racial capitalism 19–20
racial domination 10
racial inequality 8
racial ladder 66, 73, 74, 81, 83–84
racism 53, 80, 128–129, 135, 152, 159
radical humanism 14
Ramaphosa, Cyril 32
Ramose, Mogobe 45
Rancière, L. 27
rappers 56
reflexivity 33
Reiter, B.: *Constructing the Pluriverse* 129
relationality 167, 168–169, 184
religion 74, 178–181
research
  and alternative sources of knowledge 8
  collaborative research 47
  non-extractivist research 51–52
  non-Western research 129
  regulation of foreign research 30
  see also Decolonizing Methodologies: Research and Indigenous Peoples
reset 141
resistance 43
re-westernization 148
Rhodes, Cecil 71
Rhodesia 87
#RhodesMustFall movement 3, 6, 12, 29, 71, 162
Rice, Condoleezza 141–142
Riley, Boots: *Sorry to Bother You* (film) 29
Rittenhouse, Kyle 73, 81
ritual 24, 115
Robinson, Cedric 20
Rojava 153
Russia 135–136
Rwanda: foreign research 30

Sachs, Albie 107
Sage Philosophy 45
sages 55
Said, E.W. 13, 18, 26
Sarkozy, Nicolas 47
Saudi Arabia 63, 65
scholarship, decolonization of 102
science and scientists 44–45, 85
Scotland: *internal* decolonization 13
second language acquisition, psycholinguistics of 60
'second-class empire' 135
Seligmann-Silva, Márcio 182–183
semiotics 152
semi-periphery 49
Sen, Amartya 107
Senghor, Léopold Sédar 104, 118, 119
Sesanti, Simphiwe 69
Setswana divination 35
settler colonialism 13
Severo, Cristine 58
Simpson, Leanne Betasamosake: *Dancing in Our Turtle's Back* 134, 142
Smith, Ian 87
Smith, Linda Tuhiwai 4, 5–6, 8, 10, 142, 159
  Decolonizing Methodologies 10, 134, 159–181
social justice movements 10
social movements 64
social theory 18–19
socialism 117, 119
sociology 133
solidarity 58–59
South Africa 22–23, 32, 64, 70
  1996 Consitution 48
  apartheid 23, 50, 106
  COVID 30
  foreign research 30
  languages 98
  Ministry of Higher Education 28
  Missing and Murdered Indigenous Aboriginal Women 162
  plurinationality 149–150
  radio 98
  Rhodes Must Fall, Fees Must Fall 6, 10, 12, 29, 71, 162
  Setswana divination 35
  social sciences 28
  UNISA (University of South Africa) 45, 70
Southern cosmopolitanism 21
southern epistemologies 20–21

Southern Sudan: Lord's Resistance Army 30
Southern Theory 5, 10, 18–19
Soviet Union 135
Spinoza: *conatus* 110
Spivak, G.C. 27
struggles for dignity and life 10, 45, 48, 53, 57, 58–59, 121–157
student movements 176
sudaca 125
Sufism 6
Sumak Kawsay 131, 136, 137, 138, 139
Sun Yat-Sen 31
Syria 150, 153

Tanzania 15
Ted 146–147, 150
Tembe 142, 143
Temple University: Africology and African American Studies 66
text and knowledge production in neoliberal universities 2–3
theory 27–28
  dependency theory 25
  development theory 29, 67
  'universal' theory 28
Theory from Below 16
Theory from the Margins 16
Theory from the South: decolonization 8, 10, 12–38
  imperialism as civilizing 16–18
  knowledge 25–26
  nature of theory 27–29
  North and South 15–16, 37
  transparency 33
  concluding thoughts 36–38
Third World Quarterly 45
Thomas, Clarence 76
Timossi, A.J. 21
Tlostanova, Madina 135
trade 91
transindividuality 114
translanguaging 182, 185
translation 92, 96, 100, 184
transnationalization 149, 150
transparency 33
Treaty of Westphalia (1648) 141
tribes and tribalism 21, 26, 94–95, 101, 108, 112
Tropical Medicine 30
Tse, L.S. 13
Tuck, E. 15

Turkey, Republic of 135, 150
Tutu, Desmond 105

uBuntu 4, 9–10, 105–106, 108, 109, 110, 111, 115, 116, 131
  defined 117
  feminism 117–118
uBuntu, Nite and the struggle for global justice 104–119
'uBuntu and Nite Pioneers of African Philosophy' 104
Uganda
  Huawei 32
  Lord's Resistance Army 30
Ukraine 134
unconscious 133
UNISA (University of South Africa) 45, 70
United States of America 7, 13, 14, 24, 73, 184
  African Studies 29, 30–31
  anti-vaxxer movement 107
  Area Studies 30
  Black Flag movement 108
  Black Lives Matter 29, 53, 162
  Boricua communities 121
  Communism 28, 66
  critical pedagogy 122
  George Floyd 56, 128
  health 30
  Native Americans 80–81, 100
  Puerto Rican communities 121
  Red Summer (1919) 69
  Rhodes Must Fall 29
'universal' theory 28
universality 139, 140, 142
universities 29, 141, 148
University of California 68
University of South Africa (UNISA) 45, 70
upending the inhuman: decoloniality, postmodernism and Afrocentricity 9, 66–87
urgency 53

vaccines 30, 107, 114
Valleta 142
Van der Merwe, Chanel 66, 79, 86
Varna system 74
Vasco da Gama 4, 91
Veronelli, Gabriela 61
Vigoroux, Cecile 87
virus pandemics 123

Viscuso, Christopher 76
visible/invisible beings 118
Viveiros de Castro, Eduardo 168, 184
Von Humboldt, Alexander 74

wa Ngũgĩ, Mukoma 14
wa Thiong'o, Ngũgĩ 6–7, 9, 10, 57, 58, 88–103, 175, 183
  Globalectics 88
  A Grain of Wheat 88
  'On the Abolition of the English Department' 90
  The Perfect Nine (Kenda Mũiyũru) 91–92
  Petals of Blood 88
  The River Between 88
  Something Torn and New: An African Renaissance 102
  Weep Not, Child 88
Walsh, Catherine 10, 142–145, 149–151, 153–154
  Buen Vivir 131–132, 136–137
  On Decoloniality 121–124, 126, 129–130, 133
  Indisciplinar las ciencias sociales 156
Wasi, Amawtay 145
water rights 167
West, Cornel 78
Western academy 68
Western civilization 126
Westernisation 141
Whitman, Walt 94
Whorf, Benjamin Lee 7
Williams, Raymond 35
Wilson, Monica 28
witchcraft 6
Wolof 4, 104–105
women 53, 69, 75, 153–154, 177
World Social Forum 43
World Wars 7
writing 70, 152
Wynter, Sylvia 113, 115

Yang, K.W. 15, 27
Yemen 63
Yoruba 180

Zedong, Mao 147
Zimbabwe 70, 73, 87
Žižek, S. 22–23
ZTE 32

For Product Safety Concerns and Information please contact our EU Authorised Representative:

Easy Access System Europe

Mustamäe tee 50

10621 Tallinn

Estonia

gpsr.requests@easproject.com